12 SERMONS
on
FAITH

D1649066

C. H. Spurgeon

BAKER BOOK HOUSE
Grand Rapids, Michigan

Reprinted 1975 by
Baker Book House
ISBN: 0-8010-8061-4

First printing, August 1975
Second printing, November 1976
Third printing, November 1977

PHOTOLITHOPRINTED BY CUSHING - MALLOY, INC.
ANN ARBOR, MICHIGAN, UNITED STATES OF AMERICA
1977

CONTENTS

1. Life and Walk of Faith

"As ye have therefore received Christ Jesus the Lord, so walk ye in him."—
Colossians ii. 6.

OUR nature is fond of change. Although man was made in the image of God at first, it is plain enough that any trace of immutability which he may once have possessed has long ago departed. Man, unrenewed, could he possess the joys of heaven, would in time grow weary of them, and crave for change. When the children of Israel in the wilderness were fed on angels' food, they murmured for variety, and groaned out, "Our soul loatheth this light bread." It is little wonder, then, that we need cautions against shifting the ground of our hope and the object of our faith. Another evil principle will co-work with this love of change in our hearts, and produce much mischief—our natural tendency to build upon our own works. For a time that pernicious habit is cured by conviction of sin. The law, with its sharp axe, cuts down the lofty cedar of fleshly confidence, and withers all its verdure; but, since the root still remains, at the very scent of water it sprouts again, and there is good need to set the axe going with all its former edge and weight. When we think legality quite dead, it revives, and, linking hands with our love of change, it tempts us to forsake our simple standing upon Christ, the Rock of Ages, and urges us to advance to a something which it decorates before our eyes with fancied colours, and makes out to our feeble understandings to be better or more honourable to ourselves. Though this will certainly be again beaten down in a Christian, for he will meet with trouble after trouble when once he goeth astray from his first path, yet again the old secret desire to be something, to do something, to have some little honour by performing the works of the law, will come in, and we shall have need to hear the voice of wisdom in our hearts saying to us, "As ye have received Christ Jesus the Lord, so walk ye in him;" persevere in the same way in which ye have begun, and, as at the first Christ Jesus was the source of your life, the principle of your action, and the joy of your spirit, so let him be the same even till life's end, the same when you walk through the valley of the shadow of death, and enter into the joy and the rest which remain for the people of God.

In trying to teach this very useful, though simple lesson, I shall, in

5

the plainest possible language, first of all talk a little of the text *by way of exposition;* then, secondly, *by way of advocacy;* and then, thirdly, *by way of application.*

I. Oh that the gracious Spirit, who alone can lead us into all truth, would aid me while I endeavour to open up this verse BY WAY OF EXPOSITION.

In expounding the text, we readily break it up into two parts: here is the life of faith—receiving Christ Jesus the Lord; here is, secondly, the walk of faith—so walk ye in him.

1. The Holy Spirit here reveals to us *the life of faith*—the way by which you and I are saved, if saved at all. Remark, carefully, that it is represented as *receiving.* Now the word receiving *implies the very opposite of anything like merit.* Merit is purchasing; merit might be called making by labour, or winning by valour; but receiving is just the accepting of a thing as a gift. The eternal life which God gives his people is in no sense whatever the fruit of their exertions; it is the gift of God. As the earth drinks in the rain, as the sea receives the streams, as night accepts light from the stars, so we, giving nothing, partake freely of the grace of God. The saints are not by nature wells, or streams, they are but cisterns into which the living water flows. They are but as the empty vessel; sovereign mercy puts them under the conduit-pipe, and they receive grace upon grace till they are filled to the brim. He that talks about winning salvation by works; he that thinks he can earn it by prayers, by tears, by penance, by mortification of the flesh, or by zealous obedience to the law, makes a mistake; for the very first principle of the divine life is not giving out, but receiving. It is that which comes from Christ into me which is my salvation; not that which springs out of my own heart, but that which comes from the divine Redeemer and changes and renews my nature. It is not what I give out, but what I receive, which must be life to me.

The idea of receiving, again, seems to imply in it *a sense of realization,* making the matter *a reality.* One cannot very well receive a shadow; we receive that which is substantial. Gold, silver, precious stones—such things we can receive; estates, riches, bread, water, food, raiment—all these are things which are substances to us, and therefore it becomes possible for us to receive them. We do not receive a dream; we do not receive, again I say, a shadow; we do not speak of receiving a spectre; we do not receive a phantom. There is something real in a thing that is received. Well now so is it also in the life of faith; we realize Christ. While we are without faith, Christ is a name to us, a person that may have lived a long while ago, so long that his life is only a history to us now! By an act of faith Christ becomes a real person in the consciousness of our heart, as real to us as our own flesh, and blood, and bones, and we speak of him and think of him as we would of our brother, our father, our friend. Our faith gives a substance to the history and idea of Christ, puts real solidity into the spirit and name of Christ, and that which to the worldly man is but a phantom, a thing to hear about, and talk about, becomes to us a thing to taste, and handle, to lay hold upon, and to receive as real and true. I know, ye that are unconverted, that ye think all these things an idle tale; but you that are saved, you who

6

have received Christ, you know that there is substance here, and shadow everywhere else. This has become to you the one grand reality, that God is in Christ reconciling you unto himself.

But receiving means also a third thing, that is *getting a grip of it, grasping it.* The thing which I receive becomes my own. I may believe it to be real, but that is not receiving it. I may believe, also, that if I ever do get it it must be given to me, and that I cannot earn it for myself, but still that is not receiving it. Receiving is the *bona fide* taking into my hand and appropriating to myself as my own property that which is given to me. Now this is what the soul doth when it believes on Christ. Christ becomes *my* Christ; his blood cleanses my sin, and it is cleansed; his righteousness covers me, and I am clothed with it; his Spirit fills me, and I am made to live by it. He becomes to me as much mine as anything that I can call my own; nay, what I call my own here on earth is not mine; it is only lent to me, and will be taken from me; but Christ is so mine, that neither life, nor death, nor things present, nor things to come, shall ever be able to rob me of him. Oh! I hope, dear friends, you have that blessed appropriating faith which says, "Yes, he is not another man's Christ, he is my Christ," I hope you can look into his face to-day and say, "*My* beloved, who loved *me*, and gave himself for *me.*" I hope you do not talk of these things as I might talk of my lord So-and-So's park, and admire its beauties, while I myself have no right to one acre of the many thousands within the park-fence; but I trust, on the other hand, you can say— "The blessings and promises of the Lord my God are all my own; whatever I read of in the covenant of grace that is good, that is comely, that is desirable, I have heard a voice say in my ears, 'Lift up now thine eyes, and look to the north, and the south, to the east, and the west— all this have I given *thee* to be thy possession for ever and ever by a covenant of salt.'" Now put these three things together, and I think you have the idea of receiving Christ. To receive him is to have him as the result of God's free gift; to realize him; and then to appropriate him to yourselves.

The word "receive" is used in some ten or a dozen senses in holy Scripture; five of them will suffice my purpose just now. To receive is often used for *taking.* We read of receiving a thousand shekels of silver, and of receiving money, garments, olive-yards, sheep, and oxen. Perhaps in this sense we understand the words of the Master—"No man can receive anything unless it be given him from above," and that other sentence—"To as many as received him, to them gave he power to become the sons of God." We take Christ into us—to return to my old simile—as the empty vessel takes in water from the stream; so we receive Christ. The love, life, merit, nature, and grace of Jesus freely flow into us, as the oil into the widow's vessels. But the word is also used in Scripture to signify *holding that which we take in;* indeed, a vessel without a bottom could hardly be said to receive water. I do not suppose any one would talk of a sieve receiving water, except in a mock sense. But the life of faith consists in holding within us that which Christ hath put into us, so that Jesus Christ is formed in us the hope of glory. By faith it comes in; by faith it is kept in; faith gives me what

7

I have; faith keeps what I have; faith makes it mine; faith keeps it mine; faith gets hold of it with one hand, and then clasps it with both hands with a grasp that neither death nor life can loose. Then, receiving sometimes means in Scripture simply *believing*. " He came unto his own and his own received him not." We read of receiving false prophets, that is, believing them. Now, to receive Christ is to believe him. He says, "I can save you."—I receive that. He says, "I will save you."—I receive that. He says, "Trust me and I will make you like myself."—I receive that. Whatever Jesus says, I believe him, and receive him as true. I make his word so true to myself that I act upon it as being true, and regard it not as a word that may possibly be true, but which must be true, even if heaven and earth should pass away. This is receiving Christ—believing what he has said. Receiving, also, often signifies in Scripture *entertaining*. Thus the barbarous people at Melita received Paul and his companions kindly, and kindled a fire. Ah! after we have once found all in Christ to be our own, and have received him into ourselves by faith, then we entreat the Lord to enter our hearts and sup with us. We give him the best seat at the table of our souls; we would feast him on the richest dainties of our choicest love. We ask him to abide with us from morn till eve; we would commune with him every day, and every hour of the day. We entertain him; we have a reception-chamber in our hearts, and we receive Christ. And then, once again, receiving in Scripture often signifies *to enjoy*. We hear of receiving a crown of life which fadeth not away; that is, enjoying it, enjoying heaven, and being satisfied with all its bliss. Now, dear friends, when we receive Christ, there is intended in this an enjoying of it. I am only now talking the simplicities of our faith, but I do want to make them very personal to you. Are you thus enjoying Christ? If you had a crown you would wear it; you have a Christ—feed on him. If you were hungry and there were bread on the table, you would eat. Oh! eat and drink, beloved, of your Lord Jesus Christ. If you have a friend, you enjoy his company: you have a friend in Christ; Oh! enjoy his conversation. Do not leave him, like a bottle of cordial for the fainting, sealed up from us; let him not be as some choice dainty all untasted, while you are hungry. Oh! receive Christ, for this is the very heaven and rest of the soul. His flesh is meat indeed, his blood is drink indeed. Never did angels taste such divine fare. Come hither saints and satiate yourselves in him. To take him into one's self, to hold him there, to believe every word he says, to entertain him in our hearts, and to enjoy the luscious sweetness which he must confer upon all those who have eaten his flesh, and have been made to drink of his blood—this it is to receive Christ.

But we have not brought out the real meaning of this life of faith yet till we dwell upon another word. As ye have received. Received what? Salvation may be described as the blind receiving sight, the deaf receiving hearing, the dead receiving life; but beloved, beloved, here is a thought here—oh that you may get hold of it! We have not only received these things, but we have received CHRIST. " As ye have received *Christ Jesus the Lord*." Do you catch it? It is true that He gave us life from the dead? He gave us pardon of sin; He gave us imputed righteousness. These are all precious things, but you see we are not content with them; we have received *Christ himself.* The Son of God has been poured out into us, and we have received him, and appropriated him. Mark, I say, not merely the blessings of the covenant, but *himself;* not merely the purchase of his blood, but he himself from whose veins the blood hath flowed has become ours; and every soul that hath eternal life is this day a possessor of Christ Jesus the Lord. Now we will put this, also, personally to you. Have I received *Christ,* that is the *anointed?* My soul, hast thou seen Christ as the anointed of the Father in the divine decree to execute his purposes? Hast thou seen him coming forth in the fulness of time wearing the robes of his priesthood, the anointed of the Father? Hast thou seen him standing at the altar offering himself as a victim, an anointed priest, anointed with the sacred oil by which God has made him a priest for ever after the order of Melchisedec? My soul, hast thou seen Jesus going within the veil and speaking to thy Father and to his Father as one whom the Father has accepted, of whom we can speak, in the language of David, as our shield and God's anointed? Oh! it is a delight indeed to receive Christ not as an unsent prophet, not as a man who came of his own authority, not as a teacher who spoke his own word, but as one who is *Christos,* the anointed, the anointed of God, ordained of the Most High, and therefore most certainly acceptable, as it is written, "*I* have laid help upon one that is mighty; *I* have exalted one chosen out of the people. It pleased the *Father* to bruise him; *he* hath put him to grief." Delightful is the contemplation of Christ under that aspect! Soul, dost thou thus receive the Messias of God? But the text says, "Christ *Jesus.*" Now Jesus means a Saviour. *Christ* is his relation to God, *Jesus* his relation to me. Have I received Christ in his relationship to me as a Saviour? My soul, has Christ saved thee? Come, no "ifs" and "ans" about it. Hast thou received him as thy Saviour? Couldest thou say in that happy day when thy faith closed with him, "Yes, Jesus, thou hast saved me!" Oh! there are some professors of religion who do not seem to have received Christ as *Jesus.* They look upon him as one who may help them to save themselves, who can do a great deal for them, or may begin the work but not complete it. Oh! beloved, we must get a hold of him as one that has saved us, that has finished the work. What, know ye not that ye are this day whiter than the driven snow because his blood has washed you? Ye are this day more acceptable to God than unfallen angels ever were, for ye are clothed in the perfect righteousness of a divine one. Christ has wrapped you about with his own righteousness; you are saved; you have received him as God's anointed, see that you receive him as Jesus your Saviour.

Then, again, it is clear that saving faith consisteth also in receiving him *as he is in himself, as the divine Son.* "Ye have received Christ Jesus *the Lord.*" Those who say they cannot believe in his Deity have not received him. Others theoretically admit him to be divine, but he is never a subject of confidence as such; *they* have not received him. But I trust I speak to many hundreds this morning who willingly accept his Godhead, and say, "I entertain no doubt about his Deity, and, moreover, on that I risk my soul; I do take him into my heart as

9

being God over all, blessed for ever, Amen; I kiss his feet while I see his humanity; but I believe that, since those feet could tread the waters, he is divine. I look up to his hands, and as I see them pierced I know that he is human; but as I know that those hands multiplied the loaves and fishes till they fed five thousand, I know that he is divine. I look upon his corpse in the tomb, and I see that he is man; I see him in the resurrection, and I know that he is God. I see him on the cross, suffering, and I know that he is bone of my bone, and flesh of my flesh; but I hear a voice which saith, 'Let all the angels of God worship him;' 'Thy throne, O God, is for ever and ever;' and I bow before him and say, 'Oh Lord, thou Son of God and son of Mary, I receive thee as Christ Jesus *the Lord.*'"

Now this is all very plain talking you will say; and I remind you that souls are saved by very plain truths, and the dealings of men's souls with Christ are not carried on in learned or metaphysical terms. We do believe, and so take Christ Jesus the Lord into us, and by that act of faith, without any doing of our own, we are completely saved.

I shall only make this further remark here, that the apostle speaks of this *as a matter of certainty*, and goes on to argue from it. Now we do not argue from a supposition. I must have you clear, dearly beloved in the Lord, that this is a matter of certainty *to you*. We can hardly get to the next point unless you can say, "I have received Jesus." The verse runs, "As or since *ye have* received Christ Jesus the Lord so walk ye in him." We must not alter it into, "Since *I hope* I have," "Since *I trust* I have." Ye either have or have not; if ye have not, humble yourselves under the mighty hand of God, and cry to him for his great gift; but if you have, O, dear friends, do not let it be a question with you, but say "Yes, yes, yes, I can say, once for all, I have received him; poor, weak, and worthless though I am, I do put my humble seal to the fact that God is true, and I trust in him who is able to save unto the uttermost them that come unto God by him." This is the life of faith.

2. Now, in expounding the text, our second point was *the walk of faith.* "Since ye have received him, walk in him." Walk implies, first of all, *action.* Do not let your reception of Christ be a mere thing of thought to you, a subject only for your chamber and your closet, but act upon it all. If you have really received Christ, and are saved, act as if you were saved, with joy, with meekness, with confidence, with faith, with boldness. Walk in him; do not sit down in indolence, but rise and act in him. Walk in him; carry out into practical effect that which you believe. See a man who has received an immense fortune, his purse is bursting, and his caskets are heavy; what does he do? Why, he behaves like a rich man; he sees a luxury which pleases him, and he buys it; there is an estate he desires, and he purchases it; he acts like a rich man. Beloved brethren, you have received Christ—act upon it. Do not play the beggar now that boundless wealth is conferred upon you. Walking, again, implies *perseverance*, not only being in Christ to-day, that would be standing in him and falling from him; but being in him to-morrow, and the next day, and the next, and the next, and the next; walking in him all your walk of life. I remember Matthew Henry, speaking about Enoch walking with God, says he did not only take a

turn or two up and down with God, and then leave him, but he walked with God four hundred years. This implies perseverance. You have received Christ—persevere in receiving him; you have come to trust him —keep on trusting him; you hang about his neck as a poor, helpless sinner—remain hanging there; in other words abide in him. Walking implies *habit*. When we speak of a man's walk and conversation, we mean his habits, the constant tenor of his life. Now, dear friends, if you and I sometimes enjoy Christ, and then forget him; sometimes say he is ours, and anon loose our hold, that is not a habit; we do not *walk* in him. But if you have received him, let it be your habit to live upon him; keep to him; cling to him; never let him go, but live and have your being in Him. This walking implies *a continuance*. There is no notice given in the text of the suspension of this walking, but there must be a continual abiding in Christ. How many Christians there are who think that in the morning and evening they ought to come into the company of Christ, and then they may be in the world all the day. Ah! but we ought always to be in Christ, that is to say, all the day long, every minute of the day; though worldly things may take up some of my thoughts, yet my soul is to be in a constant state of being in Christ; so that if I am caught at any moment, I am in him; at any hour if any one should say to me, "Now, are you saved?" I may be able still to say, "Yes." And if they ask me for an evidence of it, I may, without saying so, prove it to them by the fact that I am acting like a man who is in Christ, who has Christ in him, has had his nature changed by receiving Christ's nature, and has Christ to be his one end and aim. I suppose, also, that walking signifies *progress*. So walk ye in him; proceed from grace to grace, run forward until you reach the uttermost limit of knowledge that man can have concerning our Beloved. "As ye have received him walk in him."

But now I want you to notice just this; it says, "Walk ye *in him*." Oh! I cannot attempt to enter into the mystery of this text—"Walk *in* him!" You know if a man has to cross a river, he fords it quickly and is out of it again at once, but you are to suppose a person walking *in* a certain element always, in Christ. Just as we walk in the air, so am I to walk in Christ; not sometimes, now and then coming to him and going away from him, but walking in him as my element. Can you comprehend that? Not a soul here can make anything out of that but the most silly jargon, except the man who having received the inner spiritual life, understandeth what it is to have fellowship with the Father and with his Son Jesus Christ. Dear friends, in trying to open up that point just for a moment, let us notice what this walking in Christ must mean. As Christ was at first when we received him *the only ground of our faith;* so as long as we live, we are to stand to the same point. Did you not sing the other day when you first came to him—

> "I'm a poor sinner and nothing at all,
> But Jesus Christ is my all in all?"

Well, that is how you are to continue to the end. We commence our faith with—

> "Nothing in my hands I bring,
> Simply to the cross I cling."

11

When thou art hoary with honours, when thou art covered with fame, when thou hast served thy Master well, still come in just the same way with—

> " A guilty weak and helpless worm,
> On Christ's kind arms I fall,
> He is my strength and righteousness,
> My Jesus and my all."

Let not your experience, your sanctification, your graces, your attainments, come in between you and Christ, but just as you took him to be the only pillar of your hope at first, so let him be even to the last. You received Christ, again, as *the substance of your faith.* The infidel laughed at you, and said you had nothing to trust to; but your faith made Christ real to you. Well, now, just as the first day when you came to Jesus you no more doubted the reality of Christ than you did your own existence, so walk ye in him. Well can I recollect that first moment when these eyes looked to Christ! Ah! there was never anything so true to me as those bleeding hands, and that thorn-crowned head. I wish it were always so, and indeed it ought to be. As ye have received Christ really, so keep on realising and finding substance in him. And that day, beloved, Christ became to us *the joy of our souls.* Home, friends, health, wealth, comforts—all lost their lustre that day when He appeared, just as stars are hidden by the light of the sun. He was the only Lord and giver of life's best bliss, the one well of living water springing up unto everlasting life. I know that the first day it mattered not to me whether the day itself was gloomy or bright. I had found Christ; that was enough for me. He was my Saviour; he was my all. I do think that that day I could have stood upon the faggots of Smithfield to burn for him readily enough. Well now, just as you received him at first as your only joy, so receive him still, walking in him, making him the source, the centre, ay, and the circumference too of all your souls' range of delight, having your all in him. So, beloved, that day when we received him, we received him as *the object of our love.* Oh! how we loved Christ then! Had we met him that day, we would have broken the alabaster box of precious ointment, and poured it upon his head; we would have washed his feet with our tears, and wiped them with the hairs of our head. Ah! Jesus, when I first received thee, I thought I should have behaved far better than I have; I thought I would spend and be spent for thee, and should never dishonour thee or turn aside from my faith, and devotedness, and zeal; but ah! brethren, we have not come up to the standard of our text —walking in him as we have received him. He has not been by us so well beloved as we dreamed he would have been.

I take it then to be the meaning of our text, as Christ Jesus the Lord was at the first All-in-All to you, so let him be while life shall last.

II. I shall be very brief upon THE ADVOCACY OF THIS PRINCIPLE, for surely you need no urgent persuasion to cleave unto such a Lord as yours.

In advocating this principle, I would say, first of all, suppose, my brethren, you and I having been so far saved by Christ, should now begin to walk in some one else, what then? Why, *what dishonour to our Lord.* Here is a man who came to Christ and says he found salvation in him, but after relying upon the Lord some half-a-dozen years, he came to find it was not a proper principle, and so now he has begun to walk by feelings, to walk by sight, to walk by philosophy, to walk by carnal wisdom. If such a case could be found, what discredit would it bring upon our Holy Leader and Captain. But I am certain no such instance will be found in you, if you have tasted that the Lord is gracious. Have you not up till now found your Lord to be a compassionate and generous friend to you, and has not simple faith in him given you all the peace your spirit could desire? I pray you, then, unless you would stain his glory in the dust, as you have received Christ, so walk in him.

Besides, *what reason have you to make a change?* Has there been any argument in *the past?* Has not Christ proved himself all-sufficient! He appeals to you to-day—"Have I been a wilderness unto you?" When your soul has simply trusted Christ, have you ever been confounded? When you have dared to come as a guilty sinner and believed in him, have you ever been ashamed? Very well, then, let the past urge you to walk in him. And as for *the present,* can that compel you to leave Christ? Oh! when we are hard beset with this world or with the severer trials within the Church, we find it such a sweet thing to come back and pillow our head upon the bosom of our Saviour. This is the joy we have to-day, that we are in him, that we are saved in him, and if we find this to-day to be enough, wherefore should we think of changing? I will not forswear the sunlight till I find a better, nor leave my Lord until a brighter Lover shall appear; and, since this can never be, I will hold him with a grasp immortal, and bind his name as a seal upon my arm. As for *the future,* can you suggest anything which can arise that shall render it necessary for you to tack about, or strike sail, or go with another captain in another ship? I think not. Suppose life to be long—He changes not. Suppose you die; is it not written that "neither death, nor life, nor things present, nor things to come, shall be able to separate us from the love of God, which is in Christ Jesus our Lord!" You are poor; what better than to have Christ who can make you rich in faith? Suppose you are sick; what more do you want than Christ to make your bed in your sickness? Suppose you should be maltreated, and mocked at, and slandered for his sake—what better do you want than to have him as a friend who sticketh closer than a brother? In life, in death, in judgment, you cannot conceive anything that can arise in which you would require more than Christ bestows.

But, dear friends, it may be that you are tempted by something else to change your course for a time. Now what is it? Is it the wisdom of this world, the cunning devices and discoveries of man? Is it that which our apostle mentions as philosophy? The wise men of the world have persuaded you to begin questioning; they have urged you to put the mysteries of God to the test of common-sense, reason, and so forth, as they call it, and not lean on the inspiration of God's Word. Ah! well, beloved, it is wisdom, I suppose, which philosophy offers you.

Well, but have you not that in Christ, in whom are hid all the treasures of wisdom and knowledge? You received Christ at first, I thought, as being made of God unto you wisdom, and sanctification, and righteousness, and so on; well, will you cast him off when you have already more than all the wisdom which this philosophy offers?

Is it *ceremonies* that tempt you? Has the priest told you that you ought to attend to these, and then you would have another ground of confidence? Well, but you have that in Christ. If there is anything in the circumcision of the Jews, you have that, for you are circumcised in him. If there be anything in baptism, as some think that to be a saving ordinance, you have been buried with him in baptism; you have that. Do you want life? your life is hid with him. Do you want death? You are dead with Christ, and buried with him. Do you want resurrection? he hath raised you up with him. Do you want heaven? he hath make you sit together in heavenly places in him. Getting Christ, you have all that everything else can offer you; therefore be not tempted from this hope of your calling, but as ye have received Christ, so walk in him.

And then, further, do you not know this? that your Jesus is the Lord from heaven? *What can your heart desire* beyond God? God is infinite; you cannot want more than the infinite. "In Him dwelleth all the fulness of the Godhead bodily." Having Christ you have God, and having God you have everything. Well might the apostle add to that sentence, "And ye are complete in him!" Well, then, if you are complete in Christ, why should you be beguiled by the bewitcheries of this world to want something besides Christ? If resting upon him, God is absolutely yours, and you are, therefore, full to the brim with all that your largest capacity can desire, oh! wherefore should you thus be led astray, like foolish children, to seek after another confidence and another trust? Oh! come back, thou wanderer; come thou back to this solid foundation, and sing once again with us—

> " On Christ the solid rock I stand,
> All other ground is sinking sand."

III. And now, last of all, a few words BY WAY OF APPLICATION.

"So walk ye in him." One of the first applications shall be made with regard to some who complain of a want of communion, or rather, of those of whom WE ought to complain, since they injure us all by their distance from Christ. There are some of you who never have much communion with Christ. You are members of the Church, and very decent people, I dare say, in your way; but you do not have communion with Christ. Ask some professors—" Do you ever have communion with Christ?" They would be obliged to say— " Well, I do not know that my life is inconsistent; I do not think anybody could blame me for any wrong act towards my fellow-man; but if you come to that, whether I have ever had communion with Christ, I am compelled to say that I ha e had it now and then, but it is very seldom; it is like the angels' visits, few and far between." Now, brethren, you have received Christ, have you not? Then the application of the principle is, as you have received him, so walk in him. If it were worth while for you to come to him at first, then it is worth while for you always to keep to him. If it were really a safe thing for you to come to him and say, "Jesus, thou art the way," then it is a safe thing for thee to do now; and if that was the foundation of blessedness to thee, to come simply to Christ, then it will be the fountain of blessedness to thee to do the same now. Come, then, to him *now*. If thou wert foolish in trusting him at the first, then thou art wise in leaving off doing so now. If thou wert wise, however, in approaching to Christ years gone by, thou art foolish in not standing by Christ now. Come, then, let the remembrance of thy marriage unto the Lord Jesus rebuke thee; and if thou hast lost thy fellowship with Jesus, come again to his dear body wounded for thy sake, and say, "Lord Jesus, help me from this time forth as I have received thee, day by day to walk in thee."

There are many of you who complain of *a want of comfort*. You are not so comfortable as you would like to be, and why? Why you have sinned. Yes, yes, but how did you receive Christ. As a saint? "No, no," say you, "I came to Christ as a sinner." Come to him as a sinner now, then. "Oh! but I feel so guilty." Just so, but what was your hope at first? Why, that guilty though you were, he had made an atonement, and you trusted in him. Well, you are guilty still; do the same as you did at first; walk in him, and I cannot imagine a person without comfort who continually makes this the strain of his life, to rest on Christ as a poor sinner, just as he did at first. Why, Lord, thou knowest the devil often says to me, "Thou art no saint." Well then if I be not a saint, yet I am a sinner, and it is written "Jesus Christ came into the world to save sinners." Then

> "Just as I am, and waiting not,
> To rid my soul of one foul spot,
> To him whose blood can cleanse each blot,
> O Lamb of God, I come, I come."

Why, you cannot help having comfort if you walk with your Surety and Substitute as you did at the first, resting on Him, and not in feelings, nor experience, nor graces, nor anything of your own; living and resting alone on him who is made of God unto you all that your soul requires.

There is yet another thing. There are many Christians whose lives really *are not consistent*. I cannot understand this if they are walking in Christ; in fact, if a man could completely walk in Christ he would walk in perfect holiness. We hear an instance, perhaps, of a little shopkeeper who puffs and exaggerates as other shopkeepers do—he does not exactly tell a lie, but something very near it. Now I want to know whether that man was walking in Christ when he did that. If he had said to himself, "Now I am in Christ," do you think he would have done it? We hear of another who is constantly impatient, always troubled, fretting, mournful. I want to know whether that man is really walking in Christ as he walked at first, when he is doubting the goodness, the providence, the tenderness of God. Surely he is not. I have heard of hard-hearted professors who take a Christian brother by the throat with, "Pay me what thou owest." Do you think they are walking in Christ when they do that? We hear

15

of others, when their brothers have need, shut up the bowels of their compassion; are mean and stingy; are they walking in Christ when they do that? Why, if a man walks in Christ, then he so acteth as Christ would act; for Christ being in him, his hope, his love, his joy, his life, he is the reflex of the image of Christ; he is the glass into which Christ looks; and then the image of Christ is reflected, and men say of that man, "He is like his Master; he lives in Christ." Oh! I know, dear brethren, if we lived now as we did the first day we came to Christ, we should live very differently from what we do. How we felt towards him that day! We would have given all we had for him! How we felt towards sinners that day! Lad that I was, I wanted to preach, and

> " Tell to sinners round,
> What a dear Saviour I had found."

How we felt towards God that day! When we were on our knees what pleading there was with him, what a nearness of access to him in prayer! Oh! how different; how different with some now! This world has with rude hand brushed the bloom from the young fruit. Is it true that flowers of grace, like the flowers of nature, die in the autumn of our piety? As we all get older, ought we to be more worldly? Should it be that our early love, which was the love of our espousals, dies away? Forgive, O Lord, this evil, and turn us anew unto thee.

> " Return, O holy Dove! return,
> Sweet messenger of rest!
> We hate the sins that made thee mourn,
> And drove thee from our breast.
>
> The dearest idol we have known,
> Whate'er that idol be,
> Help us to tear it from thy throne,
> And worship only thee.
>
> So shall our walk be close with God,
> Calm and serene our frame;
> So purer light shall mark the road
> That leads us to the Lamb."

"As ye have received him walk in him," and if ye have not received him, oh! poor sinner, remember he is free and full, full to give thee all thou needest, and free to give it even to thee. Let the verse we sung be an invitation to thee :

> " This fountain, though rich, from charge is quite clear;
> The poorer the wretch, the welcomer here :
> Come, needy and guilty; come, loathsome and bare ;
> Though leprous and filthy, come just as you are.

Trust in God's anointed—that is receive him—and then, having trusted him, continue still to trust him. May his Spirit enable you to do it, and to his name shall be glory for ever and ever.

2. Faith and Life

> "Simon Peter, a servant and an apostle of Jesus Christ, to them that have obtained like precious faith with us through the righteousness of God and our Saviour Jesus Christ; grace and peace be multiplied unto you through the knowledge of God, and of Jesus our Lord, according as his divine power hath given unto us all things that pertain unto life and godliness, through the knowledge of him that hath called us to glory and virtue : whereby are given unto us exceeding great and precious promises : that by these ye might be partakers of the divine nature, having escaped the corruption that is in the world through lust."—2 Peter i. 1—4.

THE two most important things in our holy religion are *faith* and *life*. He who shall rightly understand these two words is not far from being a master in experimental theology. Faith and life! these are vital points to a Christian. They possess so intimate a connection with each other that they are by no means to be severed; God hath so joined them together, let no man seek to put them asunder. You shall never find true faith unattended by true godliness; on the other hand, you shall never discover a truly holy life which has not for its root and foundation a living faith upon the righteousness of our Lord Jesus Christ. Woe unto those who seek after the one without the other! There be some who cultivate faith and forget holiness; these may be very high in orthodoxy, but they shall be very deep in damnation, in that day when God shall condemn those who hold the truth in unrighteousness, and make the doctrine of Christ to pander to their lusts. There are others who have strained after holiness of life, but have denied the faith; these are comparable unto the Pharisees of old, of whom the Master said, they were " whitewashed sepulchres;" they were fair to look upon externally, but inwardly, because the living faith was not there, they were full of dead men's bones and all manner of uncleanness. Ye must have faith, for this is the foundation; ye must have holiness of life, for this is the superstructure. Of what avail is the mere foundation of a building to a man in the day of tempest? Can he hide himself among sunken

17

stones and concrete? He wants a house to cover him, as well as a foundation upon which that house might have been built; even so we need the superstructure of spiritual life if we would have comfort in the day of doubt. But seek not a holy life without faith, for that would be to erect a house which can afford no permanent shelter, because it has no foundation on a rock—a house which must come down with a tremendous crash in the day when the rain descends, and the floods come, and the winds blow, and beat upon it. Let faith and life be put together, and, like the two abutments of an arch, they shall make your piety strong. Like the horses of Pharaoh's chariot, they pull together gloriously. Like light and heat streaming from the same sun, they are alike full of blessing. Like the two pillars of the temple, they are for glory and for beauty. They are two streams from the fountain of grace; two lamps lit with holy fire; two olive-trees watered by heavenly care; two stars carried in Jesus' hand. The Lord grant that we may have both of these to perfection, that his name may be praised.

Now, it will be clear to all, that in the four verses before us, our apostle has most excellently set forth the necessity of these two things—twice over he insists upon the faith, and twice over upon holiness of life. We will take the first occasion first.

I. Observe, in the first place, what he says concerning the *character and the origin of faith*, and then concerning the *character and origin of spiritual life*.

"Simon Peter, a servant and an apostle of Jesus Christ, to them that have obtained like precious faith with us through the righteousness of God and our Saviour Jesus Christ." So far *the faith*. "Grace and peace be multiplied unto you through the knowledge of God, and of Jesus our Lord, according as his divine power hath given unto us all things that pertain unto life and godliness, through the knowledge of him that hath called us to glory and virtue." These two verses, you see, concern the *spiritual life* which comes with the faith.

Let us begin where Peter begins, with the FAITH. You have here a description of true saving faith.

First, you have a description of its *source*. He says, "to them that *have obtained* like precious faith." See, then, my brethren, faith does not grow in man's heart by nature; it is a thing which is *obtained*. It is not a matter which springs up by a process of education, or by the example and excellent instruction of our parents; it is a thing which has to be obtained. Not imitation, but regeneration; not development, but conversion. All our good things come from without us, only evil can be educed from within us. Now, that which is *obtained* by us must be given to us; and well are we taught in Scripture that "faith is not of ourselves, it is the gift of God." Although faith is the act of man, yet it is the work of God. "With the heart man believeth unto righteousness;" but that heart must, first of all, have been renewed by divine grace before it ever can be capable of the act of saving faith. Faith, we say, is man's act, for we are commanded to "believe on the Lord Jesus Christ," and we shall be saved. At the same time, faith is God's gift, and wherever we find it, we may know that it did not come there from the force of nature, but from a work of divine grace. How this magnifies the grace of God, my brethren, and how low this casts human nature! Faith. Is it not one of the simplest things? Merely to depend upon the blood and righteousness of the Lord Jesus Christ, does it not seem one of the easiest of virtues? To be nothing, and to let him be everything—to be still, and to let him work for me, does not this seem to be the most elementary of all the Christian graces? Indeed, so it is; and yet, even to this first principle and rudiment, poor human nature is so fallen and so utterly undone, that it cannot attain unto! Brethren, the Lord must not only open the gates of heaven to us at the last, but he must open the gates of our heart to faith at the first. It is not enough for us to know that *he* must make us perfect in every good work to do his will, but we must be taught that *he* must even give us a desire afte. Christ; and when this is given, he must enable us to give the grip of the hand of faith whereby Jesus Christ becomes our Saviour and Lord. Now, the question comes (and we will try and make the text of to-day, a text of examination all the way through) have we obtained this faith? Are we conscious that we have been operated upon by the Holy Spirit? Is there a vital principle in us which was not there originally? Do we know to-day the folly of carnal confidence? Have we a hope that we have been enabled through divine grace to cast away all our own righteousness and every dependence, and are we now, whether we sink or swim, resting entirely upon the person, the righteousness, the blood, the intercession, the precious merit of our Lord Jesus Christ? If not, we have cause enough to tremble; but if we have, the while the apostle writes, "Unto them that have obtained like precious faith," he writes to us, and across the interval of centuries his benediction comes as full and fresh as ever, "Grace and peace be multiplied unto you."

Peter having described the origin of this faith, proceeds to describe its *object*. The word "through" in our translation, might, quite as correctly, have been rendered "in"—"faith in the righteousness of our God and our Saviour Jesus Christ." True faith, then, is a faith in Jesus Christ, but it is a faith in Jesus Christ *as divine*. That man who believes in Jesus Christ as simply a prophet, as only a great teacher, has not the faith which will save him. Charity would make us hope for many Unitarians, but honesty compels us to condemn them without exception, so far as vital godliness is concerned. It matters not how intelligent may be their conversation, nor how charitable may be their manners, nor how patriotic may be their spirit, if they reject Jesus Christ as very God of very God, we believe they shall without doubt perish everlastingly. Our Lord uttered no dubious words when he said "He that believeth not shall be damned," and we must not attempt to be more liberal than the Lord himself. Little allowance can I make for one who receives Jesus the prophet, and rejects him as God. It is an atrocious outrage upon common sense for a man to profess to be a believer in Christ at all, if he does not receive his divinity. I would undertake, at any time, to prove to a demonstration, that if Christ were not God, he was the grossest impostor who ever lived. One of two things, he was either divine or a villain. There is no stopping between the two. I cannot imagine a character more vile than that which would be borne by a man who should lead his followers to adore him as God, without ever putting in a word by way of caveat, to stop their idolatry; nay, who should have spoken in terms so ambiguous, that two thousand years after his death, there should be found millions of persons resting upon him as God. I say, if he were not God, the atrocity of his having palmed himself upon us, his disciples, as God, puts aside altogether from consideration any of the apparent virtues of his life. He was the grossest of all deceivers, if he was not "very God of very God." O beloved, you and I have found no difficulties here; when we have beheld the record of his miracles, when we have listened to the testimony of his divine Father, when we have heard the word of the inspired apostles, when we have felt the majesty of his own divine influence in our own hearts, we have graciously accepted him as "the Wonderful, the Counsellor, the mighty God, the everlasting Father;" and, as John bear witness of him and said, "The Word was in the beginning with God, and the Word was God," even so have we received him; so that at this day, he that was born of the virgin Mary, Jesus of Nazareth, the king of the Jews, is to us "God over all, blessed for ever."

> " Jesus is worthy to receive
> Honour and power divine:
> And blessings more than we can give,
> Be Lord for ever thine."

Now, beloved friends, have we heartily and joyfully received Jesus Christ as God? My hearer, if thou hast not, I pray thee seek of God the faith which saves, for thou hast it not as yet, nor art thou in the way to it. Who but a God could bear the weight of sin? Who but a God shall be the "same yesterday, to-day, and for ever?" Concerning whom but a God could it be said, "I am the Lord, I change not; therefore ye sons of Jacob are not consumed." We have to do with Christ, and we should be consumed if he changed; inasmuch, then, as he does not change, and we are not consumed, he must be divine, and our soul rolls the entire burden of its care and guilt upon the mighty shoulders of the everlasting God, who—

> "Bears the earth's huge pillars up,
> And spreads the heavens abroad."

Remark in further dwelling upon the te⁻' that the apostle has put in another word beside "God," and that is, "of God and *our Saviour*." As if the glory of the Godhead might be too bright for us, he has attempered it by gentler words "our Saviour." Now, to trust Jesus Christ as divine, will save no man, unless there be added to this a resting in him as the great propitiatory sacrifice. Jesus Christ is our Saviour because he became a substitute for guilty man. He having taken upon himself the form of manhood by union with our nature, stood in the room, place, and stead of sinners. When the whole tempest of divine wrath was about to spend itself on man, he endured it all for his elect; when the great whip of the law must fall, he bared his own shoulders to the lash; when the cry was heard, "Awake, O sword!" it was against Christ the Shepherd, against the man who was the fellow to the eternal God. And because he thus suffered in the place and stead of man, he received power from on high to become the Saviour of man, and to bring many sons into glory, because he had been made perfect through suffering. Now, have we received Jesus Christ as *our Saviour?* Happy art thou, if thou hast laid thy hand upon the head of him who was slain for sinners. Be glad, and rejoice in the Lord without ceasing, if to-day that blessed Redeemer who has ascended upon high has become *thy* Saviour, delivered *thee* from sin, passing by *thy* transgressions, and making thee to be accepted in the beloved. A Saviour is he to us when he delivers us from the curse, punishment, guilt, and power of sin, "He shall save his people from their sins." O thou great God, be thou my Saviour, mighty to save.

But be pleased to notice the word "righteousness." It is a faith in the *righteousness* of our God and our Saviour. In these days, certain divines have tried to get rid of all idea of atonement; they have taught that faith in Jesus Christ would save men, apart from any faith in him as a sacrifice. Ah, brethren, it does not say, "faith in the teaching of God our Saviour;" I do not find here that it is written, "faith in the character of God our Saviour, as our exemplar." No, but "faith in the righteousness of God our Saviour." That righteousness, like a white robe, must be cast around us. I have not received Jesus Christ at all, but I am an adversary and an enemy to him, unless I have received him as Jehovah Tsidkenu, the Lord our righteousness. There is his perfect life; that life was a life for me; it contains all the virtues, in it there is no spot; it keeps the law of God, and makes it honourable; my faith takes that righteousness of Jesus Christ, and it is cast about me, and I am then so beauteously, nay, so perfectly arrayed, that even the eye of God can see neither spot nor blemish in me. Have we, then, to-day a faith in the righteousness of God our Saviour? For no faith but this can ever bring the soul into a condition of acceptance before the Most High. "Why," saith one, "these are the very simplicities of the gospel." Beloved, I know they are, and, therefore, do we deal them out this morning, for, thanks be to God, it is the simplicities which lie at the foundation; and it is rather by simplicities than by mysteries that a Christian is to try himself and to see whether he be in the faith or no. Put the question, brethren, have we, then, this like precious faith in God and our Saviour Jesus Christ?

Our apostle has not finished the description, without saying that it is "*like* precious faith." All faith is the same sort of faith. Our faith may not be like that of Peter, in degree, but if it be genuine, it is like it as to its nature, its origin, its objects, and its results. Here is a blessed equality. Speak of "liberty, equality, and fraternity," you shall only find these things carried out within the Church of Christ. There is indeed a blessed equality here, for the poorest little-faith who ever crept into heaven on its hands and knees, has a *like* precious faith with the mighty apostle Peter. I say, brethren, if the one be gold, so is the other; if the one can move mountains, so can the other; for remember, that the privileges of mountain-moving, and of plucking up the trees, and casting them into the sea, are not given to great faith, but "if ye have faith as a grain of mustard seed," it shall be done. Little faith has a royal descent and is as truly of divine birth as is the greatest and fullest assurance which ever made glad the heart of man, hence it ensures the same inheritance at the last, and the same safety by the way. It is "like precious faith."

He tells us too, that faith is "*precious;*" and is it not precious? for it deals with precious things, with precious promises, with precious blood, with a precious redemption, with all the preciousness of the person of our Lord and Saviour Jesus Christ. Well may that be a precious faith which supplies our greatest want, delivers us from our greatest danger, and admits us to the greatest glory. Well may that be called "precious faith," which is the symbol of our election, the evidence of our calling, the root of all our graces, the channel of communion, the weapon of prevalence, the shield of safety, the substance of hope, the evidence of eternity, the guerdon of immortality, and the passport of glory. O for more of this inestimably precious faith. Precious faith, indeed it is.

When the apostle, Simon Peter, writes "to them that have obtained like precious faith with us, through the righteousness of God, and our Saviour Jesus Christ," does he write to *you?* does he write to me? If not, if we are not here addressed, remember that we can never expect to hear the voice which says, "Come ye blessed of my Father;" but we are to-day in such a condition, that dying as we now are, "Depart ye cursed" must be the thunder which shall roll in our ears, and drive us down to hell. So much, then, concerning faith.

Now we shall turn to notice with great brevity, the LIFE. "Grace and peace be multiplied unto you through the knowledge of God and of Jesus our Lord, according as his divine power hath given unto us all things that pertain unto life and godliness, through the knowledge of him that hath called us to glory and virtue." Here we have, then, brethren, the *fountain and source* of our spiritual life. Just as faith is a boon which is to be obtained, so you will perceive that our spiritual life is a principle which is *given*. A thing which is given to us, too, by divine power—"according as his *divine power* hath given unto us all things that pertain unto life and godliness." To give life at all is the essential attribute of God. This is an attribute which he will not alienate; to save and to destroy belong unto the Sovereign of heaven. "He can create, and he destroy," is one of the profoundest notes in the ascription of our praise. Suppose a corpse before us. How great a pretender would he be who should boast that it was in his power to restore it to life Certainly, it would be even a greater pretence if anyone should say that! he could give to himself or to another the divine life, the spiritual life by which a man is made a Christian. My brethren, you who are partakers of the divine nature, know that by nature you were dead in trespasses and sins, and would have continued so until this day if there had not been an interposition of divine energy on your behalf. There you lay in the grave of your sin, rotten, corrupt. The voice of the minister called to you, but you did not hear. You were often bidden to come forth, but ye did not and could not come. But when the Lord said, " Lazarus, come forth," then Lazarus came forth; and when he said to you, " Live," then you lived also, and the spiritual life beat within you, with joy and peace through believing. This we ought never to forget, because, let us never fail to remember, that if our religion is a thing which sprang from ourselves, it is of the flesh, and must die. That which is born of the flesh in its best and most favourable moments, is flesh, and only that which is born of the Spirit is spirit. " Ye must be born again." If a man's religious life be only a refinement of his ordinary life, if it be only a high attainment of the natural existence, then is it not the spiritual life, and does not prepare him for the eternal life before the throne of God. No, we must have a supernatural spark of heavenly flame kindled within us. Just as nothing but the soul can quicken the body and make it live, so the Spirit alone can quicken the soul and make the soul live. We must have the third master-principle infused, or else we shall be but natural men, made after the image of the first Adam. We must have, I say, the new spirit, or else we shall not be like the second Adam, who was made a quickening spirit. Only of the Christian can we say that he is spirit, soul, and body; the ungodly man has only soul and body, and as to spiritual existence, he is as dead as the body would be if there were no soul. Now the implantation of this new principle, called the spirit, is a work of divine power. *Divine power!* what stupendous issues are grasped in that term, divine power! It was this which digged the deep foundations of the earth and sea Divine power, it is this which guides the marches of the stars of heaven! Divine power! it is this which holds up the pillars of the universe, and which one day shall shake them, and hurry all things back to their native nothingness. Yet the selfsame power which is required to create a world and to sustain it, is required to make a man a Christian, and unless that power be put forth, the spiritual life is not in any one of us.

You will perceive, dear friends, that the apostle Peter wished to see this divine life in a healthy and vigorous state, and therefore he prays that *grace and peace may be multiplied.* Divine power is the foundation of this life; grace is the food it feeds upon, and peace is the element in which it lives most healthily. Give a Christian much grace, and his spiritual life will be like the life of a man who is well clothed and nurtured; keep the spiritual life without abundant grace, and it becomes lean, faint, and ready to die; and though die it cannot, yet will it seem as though it gave up the ghost, unless fresh grace be bestowed. Peace, I say, is the element in which it flourishes most. Let a Christian be much disturbed in mind, let earthly cares get into his soul, let him have doubts and fears as to his eternal safety, let him lose a sense of reconciliation to God, let his adoption be but dimly before his eyes, and you will not see much of the divine life within him. But oh!

23

if God shall smile upon the life within you, and you get much grace from God, and your soul dwells much in the balmy air of heavenly peace, then shall you be strong to exercise yourself unto godliness, and your whole life shall adorn the doctrine of God your Saviour.

Observe, again, that in describing this life, he speaks of it as one which was conferred upon us by our being *called*. He says, " We were called unto glory and virtue." I find translators differ here. Many of them think the word should be " By "—" We are called by the glory and virtue of God "—that is, there is a manifestation of all the glorious attributes of God, and of all the efficacious virtue and energy of his power in the calling of every Christian. Simon Peter himself was at his fishing and in his boat, but Jesus said to him, " Follow me;" and at once he followed Christ. He says there was in that calling, the divine glory and virtue; and, doubtless, when you and I shall get to heaven, and see things as they are, we shall discover in our effectual calling of God to grace, a glory as great as in the creation of worlds, and a virtue as great as in the healing of the sick, when virtue went from the garments of a Saviour. Now, can we say to-day, that we have a life within us which is the result of divine power, and have we, upon searching ourselves, reason to believe, dear friends, that there is that within us which distinguishes us from other men, because we have been called out of mankind by the glory and energy of the divine power? I am afraid some of us must say "*Nay.*" Then the Lord in his mercy yet bring us into the number of his people. But if we can, however, tremblingly say " Yes, I trust there is something of the life in me;" then as Peter did so, do I wish for you that benediction, " Grace and peace be multiplied unto you through the knowledge of our Lord and Saviour Jesus Christ." O brethren, whatever men may say against the faith of God, there is nothing in the world which creates virtue like true faith. Wherever true faith enters, though it be into the heart of a harlot or of a thief, what a change it makes! See her there; she has polluted herself many times; she has gone far into sin. Mary has been a sinner; she hears the preaching of the Saviour; standing in the crowd she listens to him one day as he preaches concerning the prodigal, and how the loving father pressed him to his bosom; she comes to Jesus and she finds forgiveness. Is she a harlot any longer? Nay, there she is, washing his feet with her tears, and wiping them with the hairs of her head. The woman who was a sinner, hates her evil ways and loves her gracious Lord. We may say of her, " But she is washed, but she is sanctified, but she is saved." Take Saul of Tarsus. Foaming with blood, breathing out threatenings, he is going to Damascus to drag the saints of God to prison. On the road he is struck down; by divine mercy he is led to put his trust in Jesus. Is he a persecutor any longer? See that earnest apostle beaten with rods—shipwrecked—in labours more abundant than all the rest of them—counting not his life dear unto him, that he may win Christ and be found in him. Saul of Tarsus becomes a majestic proof of what the grace of God can do. See Zaccheus, the grasping publican, distributing his wealth, the Ephesians burning their magical books, the gaoler washing the apostle's stripes. Take the case of many now present. Let memory refresh itself this morning, with the recollection of the change which has been wrought in you. We have

24

nothing to boast of; God forbid that we should glory, save in the cross of Christ, but yet some of us are wonderful instances of renewing grace. We were unclean, our mouths could utter blasphemy; our temper was hot and terrible; our hands were unrighteous; we were altogether as an unclean thing, but how changed now! Again, I say, we boast of nothing which we now are, for by the grace of God we are what we are, yet the change is something to be wondered at. Has divine grace wrought this change in you? Be not weary with my reiteration of this question. Let me put it again to you till I get an answer; nay, till I force you to an answer: Have you this precious faith? Can you not answer the question? Then, have you not that divine life, that life which is given by divine calling? If you have the one, you have the other; and if you have not both, you have neither; for where there is the one, the other must come, and where the one has come, the other has been there.

II. I have thus fully but feebly brought the subject before you, allow me to remind you that another verse remains which handles the same topics. In the fourth verse, he deals with the privileges of faith, and also with the privileges of the spiritual life.

Notice the PRIVILEGE OF FAITH first. "Whereby are given unto us exceeding great and precious promises"—here is the faith, "That by these ye might be partakers of the divine nature, having escaped the corruption that is in the world through lust." Here is the life resulting from the faith. Now, the *privileges of faith* first. The privileges of faith are, that we have given to us "Exceeding great and precious promises." "Great and precious"—two words which do not often come together. Many things are great which are not precious, such as great rocks, which are of little value; on the other hand, many things are precious which are not great—such as diamonds and other jewels, which cannot be very great if they be very precious. But here we have promises which are so great, that they are not less than infinite, and so precious, that they are not less than divine. I shall not attempt to speak about their greatness or their preciousness, but just give a catalogue of them, and leave you to guess at both. We have some of them which are like birds in the hand—we have them already; other promises are like birds in the bush, only that they are just as valuable and as sure as those which are in the hand.

Note here, then, we have received by precious faith the promise and *pardon*. Hark thee, my soul, all thy sins are forgiven thee. He who hath faith in Christ hath no sin to curse him, his sins are washed away, they have ceased to be; they have been carried on the scape-goat's head into the wilderness; they are drowned in the Red Sea; they are blotted out; they are thrown behind God's back; they are cast into the depths of the sea. Here is a promise of perfect pardon. Is not this great and precious?—as great as your sins are; and if your sins demanded a costly ransom, this precious promise is as great as the demand.

Then comes the *righteousness* of Christ: you are not only pardoned, that is, washed and made clean, but you are dressed, robed in garments such as no man could ever weave. The vesture is divine. Jehovah himself has wrought out your righteousness for you; the holy life of Jesus the Son of God, has become your beauteous dress, and you are covered with it. Christian, is not this an exceeding great and precious promise? The law was great—this righteousness is as great as the law. The law asked a precious revenue from man, more than humanity could pay—the righteousness of Christ has paid it all. Is it not great and precious?

Then next comes *reconciliation.* You were strangers, but you are brought nigh by the blood of Christ. Once aliens, but now fellow-citizens with the saints and of the household of God. Is not this great and precious?

Then comes your *adoption.* "Beloved, now are we the sons of God, and it doth not yet appear what we shall be: but we know that, when he shall appear, we shall be like him; for we shall see him as he is." "And if children, then heirs, heirs of God, joint heirs with Jesus Christ, if so be we suffer with him that we may be glorified together." Oh, how glorious is this great and precious promise of adoption!

Then we have the promise of *providence:* "all things work together for good to them that love God, to them that are called according to his purpose." "Thy place of defence shall be the munitions of rocks." "Thy bread shall be given thee and thy waters shall be sure." "As thy days thy strength shall be." "Fear not, I am with thee ; be not dismayed, I am thy God." "When thou passest through the rivers, I will be with thee, the floods shall not overflow thee. When thou goest through the fire, thou shalt not be burned, neither shall the flame kindle upon thee." When I think of providence, the greatness of its daily gifts, and the preciousness of its hourly boons, I may well say, here is an exceeding great and precious promise.

Then you have the promise too, that you shall never taste of death but shall only sleep in Jesus. "Write, blessed are the dead which die in the Lord from henceforth. Yea, saith the Spirit, that they cease from their labours; and their works do follow them." Nor does the promise cease here, you have the promise of a *resurrection.* "For the trumpet shall sound, and the dead shall be raised incorruptible, and we shall be changed. For this corruptible must put on incorruption, and this mortal must put on immortality." Beloved, we know that if Christ rose from the dead, so also them who sleep in Jesus, will the Lord bring with him. Nor is this all, for we shall *reign with Jesus;* at his coming, we shall be glorified with him, we shall sit upon his throne, even as he has overcome and sits with his Father upon his throne. The harps of heaven, the streets of glory, the trees of paradise, the river of the water of life, the eternity of immaculate bliss—all these, God hath promised to them who love him. "Eye hath not seen, nor ear heard, the things which God hath prepared for them that love him, but he hath revealed them unto us by his Spirit;" and by our faith we have grasped them, and we have to-day "the substance of things hoped for, and the evidence of things not seen." Now, beloved, see how rich faith makes you!—what treasure!—what a costly regalia!—what gold mines!—what oceans of wealth!—what mountains of sparkling treasures has God conferred upon you by faith!

But we must not forget the *life,* and with that we close. The text says, he has given us this promise, "*that*"—"in order that." What then? What are all these treasures lavished for? For what these pearls? For what these jewels? For what, I say, these oceans of treasure? For what? Is the end worthy of the means? Surely God never giveth greater store than the thing which he would purchase will be worth. We may suppose, then, the end to be very great when such costly means have been given; and what is the end? Why, "that by these ye might be partakers of the divine nature, having escaped the corruption that is in the world through lust." O, my brethren, if you have these mercies to-day by faith, do see to it that the result is obtained. Be not content to be made rich in these great and precious promises, without answering God's design in your being thus enriched. That design, you perceive, is twofold; it is first that you may be partakers of the divine nature; and, secondly, that you may escape the corruption which is in the world.

To be a partaker of the divine nature is not, of course, to become God. That cannot be. The essence of Deity is not to be participated in by the creature. Between the creature and the Creator there must ever be a gulf fixed in respect of essence; but as the first man Adam was made in the image of God, so we, by the renewal of the Holy Spirit, are in a yet diviner sense made in the image of the Most High, and are partakers of the divine nature. We are, by grace, made like God. "God is love;" we become love—"He that loveth is born of God." God is truth; we become true, and we love that which is true, and we hate the darkness and the lie. God is good, it is his very name; he makes us good by his grace, so that we become the pure in heart who shall see God. Nay, I will say this, that we become partakers of the divine nature in even a higher sense than this—in fact, in any sense, anything short of our being absolutely divine. Do we not become members of the body of the divine person of Christ? And what sort of union is this—"members of his body, of his flesh, and of his bones?" The same blood which flows in the head flows in the hand, and the same life which quickens Christ, quickens his people; for, "Ye are dead, and your life is hid with Christ in God." Nay, as if this were not enough, we are married into Christ. He hath betrothed us unto himself in righteousness and in faithfulness; and as the spouse must, in the nature of things, be a partaker of the same nature as the husband, so Jesus Christ first became partaker of flesh and blood that they twain might be one flesh; and then he makes his Church partakers of the same spirit, that they twain may be one spirit; for he who is joined unto the Lord is one spirit. Oh, marvellous mystery! we look into it, but who shall understand it? One with Jesus, by eternal union one, married to him; so one with him that the branch is not more one with the vine than we are a part of the Lord, our Saviour, and our Redeemer. Rejoice in this, brethren, ye are made partakers of the divine nature, and all these promises are given to you in order that you may show this forth among the sons of men, that ye are like God, and not like ordinary men; that ye are different now from what flesh and blood would make you, having been made participators of the nature of God.

Then the other result which follows from it, was this, "Having escaped the corruption that is in the world through lust." Ah, beloved, it were ill that a man who is alive should dwell in corruption. "Why seek ye the living among the dead?" said the angel to Magdalene.

Should the living dwell among the dead? Should divine life be found amongst the corruptions of worldly lusts? The bride of Christ drunken! Frequenting the ale-house! A member of Christ's body found intoxicated in the streets, or lying, or blaspheming, or dishonest! God forbid. Shall I take the members of Christ, and make them members of a harlot? How can I drink the cup of the Lord, and drink the cup of Belial? How can it be possible that I can have life, and yet dwell in the black, dark, foul, filthy, pestiferous tomb of the world's lusts? Surely, brethren, from these open lusts and sins ye have escaped: have ye also escaped from the more secret and more delusive lime-twigs of the Satanic fowler? O, have ye come forth from the lust of pride? Have ye escaped from slothfulness? Have ye clean escaped from carnal security? Are we seeking day by day to live above worldliness, the love of the things of the world, and the ensnaring avarice which they nourish? Remember, it is for this that you have been enriched with the treasures of God. Do not, oh, I conjure you, do not, chosen of God and beloved by him, and so graciously enriched, do not suffer all this lavish treasure to be wasted upon you.

There is nothing which my heart desires more than to see you, the members of this Church, distinguished for holiness: it is the Christian's crown and glory. An unholy Church! it is of no use to the world, and of no esteem among men. Oh! it is an abomination, hell's laughter, heaven's abhorrence. And the larger the Church, the more influential, the worse nuisance does it become, when it becomes dead and unholy. The worst evils which have ever come upon the world, have been brought upon her by an unholy Church. Whence came the darkness of the dark ages? From the Church of Rome. And if we want to see the world again sitting in Egyptian darkness, bound with fetters of iron, we have only to give up the faith, and to renounce holiness of life, and we may drag the world down again to the limbo of superstition, and bind her fast in chains of ignorance and vice. O Christian, the vows of God are upon you. You are God's priest: act as such. You are God's king: reign over your lusts. You are God's chosen: do not associate with Belial. Heaven is your portion; live like a heavenly spirit, so shall you prove that you have the true faith; but except ye do this, your end shall be to lift up your eyes in hell, and find yourself mistaken when it will be too late to seek or find a remedy. The Lord give us the faith and the life, for Jesus' sake. Amen.

3. Life by Faith

THE apostle quotes from the Old Testament, from the second chapter of Habakkuk, at the fourth verse, and thus confirms one inspired statement by another. Even the just are not justified by their own righteousness, but live by faith; it follows then most conclusively, that no man is justified by the law in the sight of God. If the best of men find no justification coming to them through their personal virtues, but stand accepted only by faith, how much more such imperfect beings, such frequent sinners as ourselves?

Men who are saved by faith become just. The operation of faith upon the human heart is to produce love, and through love, obedience, and obedience to the divine law is but another name for morality, or, what is the diviner form of it, holiness; and yet, wherever this holiness exists, we may make sure that the holiness is not the cause of spiritual life and safety, but faith is still the wellspring of all. You saw, a few weeks ago, the hawthorn covered with a delicious luxuriance of snow-white flowers, loading the air with fragrance; now, no one among the admiring gazers supposed that those sweet May blossoms caused the hawthorn to live. After awhile you noticed the horse chestnut adorned with its enchanting pyramids of flowers, but none among you foolishly supposed that the horse chestnut was sustained and created by its bloom: you rightly conceived these forms of beauty to be the products of life and not the cause of it. You have here, in nature's emblems, the true doctrine of the inner life. Holiness is the flower of the new nature. It is inexpressibly lovely and infinitely desirable; nay, it must be produced in its season, or we may justly doubt the genuineness of a man's profession; but the fair graces of holiness do not save, or give spiritual life, or maintain it—these are rills from the fount, and not the fountain itself. The most athletic man in the world does not live by being athletic, but is athletic because he lives and has been trained to a perfection of animal vigour. The most enterprising merchant holds his personal property not on account of his character or deservings, but because of his civil rights as a citizen. A man may cultivate his land up to the highest point of production, but his right to his land does not depend upon the mode of culture, but upon his title deeds. So the Christian man should aim after the highest degree of spiritual culture and of heavenly perfection, and yet his salvation, as to its justness and security, depends not on his attainments, but rests upon his faith in a crucified Redeemer, as it is written in the text, "The just shall live by faith." Faith is the fruitful root, the inward channel of sap, the great life-grace in every branch of the vine. In considering the text, this morning, we shall use it perhaps somewhat apart from the connection in which it stands, and yet not apart from the mind of the Spirit, nor apart from the intention of the apostle, if not here yet in other places.

I. In the first place, IN THE PUREST SPIRITUAL SENSE IT IS TRUE THAT THE JUST SHALL LIVE BY FAITH.

It is through faith that a man becomes just, for otherwise, before the law of God he is convicted of being unjust : being justified by faith, he is enrolled among the just ones. It is through faith that he is at first quickened and breathes the air of heaven, for naturally he was dead in trespasses and sins. Faith is the first sure sign of the spiritual life within the human breast. He repents of sin and looks to Jesus, because he believes the testimony of God's Son ; he believes that testimony because he has received a new life. He depends upon the atoning blood of Jesus because his heart has received the power to do so by the Holy Ghost's gift of spiritual life. Ever afterwards you shall judge of the vigour of the man's inner life by the state of his faith : if his faith groweth exceedingly, then his life also is increasing in power ; if his faith diminishes, then depend upon it the vital spark burns low. Let faith ebb out, and the life-floods are ebbing too ; let faith roll in with a mighty sweep, in a floodtide of full assurance, then the secret life-floods within the man are rising and filling the man with sacred energy. Were it possible for faith to die, the spirit-life must die too ; and it is very much because faith is imperishable that the new life is incorruptible. You shall find men only live before God as they believe in God and rest in the merit of his dear Son ; and in proportion, also, as they do this you shall find they live in closer fellowship with heaven. Great saints must be great believers : Little-faith never can be a matured saint.

Observe that this truth proves itself in all the characteristics of spiritual life. The *nobility* of the inner life—who has not noticed it ? A man whose life is hid with Christ in God is one of the aristocrats of this world. He who knows nothing of the inner life is but little above a mere animal, and is by no means comparable to the sons of God, to whom is given the royal priesthood, the saintly inheritance. In proportion as the spiritual life is developed, the man grows in dignity, becoming more like the Prince of glory, yet the very root and source of the dignity of the holy life lies in faith. Take an instance. The life of Abraham is remarkable for its placid nobility. The man appears at no time to be disturbed. Surrounded by robber bands, he dwells in his tent as quietly as in a walled city. Abraham walked with God, and does not seem to have quickened or slackened his pace ; he maintained a serene, obedient walk, never hastening through fear, nor loitering through sloth ; he kept sweet company with his God—and what a noble life was his ! The father of the faithful was second to no character in history ; he was a kingly man, yea, a conqueror of kings, and greater than they. How calm is his usual life ! Lot following his carnal prudence is robbed in Sodom, and at last loses all : Abraham following his faith, abides as a pilgrim, and is safe. Lot is carried away captive out of a city, but Abraham remains securely in a tent, because he cast himself on God. When does Abraham fail ? When does that mighty eagle suddenly drop as with wounded wing? It is when the arrow of unbelief has pierced him: he begins to tremble for Sarah his wife; she is fair, perhaps the Philistine king will take her from him; then in an unbelieving moment, he says, "She is my sister." Ah! Abraham, where is thy nobility now? The man who so calmly and confidently walked with God while he believed, degrades himself to utter the thing that is not, and so falls to the common level of falsehood. Even so will you, so shall each of us, be strong or weak, noble or fallen according to our faith. Walking confidently with God, and leaning upon the everlasting arm, you shall be as a celestial prince surrounded by ministering spirits, your life shall be happy and holy, and withal glorious before the Lord; but the moment you distrust your God, you will be tempted to follow degrading methods of evil policy, and you will pierce yourself through with many sorrows.

As the dignity, so *the energy* of the spiritual life depends upon faith. Spiritual life when in sound health is exceedingly energetic; it can do all things. Take the apostles, as an instance, and see how over sea and land, under persecutions and sufferings, they nevertheless pressed forward in the Holy War, and declared Christ throughout all nations. Wherever the spiritual life fairly pervades man, it is a force which cannot be bound, fettered, or kept under; it is a holy fury, a sacred fire in the bones. Rules, and customs, and proprieties, it snaps as fire snaps bonds of tow. But its energy depends under God the Holy Ghost, entirely upon the existence and power of faith. Let a man be troubled with doubts as to the religion which he has espoused, or concerning his own interest in the privileges which that religion bestows, and you will soon find that all the energy of his spiritual life is gone—he will have little more than a name to live, practically he will be powerless. Take Abraham again. Abraham finds that certain kings from the east have pounced upon the cities of the plain. He cares very little for Sodom or Gomorrha, but among the prisoners his nephew Lot has been carried away. Now, he has a great affection for his kinsman, and resolves to do his duty and rescue him. Without stopping to enquire whether his little band was sufficient, he relies entirely upon the Lord his God, and with his servants and neighbours hastens after the spoilers, nothing doubting, but expecting aid from the Most High God. That day did Jehovah, who raised up the righteous man from the east, give his enemies to his sword, and as driven stubble to his bow, and the patriarch returned from the slaughter of the kings laden with the spoil. He could not but fight while he believed. It was impossible for him to sit still and yet believe in God; but if he had not believed, then had he said, "The matter must go by default; it is a sorrowful misfortune, but my nephew Lot must bear it: perhaps God's providence will interpose for him." Faith believes in providence, but she is full of activity, and her activity excited by reliance upon providence leads like wheel within a wheel to the fulfilment of the providential decree. My brethren, it is necessary for us to believe much in God, or we shall do but little for him. Believe that God is with you, and you will have an insatiable ambition to extend the Saviour's kingdom. Believe in the power of the truth, and in the power of the Holy Ghost who goes with the truth, and you will not be content with the paltry schemes of modern Christendom, but you will glow and burn with a seraph's ardour, longing and desiring even to do more than you can do, and practically carrying out with your utmost ability what your heart desireth for the glory of the Lord.

Further, it is quite certain that all *the joy* of the spiritual life depends upon faith. You all know that the moment your faith ceases to hang simply upon Jesus, or even if it suffers a little check, your joy evaporates. Joy is a welcome angel, but it will not tarry where faith does not entertain it. Spiritual joy is a bird of paradise, which will build its nest only among the boughs of faith. Faith must pipe, or joy will not dance. Unbelieving Jacob finds his days few and evil, but believing Abraham dies an old man, and full of years. If you would anoint your head and wash your face, and put away the ashes and the sackcloth, you must trust more firmly in the faithfulness of the Lord your God. Doubts and fears never could strike so much as a spark with which to light the smallest candle to cheer a Christian; but simple trust in Jesus makes the sun to rise in his strength with healing beneath his wings, even upon those that sit in the valley of the shadow of death. In proportion as you lean on Christ, in that proportion shall life's burden grow light, heaven's joys grow real, and your whole being more elevated.

I might thus continue to mention each point in the secret life, but I rather choose to proceed in order to observe only, that all our *growth* in the spiritual life depends upon our faith. True life must grow in its season. You can tell the difference between two stakes, which are driven into the ground: the one may happen to have life in it, and if so, before long it sprouts, while the dead one is unchanged. So with the Christian. If he be living he will grow. He must make advances. It is not possible for the Christian to sit still and remain in the same state month after month; but if he is to increase in spiritual riches, he must of necessity exert a constant and increasing faith in the Lord Jesus Christ. Peter cannot walk the waters except he believes; doubting does not help him, but it sinks him. I fear me that some of my brethren and sisters try to grow in spiritual life by adopting methods which are not of faith. Some think that they will set themselves rules of self-denial or extra devotion—these plans are lawful, but they are not in themselves effective; for vows may be observed mechanically, and rules obeyed formally, and yet the heart may be drifting away yet further from the Lord; yea, these vows and rules may be a means of deluding us into the vain belief that all is well, whereas we are nearing to spiritual shipwreck. I have found in my own spiritual life, that the more rules I lay down for myself, the more sins I commit. The habit of regular morning and evening prayer is one which is indispensable to a believer's life, but the prescribing of the length of prayer, and the constrained remembrance of so many persons and subjects, may gender unto bondage, and strangle prayer rather than assist it. To say I will humble myself at such a time, and rejoice at such another season, is nearly as much an affectation as when the preacher wrote in the margin of his sermon, "cry here," "smile here." Why, if the man preached his sermon rightly, he would be sure to cry in the right place, and to smile at a suitable moment; and when the spiritual life is sound, it produces prayer at the right time, and humiliation of soul and sacred joy spring forth spontaneously, apart from rules and vows. The kind of religion which makes itself to order by the almanack, and turns out its emotions like bricks from a machine, weeping on Good Friday, and rejoicing two days afterwards, measuring its motions by the moon, is too artificial to be worthy of your imitation. The liberty of the spiritual life is a grand thing, and where that liberty is maintained constantly, and the energy is kept up, you will need much faith, for the fading of faith will be the withering of devotion, liberty will degenerate into license, and the energy of your life will drivel into confidence in yourself. Let who will bind himself with rules and regulations in order to advance himself in grace, be it ours, like Abraham, to believe God, and it shall be counted us for righteousness, and like Paul, to run the race which is set before us, looking unto Jesus. Faith enriches the soil of the heart. Faith fills our treasuries with the choicest gold, and loads our tables with the daintiest food for our souls. By faith we shall do valiantly, stopping lions' mouths, and quenching violent flames; but faith in Jesus, the Saviour, faith in the heavenly Father, faith in the Holy Spirit, this we must have, or we perish like foam upon the waters.

As the other side of all this, let me notice that some Christians appear to try to live by experience. If they feel happy to-day, they say they are saved, but if they feel unhappy to-morrow, they conclude that they are lost. If they feel at one moment a deep and profound calm overspreading their spirits, then are they greatly elevated; but if the winds blow and the waves beat high, then they suppose that they are none of the Lord's people. Ah, miserable state of suspense! To live by feeling is a dying life; you know not where you are, nor what you are, if your feelings are to be the barometer of your spiritual condition. Beloved, a simple faith in Christ will enable you to remain calm even when your feelings are the reverse of happy, to remain confident when your emotions are far from ecstatic. If, indeed, we be saved by Jesus Christ, then the foundation of our salvation does not lie within us, but in that crucified Man who now reigns in glory. When he changes, ah, then what changes must occur to us! But since he is the same yesterday, to-day, and for ever, why need we be so soon removed from our steadfastness? Believe in Jesus, dear heart, when thou canst not find a spark of grace within thyself; cast thyself as a sinner into the Saviour's arms when thou canst not think a good thought, nor uplift a good desire; when thy soul feels like a barren wilderness that yields not so much as one green blade of hope, or joy, or love, still look up to the great Husbandman, who can turn the desert into a garden. Have confident faith in Jesus at all times, for if thou believest in him thou art saved, and canst not be condemned. However good or bad thy state, this shall not affect the question; thou believest, therefore thou shalt be saved. Give up living from hand to mouth in that poor miserable way of frames and feelings, and wait thou only upon the Lord, from whom cometh thy salvation.

Many professors are even worse: they try to live by experiments. I am afraid a great many among Dissenters are of that kind. They must have a revival meeting once a week at least; if they do not get a grand display quite so often, they begin to fall dreadfully back, and crave an exciting meeting, as drunkards long for spirits. It is a poor spiritual life which hangs on eloquent sermons, and such like stimulants. These may be good things and comforting things: be thankful for them, but

33

I pray you do not let your spiritual life depend upon them. It is very much as though a man should, according to scriptural language, feed on the wind and snuff up the east wind; for your faith is not to stand in the wisdom of man, nor in the excellency of human speech, nor in the earnestness of your fellow Christians, but in your simple faith in him who is, and was, and is to come, who is the Saviour of sinners. A genuine faith in Christ will enable you to live happily even if you be denied the means of grace ; will make you rejoice on board ship, keep Sabbath on a sick bed, and make your dwelling-house a temple even if you find a log-hut in the far West, or a shanty in the bush of Australia. Only have faith, and thou needest not look to these excitements any more than the mountains look to the summer's sun for their stability.

Shall I need further to say, by way of caution, that I am afraid many professors live *anyhow?* I know not how otherwise to describe it. They have not enough caution to look at their inward experience, they have not enough vigour to care about excitement, but they live a kind of listless, dreamy, comatose life. I mean *some of you.* You believe that you were saved years ago. You united yourselves to a Christian church, and were baptised, and you conclude that all is right. You have written your conversion in your spiritual trade-books as a good asset, you consider it as a very clear thing. I am afraid it is rather doubtful, still you think it sure. Since that time you have kept up the habit of prayer, you have been honest, you have subscribed to church funds, have done your duty outwardly as a Christian, but there has been very little vitality in your godliness; it has been surface work, skin-deep consistency. You have not been grievously exercised about sin, you have not been bowed under the weight of inward corruption; neither have you been, on the other hand, exhilarated by a sense of divine love and a delightful recognition of your interest in it. You have gone on dreamily, as I have heard of soldiers marching when they were asleep. O for a thunderbolt to wake you, for this is dangerous living ! Of all modes of living, if you be a Christian, this is one of the most perilous; and if you be not a Christian, it is one of the most seductive ; for while the outward sinner may be got at by the preaching of the gospel, you are almost beyond the reach of gospel ministry, because you will not allow that warnings are meant for you. You wrap yourselves up and say, "It is well with me," while you are really naked, and poor. and miserable in the sight of God. Oh, if you could but get back to live by faith !

II. Secondly, "the just shall live by faith"—this means that FAITH IS OPERATIVE IN OUR DAILY LIFE.

It is operative in many ways, but three observations will suffice. Faith is *the great sustaining energy* with the just man under all his trials, difficulties, sufferings, or labours. It is a notion with some that true religion is meant to be kept shut up in churches and chapels, as a proper thing for Sundays, which ought to be attended to, since a man is not respectable if he does not take a pew somewhere, even if he does not need sit in it, or, sitting in it, pays no more attention to the word preached than to a ballad singer in the street ; there is a decent show of religion which people, as a rule, must keep up, or they cannot be received into polite society; but the idea of bringing religion down to the breakfast table, introducing it to the drawing-room, taking it into the kitchen, keeping it on hand in the shop, in the workshop, or the corn exchange, carrying it out to sea in your vessel—this is thought by some to be sheer fanaticism; and yet if there is anything taught by the revelation of the Lord Jesus Christ, it is just this: that religion is a matter of common, every-day life; and no man understands the Christian religion at all unless he has fully accepted it as not a thing for Sundays, and for certain places and certain times, but for all places and all times, and all conditions and all forms of life. An active, operative faith is by the Holy Spirit implanted in the Christian, and it is sent to him on purpose to sustain him under trial. I shall put this to some of you as a test by which you may try whether you have obtained the faith of God's elect. You have lost a large sum of money: well, are you distracted and bewildered? Do you almost lose your senses? Do you murmur against God? Then I ask you what are you better than the man who has no religion at all? Are you not an unbeliever? for if you believed that all things work together for your good, would you be so rebellious? Yet that is God's own declaration. Now is the time when your faith in God should enable you to say, " The Lord gave, and the Lord hath taken away; blessed be the name of the Lord." What do you more than others unless you can thus speak with submission and resignation—ay, even with alacrity? Where is your new nature if you cannot say, "It is the Lord, let him do as seemeth him good "? By this shall you test whether you have faith or no. Or it may be you have lost a darling child, and that loss has cut you to the very quick. You are scarcely able to reconcile yourself at present to it, yet I trust you do not so repine as to accuse your God of cruelty, but I trust your faith helps you to say, " I shall go to him, though he shall not return to me; I would not have it other than my heavenly Father has determined." Here will be a crucible for your faith. Those two instances may serve as specimens. In all positions of life a real faith is to the believer like the hair of Samson, in which his great strength lieth. It is his Moses' rod dividing seas of difficulty, his Elijah's chariot in which he mounts above the earth. So, too, in difficult labours, for instance, in labours for Christ's cause, a man who feels it his duty to do good in his neighbourhood, yet may say, " I do not know what I can do, I am afraid to commence so great a matter, for I feel so unfit, and so feeble." My dear friend, if it is your duty to do it, your not being able to do it cannot excuse you, because you have only to go and tell your heavenly Father of your weakness, and ask for strength, and he will give it liberally. Some of us who can now speak with ease were once very diffident in public. Those preachers who are now most useful, were poor stammerers before their gifts were developed; and those who are our best teachers and most successful soul-winners, were not always so; but they had faith, and they pressed forward, and God helped them. Now, if your religion is not worth an old song, you will not persevere in holy work; but if it is real and true, you will press forward through all difficulties, feeling it to be an essential of your very existence, that you should promote the Redeemer's cause. I would quite as soon not be, as live to be a useless thing. Better far to fatten the fields with one's corpse, than to lie rotting above ground in idleness. To be a soldier in Immanuel's ranks, and never fight, never carry a burden, nor uphold a banner, nor hurl a dart—ay, better that the dogs should eat my worthless carrion, than that such should be the case. Feeling this, then, you will press forward with the little power you have, and new power will come upon you, and so you will prove that your faith is sincere, because it comes to your support in the ordinary work of Christian life. Under all difficulties and labours, then, the just shall live by faith.

Furthermore, faith in ordinary life *has an effect upon the dispensations of divine providence.* It is a riddle which we cannot explain how everything is eternally fixed by divine purpose, and yet the prayer of faith moves the arm of God. Though the enigma cannot be explained, the fact is not to be denied. My brethren and sisters, I may be thought fanatical, but it is my firm belief that in ordinary matters, such as the obtaining of your living, the education of your children, the ruling of your household, you are to depend upon God as much as in the grand matter of the salvation of your soul. The hairs of your head are all numbered : go to God then about your trifles. Not a sparrow falls to the ground without your Father : cast upon the Lord your minor trials. Never think that anything is too little for your heavenly Father's love to think upon. He who rides upon the whirlwind, walks in the garden at evening in the cool breath of the zephyr; he who shakes the avalanche from its Alp, also makes the sere leaf to twinkle as it falls from the aspen; he whose eternal power directs the spheres in their everlasting marches, guides each grain of dust which is blown from the summer's threshing-floor. Confide in him for the little as well as for the great, and you shall not find him fail you. Is he God of the hills only, and not the God of the valleys ?

"Do we expect miracles then?" saith one. No, but we expect the same results as are compassed by miracles. I have sometimes thought that for God to interpose by a miracle to accomplish a purpose is a somewhat clumsy method, if I may be allowed such a word, but for him to accomplish the very same thing without interfering with the wheels of his providence, seems to me the more thoroughly God-like method. If I were hungry to-day, and God had promised to feed me, it would be as much a fulfilment of his promise if my friend here brought my food unexpectedly, as if the ravens brought it; and the bringing of it by ordinary means would all the better prove that God was there, not interrupting the machinery of providence, but making it to educe the end which he designed. God will not turn stones into bread for you, but perhaps he will give you stones to break, and you will thus earn your bread. God may not rain manna out of heaven, and yet every shower of rain falling upon your garden brings you bread. It will be the better for you to earn your food than to have it brought by ravens, or better that Christian charity should make you its care than that an inexhaustible barrel and cruse should be placed in your cupboard. Anyhow, your bread shall be given you, and your water shall be sure. My witness is, and I speak it for the honour of God, that God is a good provider. I have been cast upon the providence of God ever since I left my father's house, and in all cases he has been my Shepherd, and I have known no lack. My first income as a Christian minister was small enough in all conscience, never exceeding forty pounds, yet I was as rich then as I am now, for I had enough; and I had no more cares, nay, not half as many then as I have now; and when I breathed my prayer to God then, as I do now, for all things temporal and spiritual, I found him ready to answer me at every pinch—and pinches I have had full many. Many a pecuniary trial since then have I had in connection with the college work, which depends for funds upon the Lord's moving his people to liberality: my faith has been often tried, but God has always been faithful, and sent supplies in hours of need. If any should tell me that prayer to God was a mere piece of excitement, and that the idea of God's answering human cries is absurd, I should laugh the statement to scorn, for my experience is not that of one or two singular instances, but that of hundreds of cases, in which the Lord's inter-position, for the necessities of his work, has been as manifest as if he had rent the clouds, and thrust forth his own naked arm and bounteous hand to supply the needs of his servant. This, my testimony, is but the echo of the witness of the Lord's people everywhere. When they look back they will tell you that God is good to Israel, and that when they have walked by faith they have never found that God has failed them. The Red Sea of trouble has been divided, the waters have stood upright as a heap, and the depths have been congealed in the heart of the sea; as for their doubts and their difficulties, like the Egyptians, the depths have covered them, there has not been one of them left; and standing on the further shore to look back upon the past, the redeemed of the Lord have shouted aloud, "Sing unto the Lord, for he hath triumphed gloriously," for faith has conquered all their difficulties, and brought supplies for all their needs. Do not let me be mis-understood, however. Faith is never to be regarded as a premium for idleness. If I sit down and fold my arms, and say, "The Lord will provide;" he will most likely provide me a summons to the County Court, and a place in the parish workhouse. God has never given any promise to idle people that he will provide for them, and therefore they have no kind of right to believe that he will. To trust in God to make up for our laziness, is not faith, but wicked pre-sumption. Neither does the power of faith afford ground for fanaticism. I have no right to say, "I should like to have so-and-so, and I will ask for it, and shall have it." God has never promised to give to us everything which our whimsies may select. If we really want any good thing, we may plead the promise, "No good thing will I uphold from them that walk uprightly," but we must never dream that God will pander to our fooleries. The God of wisdom will not be art and part with our mere whims. Nor is faith to be a substitute for prudence and economy. I have known some who have, to a great degree, abstained from energetic action, because they feared to interfere with the Lord. This fear never perplexes me. My faith never leads me to believe that God will do for me what I can do for myself. I do not believe that the Lord works needlessly. Up to the highest pitch that my own prudence, and strength, and judgment can carry me I am to go, depending upon divine guidance; then I stop, for I can go no further: and I plead with my Father thus—"Now, Lord, the promise reaches further than this, it is thy business to make up the deficiency." There I pause, and God is as good as his word. But if I stop short when I might advance, how dare I ask the Lord to pander to my sloth? I believe, in Christian work, we ought for God to exert ourselves to the utmost, both in the giving of our substance and in the collecting help from our fellow Christians; and come in faith and prayer to the Lord for help. Faith is operative in the land of the unseen, not in the seen. Faith is to come to your help where creature-power fails you. Up to the point at which you can work you must work, and with God's blessing upon it, your work will not hinder your faith, but be an exhibition and display of it.

Thus with a simple faith in God, not fanatical, not idle, but going on in the path of prudence, desiring to glorify God, you shall find that all difficulties will vanish, and your doubts and fears shall fly away. Do understand that even faith itself will be no guarantee against trials and against poverty, for it is good for God's people to be tried, and there are some of them who would not glorify God if they were not poor. Therefore, you are not to suppose that you have no faith because you are in need, neither are you to expect that in answer to prayer God will necessarily keep you in easy circumstances. If it be best for you that you should not be poor, he will keep you from it; but if it be better that you should be, he will sustain you in it. Resignation should walk hand-in-hand with faith, and they each will minister to the other's beauty.

III. Lastly, THIS IS ALSO TRUE IN THE HISTORY OF THE CHRISTIAN CHURCH AS A WHOLE.

The Christian church lives by faith. She lives by faith in opposition to *speculation*. Every now and then a fit of speculative philosophy seizes the church, and then her vitality withers. In the days of the schoolmen, just before Luther's time, good men were fighting and squabbling from morning to night, gathered like so many carrion crows around the dead body of Aristotle, fighting about nobody knows what. It is said that they held sage discussions upon how many angels could poise themselves upon the point of a needle! While such foolish and unlearned questions as these were being raised, the poor people in the Christian church were starved, and the church lost all its energy, sinners were not converted, fundamental truth was despised. Then came Luther and the notable revival. In more modern days, in the period after Doddridge and Watts, amongst Dissenters, the habit of philosophising upon the Trinity was common. Brethren tried to be very exact and precise, as exact and precise as the Athanasian creed, while others combated their dogmatism, and the result was that a large proportion of the Dissenting churches fell asleep practically, degenerated doctrinally, and Socinianism threatened to eat out the very life of evangelical Dissent. Speculation is not the life of the Christian church, but faith, a reception of the Bible truth in its sublimity and authority; an obedient belief in revelation, not because we understand all its teachings, but because, not understanding, we nevertheless receive the Lord's word upon the *ipse dixit* of the Most High. Whenever the church is simple-minded enough to require no outworks to her faith, to care very little about evidences, internal or external, but just to fight the battle on the ground of divine authority, saying, " This is of God, and at your peril reject it," she has been " fair as the sun, clear as the moon, and terrible as an army with banners: " let her begin to split hairs, try to move away objections, and spend all her time upon her outworks, and then her glory departs.

In the next place, faith is the life of the church in opposition to *retiring despondency*. In our own churches, it used to be the habit for our friends to be very well content if they built a chapel in the lowest part of a town, down two courts, three alleys, and a turning; and as to attendants, the members appeared to be particularly anxious to avoid anything like the excitement of a crowd. They were a most retiring people as a rule, but as to coming out into the forefront to set their city on a hill, and make their light shine by evangelising the masses, that was a forgotten business. At the present hour, from other quarters you constantly hear expressions defiled with the most dastardly timidity, denoting the most shameful cowardice. For instance, lately we have heard that "The church is in danger!" "The church is in danger!" Christians with their Bibles, and all the truths in the Bibles; with their ministers and all their earnestness, with the Holy Spirit, with God's promises, with the foundations against which the gates of hell shall not prevail, and yet in danger! Really, such remarks and such fears are quite unworthy of the manhood of those who believe in the divinity of the Christian faith. No church can make progress till she believes enough in her God to be sure that in him she is strong. While she imagines that she is weak she is weak, fear paralyses her, dread kills her energies; but when she believes in the divine strength with which she is encein-tered as with a golden girdle, then she marches on with certainty of triumph. May we as a church always believe that resting upon the strength of God nothing can hurt us : I defy the House of Lords, the House of Commons, the Pope, the Turk, and all the nations in all the world and all the devils in hell, to put this church in danger. I do not know anything that they could take away from us, for I know of nothing which they have given us. If they had endowed and established us, they could take away what they gave, but as they have not given us a thread to a shoe-latchet, they can do whatever they please, and we shall not even call a church meeting to consider it. Yet here are other churches, with lord bishops, and deans, and pre-bends, and I know not what beside, which are horribly shaken because an arm of flesh is failing them. The pay of their preachers will by-and-by, by a gradual process, be withdrawn, and they tremble for the ark of the Lord! Shame on your little minds, to be thus afraid! Surely, you have lost confidence in truth and in God, or you would not fear because of the talents of gold which will be justly withheld from you. Remember that truth allied with earthly power has often been de-feated by error, but truth alone has always defeated error, even when that error has had physical might upon its side. Let truth have her fair chance and stand alone. She is most strong when least hampered with human strength, and most sure to be victorious when she hath no might but that which dwells in herself, or comes from her God.

In the next place, the Christian church lives by faith, that is, faith in opposition to a *squeamishness* which I see springing up nowadays as to the selection of instruments. Let me be understood. I hear it is said, "Why allow these men to preach in the street? Is it not a pity that illiterate persons should preach at all? Some of them are very un-grammatical, and really what they say at the very best is very so-so. Is it not better that none should go out but the best trained men?" Then, for missions, it is said, the very best picked men only should be sent forth. As to young men, full of zeal, not having had experience, and not having learned all the classics, and being well up in mathematics it is of no use thinking to send them. Many a church indeed thinks that all her officers ought to be rich, all her ministers learned, all her agents Masters of Arts at least, if not Doctors of Divinity. This was not so in the olden time. Thus it was not when the church of God grew mightily, for of old the church of God had faith—in what? Why, faith in weakness, faith in the things that were not. Did not she believe that "Not many noble, not many wise men after the flesh, not many mighty, are called; but God hath chosen the foolish things of the world to confound the wise; and God hath chosen the weak things of the world to confound the things which are mighty; and base things of the world, and things which are despised." It is very memorable that in the catacombs of Rome, among those remarkable inscriptions which are now preserved with so much care as the memorials of the departed saints, it is rare to find an inscription which is all of it spelt correctly, proving that the persons who wrote them, who were no doubt the very pick of the Christian flock, could neither write nor spell correctly; and yet these were the men that turned the world upside down. When Wesley began his career, our churches were nearly dead with the disease called "proprieties," but Mr. Wesley employed men, some of whom were quite unlettered, to go about to preach, and by those men this nation was revived. To this day, our Primitive Methodist friends are doing a great and noble work, for which God be thanked, because they use almost every man they have, and they use the men till they become fit to be used, trained and tutored by practice. In this church, I thank God, I have always encouraged every brother and sister to do all they can, and I do still urge all so to do. I trust there is not a young man here who can say that I ever held him back in desiring to serve his Master. If I have, I am sure I am very sorry for it. Oh! do all of you all that you can; for this church at any rate has faith in you all, that though you make a thousand blunders, yet it is better to have the gospel preached blunderingly than not at all; and while three millions and more in London are perishing for lack of knowledge, it is better that you spoil the Queen's English and make ever such mistakes, than that you should not preach Jesus Christ. God will not be angry with you for all your ignorance, if you be not ignorant of the one thing needful.

So, brethren, it comes to this, that we must not as a Christian church calculate our resources, nor take out our note books and count up how much we have to rely upon. The exchequer of the church is the liberality of God; the power of the church is the omnipotence of Jehovah; the persuasions of the church are the irresistible influences of the Holy Ghost; the destiny of the church is an ultimate conquest over all the sons of men. Advance then, every one of you to the fray, for you advance also to conquest! Rely upon him who has said, "Lo, I am with you alway, even unto the end of the world!" and you shall find that as the just you shall live by faith; while if you sit down and waste your time, or turn your backs and retire from the battle, you shall be written among the cravens whose memorial is in the dust; but if you stand fast and are immovable, "always abounding in the work of the Lord," your record shall be on high, and your portion shall be at the right hand of the Father, where Christ sitteth, and where you shall also shall sit for ever and ever. God bless these words for his name's sake. Amen.

4. Justification by Faith — Illustrated by Abram's Righteousness

"And he believed in the Lord; and he counted it to him for righteousness."—
Genesis xv. 6.

You will remember that last Lord's-day morning we spoke upon the calling of Abram, and the faith by which he was enabled to enter upon that separated life at the bidding of the Most High. We shall to-day pass from the consideration of his calling to that of his justification, that being most remarkably next in order in his history, as it is in point of theology in the New Testament; for, "whom he called, them he also justified."

Referring to the chapter before us for a preface to our subject, note that after Abram's calling his faith proved to be of the most practical kind. Being called to separate himself from his kindred and from his country, he did not therefore become a recluse, a man of ascetic habits, or a sentimentalist, unfit for the battles of ordinary life—no; but in the noblest style of true manliness he showed himself able to endure the household trouble and the public trial which awaited him. Lot's herdsmen quarrelled with the servants of Abram, and Abram with great disinterestedness gave his younger and far inferior relative the choice of pasturage, and gave up the well-watered plain of Sodom, which was the best of the land. A little while after, the grand old man who trusted in his God showed that he could play the soldier, and fight right gloriously against terrible odds. He gathered together his own household servants, and accepted the help of his neighbours, and pursued the conquering hosts of the allied kings, and smote them with as heavy a hand as if from his youth up he had been a military man. Brethren, this every-day life faith is the faith of God's elect. There are persons who imagine saving faith to be a barren conviction of the truth of certain abstract propositions, leading only to a quiet contemplation upon certain delightful topics, or a separating ourselves from all sympathy with our fellow creatures; but it is not so. Faith, restricted merely to religious exercise, is not Christian faith, it must show itself in everything. A merely religious faith may

41

be the choice of men whose heads are softer than their hearts, fitter for cloisters than markets; but the manly faith which God would have us cultivate, is a grand practical principle adapted for every day in the week, helping us to rule our household in the fear of God, and to enter upon life's rough conflicts in the warehouse, the farm, or the exchange. I mention this at the commencement of this discourse, because as this is the faith which came of Abram's calling, so also does it shine in his justification, and is, indeed, that which God counted unto him for righteousness.

Yet the first verse shows us that even such a believer as Abram needed comfort. The Lord said to him, "Fear not." Why did Abram fear? Partly because of the reaction which is always caused by excitement when it is over. He had fought boldly and conquered gloriously, and now he fears. Cowards tremble before the fight, and brave men after the victory. Elias slew the priests of Baal without fear, but after all was over, his spirit sank and he fled from the face of Jezebel. Abram's fear also originated in an overwhelming awe in the presence of God. The word of Jehovah came to him with power, and he felt that same prostration of spirit which made the beloved John fall at the feet of his Lord in the Isle of Patmos, and made Daniel feel, on banks of Hiddekel that there was no strength in him. "Fear not," said the Lord to the patriarch. His spirit was too deeply bowed. God would uplift his beloved servant into the power of exercising sacred familiarity. Ah, brethren, this is a blessed fear—let us cultivate it; for until it shall be cast out by perfect love, which is better still, we may be content to let this good thing rule our hearts. Should not a man, conscious of great infirmities, sink low in his own esteem in proportion as he is honoured with communion with the glorious Lord?

When he was comforted, Abram received on open declaration of his justification. I take it, beloved friends, that our text does not intend to teach us that Abram was not justified before this time. Faith always justifies whenever it exists, and as soon as it is exercised; its result follows immediately, and is not an aftergrowth needing months of delay. The moment a man truly trusts his God he is justified. Yet many are justified who do not know their happy condition; to whom as yet the blessing of justification has not been opened up in its excellency and abundance of privilege. There may be some of you here to-day who have been called by grace from darkness into marvellous light; you have been led to look to Jesus, and you believe you have received pardon of your sin, and yet, for want of knowledge, you know little of the sweet meaning of such words as these, "Accepted in the Beloved," "Perfect in Christ Jesus," "Complete in him." You are doubtless justified, though you scarcely understand what justification means; and you are accepted, though you have not realised your acceptance; and you are complete in Jesus Christ, though you have to-day a far deeper sense of your personal incompleteness than of the all-sufficiency of Jesus. A man may be entitled to property though he cannot read the title-deeds, or has not as yet heard of their existence; the law recognises right and fact, not our apprehension thereof. But there will come a time, beloved, when you who are called will clearly realise your justification, and will rejoice in it; it shall be intelligently understood by you, and shall become a matter of transporting delight, lifting you to a higher platform of experience, and enabling you to walk with a firmer step, sing with a merrier voice, and triumph with an enlarged heart.

I intend now, as God may help me, first to note *the means of Abram's justification;* then, secondly, *the object of the faith which justified him;* and then, thirdly, *the attendants of his justification.*

I. First, brethren, HOW WAS ABRAM JUSTIFIED?

We see in the text the great truth, which Paul so clearly brings out in the fourth chapter of his epistle to the Romans, that Abram was *not justified by his works.* Many had been the good works of Abram. It was a good work to leave his country and his father's house at God's bidding; it was a good work to separate from Lot in so noble a spirit; it was a good work to follow after the robber-kings with undaunted courage; it was a grand work to refuse to take the spoils of Sodom, but to lift up his hand to God that he would not take from a thread even to a shoe latchet; it was a holy work to give to Melchisedec tithes of all that he possessed, and to worship the Most High God; yet none of these are mentioned in the text, nor is there a hint given of any other sacred duties as the ground or cause, or part cause of his justification before God. No, it is said, "He believed in the Lord, and he counted it to him for righteousness." Surely, brethren, if Abram, after years of holy living, is not justified by his works, but is accepted before God on account of his faith, much more must this be the case with the ungodly sinner who, having lived in unrighteousness, yet believeth on Jesus and is saved. If there be salvation for the dying thief, and others like him, it cannot be of debt, but of grace, seeing they have no good works. If Abram, when full of good works, is not justified by them, but by his faith, how much more we, being full of imperfections, must come unto the throne of the heavenly grace and ask that we may be justified by faith which is in Christ Jesus, and saved by the free mercy of God!

Further, this justification came to Abram *not by obedience to the ceremonial law* any more than by conformity to the moral law. As the apostle has so plainly pointed out to us, Abram was justified before he was circumcised. The initiatory step into the outward and visible covenant, so far as it was ceremonial, had not yet been taken, and yet the man was perfectly justified. All that follows after cannot contribute to a thing which is already perfect. Abram, being already justified, cannot owe that justification to his subsequent circumcision—this is clear enough; and so, beloved, at this moment, if you and I are to be justified, these two things are certain: it cannot be by the works of the moral law; it cannot be by obedience to any ceremonial law, be it what it may—whether the sacred ritual given to Aaron, or the superstitious ritual which claims to have been ordained by gradual tradition in the Christian church. If we be indeed the children of faithful Abraham, and are to be justified in Abraham's way, it cannot be by submission to rites or ceremonies of any kind. Hearken to this carefully, ye who would be justified before God: baptism is in itself an excellent ordinance, but it cannot justify nor help to justify us; confirmation is a mere figment of men, and could not, even if commanded by God, assist in justification; and the

Lord's-supper, albeit that it is a divine institution, cannot in any respect whatsoever minister to your acceptance or to your righteousness before God. Abram had no ceremonial in which to rest; he was righteous through his faith, and righteous only through his faith; and so must you and I be if we are ever to stand as righteous before God at all. Faith in Abram's case was the alone and unsupported cause of his being accounted righteous, for note, although in other cases Abram's faith produced works, and although in every case where faith is genuine it produces good works, yet the particular instance of faith recorded in this chapter was unattended by any works. For God brought him forth under the star-lit heavens, and bade him look up. "So shall thy seed be," said the sacred voice. Abram did what? Believed the promise —that was all. It was before he had offered sacrifice, before he had said a holy word or performed a single action of any kind that the word immediately and instanter went forth, "He believed in the Lord; and he counted it to him for righteousness." Always distinguish between the truth, that living faith always produces works; and the lie, that faith and works co-operate to justify the soul. We are made righteous only by an act of faith in the work of Jesus Christ. That faith, if true, always produces holiness of life, but our being righteous before God is not because of our holiness in life in any degree or respect, but simply because of our faith in the divine promise. Thus saith the inspired apostle: "His faith was imputed to him for righteousness. Now it was not written for his sake alone, that it was imputed to him; but for us also, to whom it shall be imputed, if we believe on him that raised up Jesus our Lord from the dead; who was delivered for our offences, and was raised again for our justification."

I would have you note that *the faith which justified Abram was still an imperfect faith,* although it perfectly justified him. It was imperfect beforehand, for he had prevaricated as to his wife, and bidden Sarai, "Say thou art my sister." It was imperfect after it had justified him, for in the next chapter we find him taking Hagar, his wife's hand-maid, in order to effect the divine purpose, and so showing a want of confidence in the working of the Lord. It is a blessing for you and for me that we do not need perfect faith to save us. "If ye have faith as a grain of mustard seed, ye shall say unto this mountain, Remove hence to yonder place; and it shall remove." If thou hast but the faith of a little child, it shall save thee. Though thy faith be not always at the same pitch as the patriarch's when he staggered not at the promise through unbelief, yet if it be simple and true, if it confide alone in the promise of God—it is an unhappy thing that it is no stronger, and thou oughtst daily to pray, "Lord, increase my faith"— but still it shall justify thee through Christ Jesus. A trembling hand may grasp the cup which bears a healing draught to the lip—the weakness of the hand shall not lessen the power of the medicine.

So far, then, all is clear, Abram was not justified by works, nor by ceremonies, nor partly by works, and partly by faith, nor by the perfection of his faith—he is counted righteous simply because of his faith in the divine promise.

I must confess that, looking more closely into it, this text is too deep for me. and therefore I decline, at this present moment, to enter into the controversy which rages around it; but one thing is clear to me that if faith be, as we are told, counted to us for righteousness, it is not because faith in itself has merit which may make it a fitting substitute for a perfect obedience to the law of God, nor can it be viewed as a substitute for such obedience. For, brethren, all good acts are a duty: to trust God is our duty, and he that hath believed to his utmost hath done no more than it was his duty to have done. He who should believe without imperfection, if this were possible, would even then have only given to God a part of the obedience due; and if he should have failed, in love, or reverence, or aught beside, his faith, as a virtue and a work, could not stand him in any stead. In fact, according to the great principle of the New Testament, even faith, as a work, does not justify the soul. We are not saved by works at all or in any sense, but alone by grace, and the way in which faith saves us is not by itself as a work, but in some other way directly opposite thereto.

Faith cannot be its own righteousness, for it is of the very nature of faith to look out of self to Christ. If any man should say, "My faith is my righteousness," then it is evident that he is confiding in his faith; but this is just the thing of all others which it would be unsafe to do, for we must look altogether away from ourselves to Christ alone, or we have no true faith at all. Faith must look to the atonement and work of Jesus, or else she is not the faith of Scripture. Therefore to say that faith in and of itself becomes our righteousness, is, it seems to me, to tear out the very bowels of the gospel, and to deny the faith which has been once delivered to the saints. Paul declares, contrary to certain sectaries who rail against imputed righteousness—that we are justified and made righteous by the righteousness of Christ; on this he is plain and positive. He tells us (Romans v. 19) that, "as by one man's disobedience many were made sinners, so by the obedience of one shall many be made righteous." The Old Testament verse before us as a text this morning, gives us but as it were the outward aspect of justification; it is brought to us by faith, and the fact that a man has faith entitles him to be set down as a righteous man; in this sense God accounts faith to a man as righteousness, but the underlying and secret truth which the Old Testament does not so clearly give us is found in the New Testament declaration, that we are accepted in the Beloved, and justified because of the obedience of Christ. Faith justifies, but not in and by itself, but because it grasps the obedience of Christ. "As by the offence of one judgment came upon all men to condemnation ; even so *by the righteousness of one* the free gift came upon all men unto justification of life." To the same effect is that verse in the second epistle general of Peter (first chapter, first verse), which runs in our version as follows: "Simon Peter, a servant and an apostle of Jesus Christ, to them that have obtained like precious faith with us through the righteousness of God and our Saviour Jesus Christ." Now, everybody who is at all familiar with the original knows that the correct translation is "through the righteousness of our God and Saviour Jesus Christ." The righteousness which belongs to the Christian is the righteousness of our God and Saviour, who is "made of God unto us righteousness." Hence the beauty of the old prophetic title of the Messiah, "The Lord our Righteousness." I do not wish to

45

enter into controversy as to imputed righteousness this morning, we may discuss that doctrine another time; but we feel confident that this text cannot mean that faith in itself, as a grace or a virtue, becomes the righteousness of any man. The fact is, that faith is counted to us for righteousness because she has Christ in her hand; she comes to God resting upon what Christ has done, depending alone upon the propitiation which God has set forth; and God, therefore, writes down every believing man as being a righteous man, not because of what he is in himself, but for what he is in Christ. He may have a thousand sins, yet shall he be righteous if he have faith. He may painfully transgress like Samson, he may be as much in the dark as Jephtha, he may fall as David, he may slip like Noah; but, for all that, if he have a true and living faith, he is written down among the justified, and God accepteth him. While there be some who gloat over the faults of believers, God spieth out the pure gem of faith gleaming on their breast; he takes them for what they want to be, for what they are in heart, for what they would be if they could; and covering their sins with the atoning blood, and adorning their persons with the righteousness of the Beloved, he accepts them, seeing he beholds in them the faith which is the mark of the righteous man wherever it may be.

II. Let us pass on to consider THE PROMISE UPON WHICH HIS FAITH RELIED when Abram was justified.

Abram's faith, like ours, rested upon *a promise received direct from God.* "This shall not be thine heir; but he that shall come forth out of thine own bowels shall be thine heir. And he brought him forth abroad, and said, Look now toward heaven, and tell the stars, if thou be able to number them: and he said unto him, So shall thy seed be." Had this promise been spoken by any other, it would have been a subject of ridicule to the patriarch; but, taking it as from the lip of God, he accepts it, and relies upon it. Now, brethren, if you and I have true faith we accept the promise, "He that believeth and is baptised, shall be saved" as being altogether divine. If such a declaration were made to us by the priests of Rome, or by any human being on his own authority, we could not think it true; but, inasmuch as it comes to us written in the sacred word as having been spoken by Jesus Christ himself, we lean upon it as not the word of man, but the word of God. Beloved, it may be a very simple remark to make, but after all it is needful, that we must be careful that our faith in the truth is fixed upon the fact that God has declared it to be true, and not upon the oratory or persuasion of any of our most honoured ministers or most respected acquaintances. If your faith standeth in the wisdom of man, it is probably a faith in man; it is only that faith which believes the promise because God spake it which is real faith in God. Note that and try your faith thereby.

In the next place, Abram's faith was *faith in a promise concerning the seed.* It was told him before that he should have a seed in whom all the nations of the earth should be blessed. He recognised in this the selfsame promise which was made to Eve at the gates of Paradise, " I will put enmity between thee and the woman, between thy seed and her seed." "Abraham saw my day," says our Lord, " he saw it and was glad." In this promise Abram saw the one seed, as saith the apostle in Galatians iii. 16, " He saith not, And to seeds, as of many ; but as of one, And to thy seed, which is Christ." He saw Christ by the eye of faith, and then he saw the multitude that should believe in him, the seed of the father of the faithful. The faith which justifies the soul concerns itself about Christ and not concerning mere abstract truths. If your faith simply believeth this dogma and that, it saveth you not ; but when your faith believes that God was in Christ reconciling the world unto himself, not imputing unto them their trespasses ; when your faith turns to God in human flesh and rests in him with its entire confidence, then it justifies you, for it is the faith of Abram. Dear hearer, have you such a faith as this ? Is it faith in the promise of God ? Is it faith that deals with Christ and looks alone to him ?

Abram had faith in *a promise which it seemed impossible could ever be fulfilled.* A child was to be born of his own loins, but he was nearly a hundred years old, and Sarai also was said to be barren years before. His own body was now dead as it were, and Sarai, so far as child-bearing was concerned, was equally so. The birth of a son could not happen unless the laws of nature were reversed ; but he considered not these things, he put them all aside ; he saw death written on the creature, but he accepted the power of life in the Creator, and he believed without hesitation. Now, beloved, the faith that justifies us must be of the same kind. It seems impossible that I should ever be saved ; I cannot save myself ; I see absolute death written upon the best hopes that spring of my holiest resolutions ; "In me, that is, in my flesh, there dwelleth no good thing ; " I can do nothing ; I am slain under the law ; I am corrupt through my natural depravity ; but yet for all this I believe that through the life of Jesus I shall live, and inherit the promised blessing. It is small faith to believe that God will save you when graces flourish in your heart, and evidences of salvation abound, but it is a grand faith to trust in Jesus in the teeth of all your sins, and notwithstanding the accusations of conscience. To believe in him that justifieth not merely the godly but *the ungodly.* (Romans iv. 5.) To believe not in the Saviour of saints, but in the Saviour of sinners ; and to believe that if any man sin, we have an advocate with the Father, Jesus Christ, the righteous ; this is precious, and is counted unto us for righteousness.

This justifying faith was faith which dealt with *a wonderful promise,*

47

vast and sublime. I imagine the patriarch standing beneath the starry sky, looking up to those innumerable orbs. He cannot count them. To his outward eye, long accustomed in the land of the Chaldees to midnight observation, the stars appeared more numerous than they would to an ordinary observer. He looked and looked again with elevated gaze, and the voice said, " So shall thy seed be." Now he did not say, ' Lord, if I may be the father of a clan, the progenitor of a tribe, I shall be well content; but it is not credible that countless hosts can ever come of my barren body." No, he believed the promise; he believed it just as it stood. I do not hear him saying, "It is too good to be true." No; God hath said it—and nothing is too good for God to do. The greater the grace of the promise, the more likely it is to have come from him, for good and perfect gifts come from the Father of Lights. Beloved, does your faith take the promise as it stands in its vastness, in its height, and depth, and length, and breadth? Canst thou believe that thou, a sinner, art nevertheless a child, a son, an heir, an heir of God, joint-heir with Christ Jesus? Canst thou believe that heaven is thine, with all its ecstacies of joy, eternity with its infinity of bliss, God with all his attributes of glory? Oh! this is the faith that justifies, far-reaching, wide-grasping faith, that diminishes not the word of promise, but accepts it as it stands. May we have more and more of this large-handed faith!

Once more, Abram showed faith in *the promise as made to himself.* Out of his own bowels a seed should come, and it was in *him* and in his seed that the whole world should be blessed. I can believe all the promises in regard to other people. I find faith in regard to my dear friend to be a very easy matter, but oh! when it comes to close grips, and to laying hold for yourself, here is the difficulty. I could see my friend in ten troubles, and believe that the Lord would not forsake him. I could read a saintly biography, and finding that the Lord never failed his servant when he went through fire and through water, I do not wonder at it; but when it comes to one's own self, the wonder begins. Our heart cries, " Whence is this to me? What am I, and what my father's house, that such mercy should be mine? *I* washed in blood and made whiter than snow to-day! Is it so? *Can* it be? *I* made righteous, through my faith in Jesus Christ, perfectly righteous! O can it be? What! For me the everlasting love of God, streaming from its perennial fountain? For me the protection of a special providence in this life, and the provision of a prepared heaven in the life to come? For me a harp, a crown, a palm branch, a throne! For me the bliss of for ever beholding the face of Jesus, and being made like to him, and reigning with him! It seems impossible. And yet this is the faith that we must have, the faith which lays on Christ Jesus for itself, saying with the apostle, " He loved me, and gave himself for me." This is the faith which justifies; let us seek more and more of it, and God shall have glory through it.

III. In the third place, let us notice THE ATTENDANTS OF ABRAM'S JUSTIFICATION.

With your Bibles open, kindly observe that after it is written his faith was counted to him for righteousness, it is recorded that the Lord said to him, " I am Jehovah that brought thee out of Ur of the Chaldees, to give thee this land to inherit it." When the soul is graciously enabled to perceive its complete justification by faith, then *it more distinctly discerns its calling.* Now, the believer perceives his privileged separation and discerns why he was convinced of sin, why he was led away from self-righteousness and the pleasures of this world, to live the life of faith; now he sees his high calling and the prize of it, and from the one blessing of justification he argues the blessedness of all the inheritance to which he is called. The more clear a man is about his justification the more will he prize his calling, and the more earnestly will he seek to make it sure by perfecting his separation from the world and his conformity to his Lord. Am I a justified man? Then will I not go back to that bondage in which I once was held. Am I now accepted of God through faith? Then will I live no longer by sight, as I once did as a carnal man, when I understood not the power of trusting in the unseen God. One Christian grace helps another, and one act of divine grace casts a refulgence upon another. Calling gleams with double glory side by side with the twin star of justification.

Justifying faith receives more vividly the promises. " I have brought thee," said the Lord, " into this land to inherit it." He was reminded again of the promise God made him years before. Beloved, no man reads the promises of God with such delight and with such a clear understanding as the man who is justified by faith in Christ Jesus. "For now," saith he, "this promise is mine, and made to me. I have the pledge of its fulfilment in the fact that I walk in the favour of God. I am no longer obnoxious to his wrath; none can lay anything to my charge, for I am absolved through Jesus Christ; and, therefore, if when I was a sinner he justified me, much more, being justified, will he keep his promise to me. If when I was a rebel condemned, he nevertheless in his eternal mercy called me and brought me into this state of acceptance, much more will he preserve me from all my enemies, and give me the heritage which he has promised by his covenant of grace. A clear view of justification helps you much in grasping the promise, therefore seek it earnestly for your soul's comfort.

Abram, after being justified by faith, was *led more distinctly to behold the power of sacrifice.* By God's command he killed three bullocks, three goats, three sheep, with turtle doves and pigeons, being all the creatures ordained for sacrifice. The patriarch's hands are stained with blood;

he handles the butcher's knife, he divides the beasts, he kills the birds he places them in an order revealed to him by God's Spirit at the time; there they are. Abram learns that there is no meeting with God except through sacrifice. God has shut every door except that over which the blood is sprinkled. All acceptable approaches to God must be through an atoning sacrifice, and Abram sees this. While the promise is still in his ears, while the ink is yet wet in the pen of the Holy Spirit, writing him down as justified, he must see a sacrifice, and see it, too, in emblems which comprehend all the revelation of sacrifice made to Aaron. So, brethren, it is a blessed thing when your faith justifies you, if it helps you to obtain more complete and vivid views of the atoning sacrifice of Jesus Christ. The purest and most bracing air for faith to breathe is on Calvary. I do not wonder that your faith grows weak when you fail to consider well the tremendous sacrifice which Jesus made for his people. Turn to the annals of the Redeemer's sufferings given us in the Evangelists; bow yourself in prayer before the Lamb of God, blush to think you should have forgotten his death, which is the centre of all history; contemplate the wondrous transaction of substitution once again, and you will find your faith revived. It is not the study of theology, it is not reading books upon points of controversy, it is not searching into mysterious prophecy which will bless your soul, it is looking to Jesus crucified. That is the essential nutriment of the life of faith, and mind that you keep to it. As a man already justified, Abram looked at the sacrifice, all day long and till the sun went down, chasing away the birds of prey as you must drive off all disturbing thoughts. So must you also study the Lord Jesus, and view him in all his characters and offices, be not satisfied except you grow in grace and in the knowledge of your Lord and Saviour Jesus Christ.

Perhaps even more important was the next lesson which Abram had to learn. He was led to behold *the covenant.* I suppose that these pieces of the bullock, the lamb, the ram, and the goat, were so placed that Abram stood in the midst with a part on this side and a part on that. So he stood as a worshipper all through the day, and towards nightfall, when a horror of great darkness came over him, he fell into a deep sleep. Who would not feel a horror passing over him as he sees the great sacrifice for sin, and sees himself involved therein? There in the midst of the sacrifice he saw, moving with solemn motion, a smoking furnace and a burning lamp, answering to the pillar of cloud and fire, which manifested the presence in later days to Israel in the wilderness. In these emblems the Lord passed between the pieces of the sacrifice to meet his servant, and enter into covenant with him. This has always been the most solemn of all modes of covenanting; and has even been adopted in heathen nations on occasions of unusual solemnity. The sacrifice is divided and the covenanting parties meet between the divided pieces. The profane interpretation was, that they imprecated upon each other the curse that if they broke the covenant they might be cut in pieces as these beasts had been; but this is not the interpretation which our hearts delight in. It is this. It is only in the midst of the sacrifice that God can enter into a covenant relationship with sinful man. God cometh in his glory like a flame of fire, but subdued and tempered to us as with a cloud of smoke in the person of Jesus Christ; and he comes through the bloody sacrifice which has been offered once for all through Jesus Christ on the tree. Man meets with God in the midst of the sacrifice of Christ. Now, beloved, you who are justified, try this morning to reach this privilege which particularly belongs to you at this juncture of your spiritual history. Know and understand that God is in covenant bonds with you. He has made a covenant of grace with you which never can be broken : the sure mercies of David are your portion. After this sort does that covenant run, " A new heart also will I give them, and a right spirit will I put within them. They shall be my people, and I will be their God." That covenant is made with you over the slaughtered body of the Son of God. God and you cross hands over him who sweat, as it were, great drops of blood falling to the ground. The Lord accepts us, and we enter with him into sacred league and amity, over the victim whose wounds and death ratify the compact. Can God forget a covenant with such sanctions? Can such a federal bond so solemnly sealed be ever broken? Impossible. Man is sometimes faithful to his oath, but God is always so; and when that oath is confirmed for the strengthening of our faith by the blood of the Only-begotten, to doubt is treason and blasphemy. God help us, being justified, to have faith in the covenant which is sealed and ratified with blood.

Immediately after, God made to Abram (and here the analogy still holds) *a discovery*, that all the blessing that was promised, though it was surely his, would not come without an interval of trouble. " Thy seed shall be a stranger in a land that is not theirs, and shall serve them; and they shall afflict them four hundred years." When a man is first of all brought to Christ he often is so ignorant as to think, " Now my troubles are all over; I have come to Christ and I am saved : from this day forward I shall have nothing to do but to sing the praises of God." Alas! a conflict remains. We must know of a surety that the battle now begins. How often does it happen that the Lord, in order to educate his child for future trouble, makes the occasion when his justification is most clear to him the season of informing him that he may expect to meet with trouble! I was struck with that fact when I was reading for my own comfort the other night the fifth chapter of Romans; it runs thus—" Therefore being justified by faith, we have peace with God through our Lord Jesus Christ: by whom also we have access by faith into this grace wherein we stand, and rejoice in hope of the glory of God." See how softly it flows, a justification sheds the oil of joy upon the believer's head. But what is the next verse—" and not only so, but we glory in tribulation also: knowing that tribulation worketh patience," and so on. Justification ensures tribulation. Oh! yes, the covenant is yours; you shall possess the goodly land and Lebanon, but, like all the seed of Abraham, you must go down into Egypt and groan, being burdened. All the saints must smart before they sing; they must carry the cross before they wear the crown. You are a justified man, but you are not freed from trouble. Your sins were laid on Christ, but you still have Christ's cross to carry. The Lord has exempted you from the curse, but he has not exempted you from the chastisement. Learn that you enter on the children's discipline on the very day in which you enter upon their accepted condition.

To close the whole, the Lord gave to Abram *an assurance of ultimate success.* He would bring his seed into the promised land, and the people who had oppressed them he would judge. So let it come as a sweet revelation to every believing man this morning, that at the end he shall triumph, and those evils which now oppress him shall be cast beneath his feet. The Lord shall bruise Satan under our feet shortly. We may be slaves in Egypt for awhile, but we shall come up out of it with great abundance of true riches, better than silver or gold. We shall be prospered by our tribulations, and enriched by our trials. Therefore, let us be of good cheer. If sin be pardoned, we may well bear affliction. " Strike, Lord," said Luther, " now my sins are gone; strike as hard as thou wilt if transgression be covered." These light afflictions which are but for a moment, are not worthy to be compared with the glory which shall be revealed in us. Let us make it the first point of our care to be justified with Abraham's seed, and then whether we sojourn in Egypt or enjoy the peace of Canaan, it little matters: we are all safe if we are only justified by faith which is in Christ Jesus.

Dear friends, this last word, and I send you home. Have you believed in God? Have you trusted Christ? O that you would do so to-day! To believe that God speaks truth ought not to be hard; and if we were not very wicked this would never need to be urged upon us, we should do it naturally. To believe that Christ is able to save us seems to me to be easy enough, and it would be if our hearts were not so hard. Believe thy God, man, and think it no little thing to do so. May the Holy Ghost lead thee to a true trust. This is the work of God, that ye believe on Jesus Christ, whom he hath sent. Believe that the Son of God can save, and confide thyself alone in him, and he will save thee. He asks nothing but faith, and even this he gives thee ; and if thou hast it, all thy doubts and sins, thy trials and troubles put together, shall not shut thee out of heaven. God shall fulfil his promise, and surely bring thee in to possess the land which floweth with milk and honey.

5. Faith and Regeneration

"Whosoever believeth that Jesus is the Christ is born of God: and every one that loveth him that begat loveth him also that is begotten of him."—1 John v. 1.

FOR the preacher of the gospel to make full proof of his ministry will be a task requiring much divine teaching. Besides much care in the manner and spirit, he will need guidance as to his matter. One point of difficulty will be to preach the whole truth in fair proportion, never exaggerating one doctrine, never enforcing one point, at the expense of another, never keeping back any part, nor yet allowing it undue prominence. For practical result much will depend upon an equal balance, and a right dividing of the word. In one case this matter assumes immense importance because it affects vital truths, and may lead to very serious results unless rightly attended to; I refer to the elementary facts involved in the work of Christ for us, and the operations of the Holy Spirit in us. Justification by faith is a matter about which there must be no obscurity much less equivocation; and at the same time we must distinctly and determinately insist upon it that regeneration is necessary to every soul that shall enter heaven. "Ye must be born again" is as much a truth as that clear gospel statement, "He that believeth and is baptised shall be saved." It is to be feared that some zealous brethren have preached the doctrine of justification by faith not only so boldly and so plainly, but also so baldly and so out of all connection with other truth, that they have led men into presumptuous confidences, and have appeared to lend their countenance to a species of Antinomianism very much to be dreaded. From a dead, fruitless, inoperative faith we may earnestly pray, "Good Lord, deliver us," yet may we be unconsciously fostering it. Moreover, to stand up and cry, "Believe, believe, believe," without explaining what is to be believed, to lay the whole stress of salvation upon faith without explaining what salvation is, and showing that it means deliverance from the power as well as from the guilt of sin, may seem to a fervent revivalist to be the proper thing for the occasion, but those who have watched the result of such teaching have had grave cause to question whether as much hurt may not be done by it as

53

good. On the other hand, it is our sincere conviction that there is equal danger in the other extreme. We are most certain that a man must be made a new creature in Christ Jesus, or he is not saved ; but some have seen so clearly the importance of this truth that they are for ever and always dwelling upon the great change of conversion, its fruits, and its consequences, and they hardly appear to remember the glad tidings that whosoever believeth on Christ Jesus hath everlasting life. Such teachers are apt to set up so high a standard of experience, and to be so exacting as to the marks and signs of a true born child of God, that they greatly discourage sincere seekers, and fall into a species of legality from which we may again say, " Good Lord, deliver us." Never let us fail most plainly to testify to the undoubted truth that true faith in Jesus Christ saves the soul, for if we do not we shall hold in legal bondage many who ought long ago to have enjoyed peace, and to have entered into the liberty of the children of God.

It may not be easy to keep these two things in their proper position, but we must aim at it if we would be wise builders. John did so in his teaching. If you turn to the third chapter of his gospel it is very significant that while he records at length our Saviour's exposition of the new birth to Nicodemus, yet in that very same chapter he gives us what is perhaps the plainest piece of gospel in all the Scriptures : " And as Moses lifted up the serpent in the wilderness, even so must the Son of man be lifted up : that whosoever believeth in him should not perish, but have eternal life." So, too, in the chapter before us he insists upon a man's being born of God ; he brings that up again and again, but evermore does he ascribe wondrous efficacy to faith ; he mentions faith as the index of our being born again, faith as overcoming the world, faith as possessing the inward witness, faith as having eternal life—indeed, he seems as if he could not heap honour enough upon believing, while at the same time he insists upon the grave importance of the inward experience connected with the new birth.

Now, if such a difficulty occurs to the preacher, we need not wonder that it also arises with the hearer, and causes him much questioning. We have known many who, by hearing continually the most precious doctrine that belief in Christ Jesus is saving, have forgotten other truths, and have concluded that they were saved when they were not, have fancied they believed when as yet they were total strangers to the experience which always attends true faith. They have imagined faith to be the same thing as a presumptuous confidence of safety in Christ, not grounded upon the divine word when rightly understood, nor proved by any facts in their own souls. Whenever self-examination has been proposed to them they have avoided it as an assault upon their assurance, and when they have been urged to try themselves by gospel tests, they have defended their false peace by the notion that to raise a question about their certain salvation would be unbelief. Thus, I fear, the conceit of supposed faith in Christ has placed them in an almost hopeless position, since the warnings and admonitions of the gospel have been set aside by their fatal persuasion that it is needless to attend to them, and only necessary to cling tenaciously to the belief that all has been done long ago for us by Christ Jesus, and that godly fear and careful walking are superfluities, if not actually an offence against the gospel. On the other hand, we have known others who have received the doctrine of justification by faith as a part of their creed, and yet have not accepted it as a practical fact that the believer is saved. They so much feel that they must be renewed in the spirit of their minds, that they are always looking within themselves for evidences, and are the subjects of perpetual doubts. Their natural and frequent song is—

> "'Tis a point I long to know,
> Oft it causes anxious thought;
> Do I love the Lord, or no?
> Am I his, or am I not?"

These are a class of people to be much more pitied than condemned. Though I would be the very last to spread unbelief, I would be the very first to inculcate holy anxiety. It is one thing for a person to be careful to know that he is really in Christ, and quite another thing for him to doubt the promises of Christ, supposing that they are really made to him. There is a tendency in some hearts to look too much within, and spend more time in studying their outward evidences and their inward feelings, than in learning the fulness, freeness, and all-sufficiency of the grace of God in Christ Jesus. They too much obscure the grand evangelical truth that the believer's acceptance with God is not in himself, but in Christ Jesus, that we are cleansed through the blood of Jesus, that we are clothed in the righteousness of Jesus, and are, in a word, "accepted in the Beloved." I earnestly long that these two doctrines may be well balanced in your souls. Only the Holy Spirit can teach you this. This is a narrow path which the eagle's eye has not seen, and the lion's whelp has not trodden. He whom the Holy Ghost shall instruct will not give way to presumption and despise the Spirit's work within, neither will he forget that salvation is of the Lord Jesus Christ, "who of God is made unto us wisdom, and righteousness, and sanctification, and redemption." The text appears to me to blend these two truths in a very delightful harmony, and we will try to speak of them, God helping us.

"He that believeth that Jesus is the Christ is born of God." We shall consider this morning, first of all, *the believing which is here intended;* and then, secondly, *how it is a sure proof of regeneration;* and then, thirdly, dwelling for awhile upon the closing part of the verse we shall *show how it becomes an argument for Christian love:* "Every one that loveth him that begat loveth him also that is begotten of him."

I. WHAT IS THE BELIEVING INTENDED IN THE TEXT? We are persuaded, first of all, that *the believing here intended is that which our Lord and his apostles exhorted men to exercise,* and to which the promise of salvation is always appended in the word of God; as for instance that faith which Peter inculcated when he said to Cornelius, "To him give all the prophets witness, that through his name whosoever believeth in him shall receive remission of sins;" and which our Lord commanded when he came into Galilee, saying to men, "Repent ye, and believe the gospel" (Mark i. 15). Certain persons have been obliged to admit that the apostles commanded, and exhorted, and besought men to believe, but they tell us that the kind of believing which the apostles bade men exercise was not a saving faith. Now, God forbid we should ever in our zeal to defend a favourite position, be driven to an assertion so monstrous. Can we imagine for a moment apostles with burning zeal and ardour, inspired by the Spirit of God within them, going about the world exhorting men to exercise a faith which after all would not save them? To what purpose did they run on so fruitless an errand, so tantalising to human need, so barren of results? When our Lord bade his disciples go into all the world and preach the gospel to every creature, and added, "he that believeth and is baptised shall be saved," the faith which was to be preached was evidently none other than a saving faith, and it is frivolous to say otherwise. I must confess that I felt shocked the other day to read in a certain sermon the remark that the words of Paul to the jailor "were spoken in a conversation held at midnight under peculiar circumstances, and the evangelist who wrote them was not present at the interview." Why, had it been at high noon, and had the whole world been present, the apostle could have given no fitter answer to the question, "What must I do to be saved?" than the one he did give, "Believe in the Lord Jesus Christ, and thou shalt be saved." It is, I repeat, a mere frivolity or worse, to say that the faith enjoined by the apostles was a mere human faith which does not save, and that there is no certainty that such faith saves the soul. That cause must be desperate which calls for such a defence.

Furthermore, *the faith here intended is the duty of all men.* Read the text again : "Whosoever believeth that Jesus is the Christ is born of God." It can never be less than man's duty to believe the truth ; that Jesus is the Christ is the truth, and it is the duty of every man to believe it. I understand here by "believing," confidence in Christ, and it is surely the duty of men to confide in that which is worthy of confidence, and that Jesus Christ is worthy of the confidence of all men is certain, it is therefore the duty of men to confide in him.

Inasmuch as the gospel command, "Believe in the Lord Jesus Christ and thou shalt be saved," is addressed by divine authority to every creature, it is the duty of every man so to do. What saith John : "This is his commandment, That we should believe on the name of his Son Jesus Christ," and our Lord himself assures us, "He that believeth on him is not condemned: but he that believeth not is condemned already, because he hath not believed in the name of the only-begotten Son of God." I know there are some who will deny this, and deny it upon the ground that man has not the spiritual ability to believe in Jesus, to which I reply that it is altogether an error to imagine that the measure of the sinner's moral ability is the measure of his duty. There are many things which men ought to do which they have now lost the moral and spiritual, though not the physical, power to do. A man ought to be chaste, but if he has been so long immoral that he cannot restrain his passions, he is not thereby free from the obligation. It is the duty of a debtor to pay his debts, but if he has been such a spendthrift that he has brought himself into hopeless poverty, he is not exonerated from his debts thereby. Every man ought to believe that which is true, but if his mind has become so depraved that he loves a lie and will not receive the truth, is he thereby excused? If the law of God is to be lowered according to the moral condition of sinners, you would have a law graduated upon a sliding-scale to suit the degrees of human sinfulness ; in fact, the worst man would then be under the least law, and become consequently the least guilty. God's requirements would be a variable quantity, and, in truth, we should be under no rule at all. The command of Christ stands good however bad men may be, and when he commands all men everywhere to repent, they are bound to repent, whether their sinfulness renders it impossible for them to be willing to do so or not. In every case it is man's duty to do what God bids him.

At the same time, *this faith, wherever it exists, is in every case, without exception, the gift of God and the work of the Holy Spirit.* Never yet did a man believe in Jesus with the faith here intended, except the Holy Spirit led him to do so. He has wrought all our works in us, and our faith too. Faith is too celestial a grace to spring up in human nature till it is renewed: faith is in every believer " the gift of God." You will say to me, "Are these two things consistent?" I reply, "Certainly, for they are both true." " How consistent ? " say you. " How inconsistent ?" say I, and you shall have as much difficulty to prove them inconsistent as I to prove them consistent. Experience makes them consistent, if theory does not. Men are convinced by the Holy Spirit of sin—" of sin," saith Christ, " because they believe not on me ; " here is one of the truths ; but the selfsame hearts are taught by the same Spirit that faith is of the operation of God. (Col. ii. 12.) Brethren, be willing to see both sides of the shield of truth. Rise above the babyhood which cannot believe two doctrines until it sees the connecting link. Have you not two eyes, man? Must you needs put one of them out in order to see clearly? Is it impossible to you to use a spiritual stereoscope, and look at two views of truth until they melt into one, and that one becomes more real and actual because it is made up of two? Many men refuse to see more than one side of a doctrine, and persistently fight against anything which is not on its very surface consistent with their own idea. In the present case I do not find it difficult to believe faith to be at the same time the duty of man and the gift of God; and if others cannot accept the two truths, I am not responsible for their rejection of them ; my duty is performed when I have honestly borne witness to them.

Hitherto we have only been clearing the way. Let us advance. The faith intended in the text *evidently rests upon a person*—upon Jesus. " Whosoever believeth that Jesus is the Christ is born of God." It is not belief about a doctrine, nor an opinion, nor a formula, but belief concerning a person. Translate the words, "Whosoever believeth that Jesus is the Christ," and they stand thus : "Whosoever believeth that the Saviour is the Anointed is born of God." By which is assuredly not meant, whosoever professes to believe that he is so, for many do that whose lives prove that they are not regenerate ; but, whosoever so believes it to be the fact, as truly and in very deed to receive Jesus as God has set him forth and anointed him, is a regenerate man. What is meant by "Jesus is the Christ," or, Jesus is the Anointed? First, that he is the Prophet; secondly, that he is the Priest ; thirdly, that he is the King of the church, for in all these three senses he is the Anointed. Now, I may ask myself this question :

Do I this day believe that Jesus is the great Prophet anointed of God to reveal to me the way of salvation? Do I accept him as my teacher and admit that he has the words of eternal life? If I so believe, I shall obey his gospel and possess eternal life. Do I accept him to be henceforth the revealer of God to my soul, the messenger of the covenant, the anointed Prophet of the Most High? But he is also a priest. Now, a priest is ordained from among men to offer sacrifices; do I firmly believe that Jesus was ordained to offer his one sacrifice for the sins of mankind, by the offering of which sacrifice once for all he has finished atonement and made complete expiation? Do I accept his atonement as an atonement for me, and receive his death as an expiation upon which I rest my hope for forgiveness of all my transgressions? Do I in fact believe Jesus to be the one sole, only propitiating Priest, and accept him to act as priest for me? If so, then I have in part believed that Jesus is the Anointed. But he is also King, and if I desire to know whether I possess the right faith, I further must ask myself, "Is Jesus, who is now exalted in heaven, who once bled on the cross, is he King to me? Is his law my law? Do I desire entirely to submit myself to his government? Do I hate what he hates, and love what he loves? Do I live to praise him? Do I, as a loyal subject, desire to see his kingdom come and his will done on earth as it is in heaven?" My dear friend, if thou canst heartily and earnestly say, "I accept Jesus Christ of Nazareth to be Prophet, Priest, and King to me, because God has anointed him to exercise those three offices; and in each of these three characters I unfeignedly trust him," then, dear friend, you have the faith of God's elect, for it is written, "He that believeth that Jesus is the Christ is born of God."

Now we will go a little further. *True faith is reliance.* Look at any Greek lexicon you like, and you will find that the word πιστευειν does not merely mean to believe, but to trust, to confide in, to commit to, entrust with, and so forth; and the marrow of the meaning of faith is confidence in, reliance upon. Let me ask, then, every professor here who professes to have faith, is your faith the faith of reliance? You give credit to certain statements, do you also place trust in the one glorious person who alone can redeem? Have you confidence as well as credence? A creed will not save you, but reliance upon the anointed Saviour is the way of salvation. Remember, I beseech you, that if you could be taught an orthodoxy unadulterated with error, and could learn a creed written by the pen of the Eternal God himself, yet a mere notional faith, such as men exercise when they believe in the existence of men in the moon, or nebulæ in space, could not save your soul. Of this we are sure, because we see around us many who have such a faith, and yet evidently are not children of God.

Moreover, true faith is not a flattering presumption, by which a man says, "I believe I am saved, for I have such delightful feelings, I have had a marvellous dream, I have felt very wonderful sensations;" for all such confidence may be nothing but sheer assumption. Presumption, instead of being faith, is the reverse of faith; instead of being the substance of things hoped for, it is a mere mirage. Faith, is as correct as reason, and if her arguments are considered, she is as secure in her conclusions as though she drew them by mathematical rules. Beware, I pray you, of a faith which has no basis but your own fancy.

Faith, again, is not the assurance that Jesus died for me. I sometimes feel myself a little at variance with that verse—

> "Just as I am—without one plea
> But that thy blood was shed for me."

It is eminently suitable for a child of God, but I am not so sure as to its being the precise way for putting the matter for a sinner. I do not believe in Jesus because I am persuaded that his blood was shed for me, but rather I discover that his blood was shed especially for me from the fact that I have been led to believe in him. I fear me there are thousands of people who believe that Jesus died for them, who are not born of God, but rather are hardened in their sin by their groundless hopes of mercy. There is no particular efficacy in a man's assuming that Christ has died for him; for it is a mere truism, if it be true as some teach, that Jesus died for everybody. On such a theory every believer in a universal atonement would necessarily be born of God, which is very far from being the case. When the Holy Spirit leads us to rely upon the Lord Jesus, then the truth that God gave his only begotten Son that whosoever believeth in him might be saved, is opened up to our souls, and we see that for us who are believers, Jesus died with the special intent that we should be saved. For the Holy Spirit to assure us that Jesus shed his blood for us in particular is one thing, but merely to conclude that Jesus died for us on the notion that he died for everybody is as far as the east is from the west, from being real faith in Jesus Christ.

Neither is it faith for me to be confident that I am saved, for it may be the case that I am not saved, and it can never be faith to believe a lie. Many have concluded rashly that they were saved when they were still in the gall of bitterness. That was not the exhibition of confidence in Christ but the exhibition of a base presumption destructive to the last degree. To come back to where we started from, faith, in a word, is reliance upon Jesus Christ. Whether the Redeemer died in special and particular for me or not, is not the question to be raised in the first place; I find that he came into the world to save sinners, under that general character I come to him, I find that whosoever trusteth him shall be saved, I therefore trust him, and having done so, I learn from his word that I am the object of his special love, and that I am born of God.

In my first coming to Jesus I can have no knowledge of any personal and special interest in the blood of Jesus; but since it is written, "God hath set him forth to be a propitiation for our sins: and not for ours only, but also for the sins of the whole world," I come and trust myself to that propitiation; sink or swim I cast myself on the Saviour. Great Son of God, thou hast lived and died, thou hast bled and suffered, and made atonement for sin for all such as trust thee, and I trust thee, I lean upon thee, I cast myself upon thee. Now, whoever has such faith as this is born of God, he has true faith which is proof positive of the new birth. Judge ye, therefore, whether ye have this faith or no.

Let me tarry just one minute longer over this. The true faith is set forth in Scripture by figures, and one or two of these we will mention. It was an eminent type of faith when the Hebrew father in Egypt slew the lamb and caught the warm blood in the basin, then took a bunch of hyssop and dipped it in the blood and marked the two posts of his door, and then struck a red mark across the lintel. That smearing of the door represented faith. The deliverance was wrought by the blood ; and the blood availed through the householder's own personally striking it upon his door. Faith does that ; it takes of the things of Christ, makes them its own, sprinkles the soul, as it were, with the precious blood, accepts the way of mercy by which the Lord passes over us and exempts his people from destruction. Faith was shown to the Jews in another way. When a beast was offered in sacrifice for sin, the priest and sometimes the representatives of the tribes or the individual laid their hands upon the victim in token that they desired their sins to be transferred to it, that it might suffer for them as a type of the great substitute. Faith lays her hands on Jesus, desiring to receive the benefit of his substitutionary death.

A still more remarkable representation of faith was that of the healing look of the serpent-bitten Israelites. On the great standard in the midst of the camp Moses lifted up a serpent of brass; high overhead above all the tents this serpent gleamed in the sun, and whoever of all the dying host would but look to it was made to live. Looking was a very simple act, but it indicated that the person was obedient to God's command. He looked as he was bidden, and the virtue of healing came from the brazen serpent through a look. Such is faith. It is the simplest thing in the world, but it indicates a great deal more than is seen upon its surface :

" There is life for a look at the Crucified One."

To believe in Jesus is but to glance the eye of faith to him, to trust him with thy soul.

That poor woman who came behind our Saviour in the press offers us another figure of what faith is. She said, " If I may but touch the hem of his garment I shall be made whole." Taking no medicines, making no profession, and performing no ceremonies, she simply touched the ravelling of the Saviour's robe, and she was healed at once. O soul, if thou canst get into contact with Christ by simply trusting him, though that trust be ever so feeble, thou hast the faith of God's elect ; thou hast the faith which is in every case the token of the new birth.

II. We must now pass on to show that WHEREVER IT EXISTS IT IS THE PROOF OF REGENERATION. There never was a grain of such faith as this in this world, except in a regenerate soul, and there never will be while the world standeth. It is so according to the text, and if we had no other testimony this one passage would be quite enough to prove it. " Whosoever believeth that Jesus is the Christ is born of God." " Ah ! " I hear thee say, poor soul, " the new birth is a great mystery; I do not understand it; I am afraid I am not a partaker in it." You are born again if you believe that Jesus is the Christ, if you are relying upon a crucified Saviour you are assuredly begotten again unto a lively hope. Mystery or no mystery, the new birth is yours if you are a believer. Have you never noticed that the greatest mysteries in the world reveal themselves by the simplest indications. The simplicity and apparent easiness of faith is no reason why I should not regard its existence as an infallible indication of the new birth within. How know we that the new-born child lives except by its cry? Yet a child's cry—what a simple sound it is! how readily could it be imitated! a clever workman could with pipes and strings easily deceive us; yet was there never a child's cry in the world but what it indicated the mysteries of breathing, heart-beating, blood-flowing, and all the other wonders which come with life itself. Do you see yonder person just drawn out of the river? Does she live? Yes, life is there. Why? Because the lungs still heave. But does it not seem an easy thing to make lungs heave? A pair of bellows blown into them, might not that produce the motion? Ah, yes, the thing is easily imitated after a sort; but no lungs heave except where life is, no blood is pumped to and fro from the heart except where life is. Take another illustration. Go into a telegraph office at any time, and you will see certain needles moving right and left with unceasing click. Electricity is a great mystery, and you cannot see or feel it; but the operator tells you that the electric current is moving along the wire. How does he know? "I know it by the needle." How is that? I could move your needles easily "Yes; but do not you see the needle has made two motions to the right, one to the left, and two to the right again? I am reading a message." "But," say you, "I can see nothing in it; I could imitate that clicking and moving very easily." Yet he who is taught the art sees before him in those needles, not only electric action, but a deeper mystery still; he perceives that a mind is directing the invisible force, and speaking by means of it. Not to all, but to the initiated is it given to see the mystery hidden within the simplicity. The believer sees in the faith, which is simple as the movements of the needle, an indication that God is operating on the human mind, and the spiritual man discerns that there is an inner secret intimated thereby, which the carnal eye cannot decipher. To believe in Jesus is a better indicator of regeneration than anything else, and in no case did it ever mislead. Faith in the living God and his Son Jesus Christ is always the result of the new birth, and can never exist except in the regenerate. Whoever has faith is a saved man.

I beg you to follow me a little in this argument. A certain divine has lately said, "A man's act of believing is not the same as his being saved: it is only in the direction of being saved." This is tantamount to a denial that every believer in Christ is at once saved; and the inference is that a man may not conclude that he is saved because he believes in Jesus. Now, observe how opposed this is to Scripture. It is certain from the Word of God that *the man who believes in Jesus is not condemned.* Read John iii. 18, and many other passages. "He that believeth on Him is not condemned." Now is not every unregenerate man condemned? Is not a man who is not condemned a saved man? When you are sure on divine authority that the believer is not condemned, how in the name of everything that is rational can you deny that the believer is saved? If he is not condemned, what has he to fear? Will he not rightly conclude that being justified by faith, he has peace with God through our Lord Jesus Christ?

Note, secondly, that faith in the fourth verse of the chapter before us is said to "*overcome the world.*" "This is the victory that over-cometh the world, even our faith." What, then, does faith overcome the world in persons who are not saved? How can this be possible when the apostle saith that that which overcomes the world is born of God? Read the fourth verse: "Whatsoever is born of God overcometh the world:" but faith overcomes the world, therefore the man who has faith is regenerate; and what means that but that he is saved, and that his faith is the instrument by which he achieves victories.

Further, faith accepts the witness of God, and more, he that hath faith *has the witness in himself* to the truth of God. Read the tenth verse of the chapter: "He that believeth on the Son of God hath the witness in himself." It is not said, "He that does this or feels that," but "He that believeth hath the witness in himself," his heart bears witness to the truth of God. Has any unsaved man an experimental witness within? Will you tell me that a man's inner experience bears witness to God's gospel and yet the man is in a lost state, or only hopeful of being saved ultimately? No, sir, it is impossible. He that believeth has that change wrought in him which enables him by his own con-sciousness to confirm the witness of God, and such a man must be in a state of salvation. It is not possible to say of him that he is an un-saved man.

Again, note in this chapter, at the thirteenth verse, that wherever there is faith there is eternal life; so run the words, "these things have I written unto you that believe on the name of the Son of God; that ye may know that ye have eternal life." Our Lord himself, and his apostles, in several places have declared, "He that believeth on him hath everlasting life." Do not tell me that a sinner who believes in Jesus is to make an advance before he can say he is saved, that a man who trusts Christ is only on the way to salvation, and must wait until he has used the ordinances, and has grown in grace, before he may know that he is saved. No, the moment that the sinner's trust is placed on the finished work of Jesus he is saved. Heaven and earth may pass away, but that man shall never perish. If only one second ago I trusted the Saviour I am safe; just as safe as the man who has believed in Jesus fifty years, and who has all that while walked uprightly. I do not say that the new born convert is as happy, nor as useful, nor as holy, nor as ripe for heaven, but I do say that the words, "he that believeth on him hath everlasting life," is a truth with general bearings, and relates as much to the babe in faith as it does to the man who has attained to fulness of stature in Jesus Christ.

As if this chapter were written on purpose to meet the gross error that faith does not bring immediate salvation, it extols faith again and again, yea, and I may add, our Lord himself crowns faith, because faith never wears the crown, but brings all the glory to the dear Redeemer.

Now, let me say a word or two in reply to certain questions. But must not a man repent as well as believe? Reply: No man ever be-lieved but what he repented at the same time. Faith and repentance go together. They must. If I trust Christ to save me from sin, I am at the same time repenting of sin, and my mind is changed in relation to sin, and everything else that has to do with its state. All the fruits meet for repentance are contained in faith itself. You shall never find that a man who trusts Christ remains an enemy to God, or a lover of sin. The fact that he accepts the atonement provided is proof positive that he loathes sin, and that his mind is thoroughly changed in reference to God. Moreover, as to all the graces which are produced in the Christian afterwards, are they not all to be found in embryo in faith? "Only believe, and you shall be saved," is the cry which many sneer at, and others misunderstand; but do you know what "only believe" means? Do you know what a world of meaning lies in that word? Read that famous chapter to the Hebrews, and see what faith has done and is still able to do, and you will see that it is no trifle. Wherever there is faith in a man let it but develop itself and there will be a purging of himself from sin, a separating himself from the world, a conflict with evil, and a warring for the glory of Christ, which nothing else could produce. Faith is in itself one of the noblest of graces; it is the compendium of all virtues; and as sometimes there will lie within one single ear enough seed to make a whole garden fertile, so, within that one word "faith," there lies enough of virtue to make earth blessed; enough of grace, if the Spirit make it to grow, to turn the fallen into the perfect. Faith is not the easy and light thing men think. Far are we from ascribing salvation to the profession of a mere creed, we loathe the idea; neither do we ascribe salvation to a fond persuasion, but we do ascribe salvation to Jesus Christ, and the obtaining of it to that simple, child-like confidence which lovingly casts itself into the arms of him who gave both his hands to the nail and suffered to the death for the sins of his people. He who believes, then, is saved—rest assured of that. "Whosover believeth that Jesus is the Christ is born of God."

III. Now what flows out of this? Love is the legitimate issue! We must love if we are begotten of God all those who are also born of God. It would be an insult to you if I were to prove that a brother should love his brother. Doth not nature herself teach us that? Those, then, who are born of God ought to love all those of the same household. And who are they? Why, all those who have believed that Jesus is the Christ, and are resting their hopes where we rest ours, namely, on Christ the Anointed One of God. We are to love all such. We are to do this because we are of the family. We believe, and therefore we have been begotten of God. Let us act as those who are of the divine family; let us count it our privilege that we are received into the household, and rejoice to perform the lovely obligations of our high position. We look around us and see many others who have believed in Jesus Christ; let us love them because they are of the same kindred. "But they are some of them unsound in doctrine, they make gross mistakes as to the Master's ordinances." We are not to love their faults, neither ought we to expect them to love ours, but we are nevertheless to love their persons, for "whosoever believeth that Jesus is the Christ is born of God," and therefore he is one of the family, and as we love the Father who begat we are to love all those that are begotten of him. First, I love God, and therefore I desire to promote God's truth and to keep God's gospel free from taint. But then I am to love all those whom God has begotten, despite the infirmities and errors I see in them, being also myself compassed about with infirmities. Life is the reason for love, the common life which is indicated by the common faith in the dear Redeemer is to bind us to each other. I must confess, though I would pay every deference to every brother's conscientious judgment, I do not know how I could bring my soul as a child of God to refuse any man communion at my Master's table, who believed that Jesus is the Christ. I have proof in his doing so, if he be sincere (and I can only judge of that by his life), that he is born of God; and has not every child a right to come to the Father's table? I know in the olden times, parents used to make children go without their meals as a punishment, but everybody tells us now that this is cruel and unwise, for it injures the child's constitution to deprive it of necessary food. There are rods in the Lord's house, and there is no need to keep disobedient children away from the supper. Let them come to the Lord's table, and eat and drink with the Lord Jesus and with all his saints, in the hope that when their constitution bestows stronger they will throw out the disease which now they labour under, and come to be obedient to the whole gospel, which saith, " He that believeth and is baptised shall be saved."

Let me beg the members of this church to exhibit mutual love to one another. Are there any feeble among you ? Comfort them. Are there any who want instruction ? Bring your knowledge to their help. Are there any in distress ? Assist them. Are they backsliding? Restore them. " Little children, love one another," is the rule of Christ's family, may we observe it. May the love of God which has been shed abroad in our hearts by the Holy Ghost which is given unto us, reveal itself by our love to all the saints. And, remember, other sheep he has which are not yet of his fold ; them also he must bring in. Let us love those who are yet to be brought in, and lovingly go forth at once to seek them ; in whatever other form of service God has given us, let us with loving eyes look after our prodigal brothers, and who knows, we may bring into the family this very day some for whom there will be joy in the presence of the angels of God, because the lost one has been found. God bless and comfort you, for Jesus Christ's sake. Amen.

6. The Life, Walk, and Triumph of Faith

" And when Abram was ninety years old and nine, the LORD appeared to Abram, and said unto him, I am the Almighty God ; walk before me, and be thou perfect. And I will make my covenant between me and thee, and will multiply thee exceedingly."—Genesis xvii. 1, 2.

BELOVED, all Scripture is the word of God, but some Scripture is expressly so. Much of its teaching comes through inspired men, but some of it was spoken by God's own mouth, directly and without instrumentality: such are the words now before us which were of old spoken into Abram's ear by the Almighty God. These sentences ought for this reason to be regarded with peculiar reverence, and considered with double attention. The glow of Divinity is fresh upon the lines, bend then your souls to the understanding of them. If a letter were written to you when you were far from home, you would value every line of it if your fond mother had asked a friend to write it in her name, and had dictated the expressions which he should employ ; but if there were inserted in the body of the letter several sentences with this preface, "and your mother expressly says"—then you would treasure up the exact words, and repeat them to yourself again and again; would you not ? All God's words in Scripture are pearls, but this is one of the fairest of them. They are all diamonds, but such words as God speaks from his own mouth I may call the Koh-i-noors of Scripture.

Look, then, at the text. We will read it again: " When Abram was ninety years old and nine, the Lord appeared to Abram, and said unto him, I am the Almighty God; walk before me, and be thou perfect. And I will make my covenant between me and thee, and will multiply thee exceedingly." Happy was Abram to have such intimate intercourse with God ! These sacred visitations were the grand events of his life; but we need not envy him, for God has appeared unto us in a yet more glorious manner, and the appearance is abiding. Behold, in the person of the Lord Jesus Christ the tabernacle of God is among men, and he doth dwell among them ; and, in the indwelling of the

Holy Ghost, the believer has obtained an intimacy with God, which none of the older dispensation attained unto. The Lord was to the former saints as a wayfaring man who tarried but for a night; but it is our privilege to pray, "Abide with us," and our joy to know that wherever two or three are met together in the name of our Lord, he is there and will manifest himself unto them. Permit me, therefore, to encourage you to pray that the words of the Lord to Abram may be words for you, pressed home upon your own spirit, and sounded in your souls with power, as from the lips of the Lord himself. Then shall our meditations be sweet indeed, and we shall be blessed with faithful Abraham. O, Spirit Divine, make it so we entreat thee!

I. The first thing we shall speak about, upon this occasion, is SURE RELIANCE. The foundation of it is laid before us in the text. True confidence leans alone upon God, who declares himself to be Almighty God, or God All-sufficient—for such is an equally correct rendering of the passage.

All true faith hangs upon God, as the vessel upon the nail. Strong faith realises the all-sufficiency of God, and that is the secret of its strength, the hidden manna on which it feeds and becomes vigorous. The Lord is all-sufficient in power to accomplish his own purposes, all-sufficient in wisdom to find his own way through difficulties which to us may appear to be like a maze, but which to him are plain enough; and he is all-sufficient in love, so that he will never fail us for want of mercy in his heart, or pity in his bosom. God is God All-sufficient; simple as that truth is for us to speak, and for you to hear, it is a deep unfathomable, and did we really grasp its truth and dwell upon it, it would have a very wonderful effect upon our whole conduct.

Remember, that Abram was ninety years old and nine, and as yet had no child by his wife Sarah; yet he had received a promise from God that there should be a seed which should spring out of his loins. He was long past the natural term of life in which it was likely that he would be the father of a son. So, also, was it with his wife Sarah. Abram, for a while overcome by unbelief, thought it best to take to himself, at the suggestion of his wife Sarah, her handmaid Hagar; and now, for some few years, Abram had possessed a son named Ishmael, and it is probable that he thought that this son would answer to God's promise, and that somehow or other the blessing would come through him. But the Lord had not so determined. He took no pleasure in the carnal policy which led to Ishmael's birth. The Lord meant the language before us to be a gentle but unmistakable rebuke for him, for he said in effect, "I am God All-sufficient—quite sufficient to fulfil my own purposes without Abram's help—quite able to achieve my own designs without such a questionable expedient as that of Hagar and her son Ishmael." That is, no doubt, the divine intent in the declaration of all-sufficiency. Hear ye, then, these words if ye also have been at any time distrustful, and let them sink into your souls,—" I am God All-sufficient." If any of you are tempted at this time to do what is questionable, because you cannot see how God's promise to you will be effected without it, the Lord tells you he wants no help of yours to achieve his own designs. "I am God Almighty," saith he; "Is anything too hard for me? Dost thou think I need thy wisdom to set me right, or thy puny arm to strengthen me? Do I want thy help to achieve my purposes, which stand fast as my eternal throne?" It was a tender rebuke of Abram's very gross mistake, and it is to us a hint that we are never to put forth our hand unto iniquity, or to do any-thing that is doubtful in any form or shape, under the notion that we are thus effecting the purposes of God. Look at Rebekah. She little understood the all-sufficiency of God. God had promised her that Jacob should have the covenant-blessing, but she seems to think that God cannot keep his word and cause Jacob to inherit the promises unless she, has a finger in it. Father Isaac has sent out Esau a-hunting, to bring home savoury meat, and has promised that he will give him the blessing when he returns. And now Rebekah thinks God will be defeated, the anxious mother imagines the Most High to be in a dilemma, and his purposes to be likely to fail unless her inherited craftiness can devise a stratagem to eke out the divine wisdom. Rebekah must tell lies, and Jacob must tell lies too; and poor old Isaac must be deceived, or else God's purposes will not be accomplished. O foolish Rebekah! Ere we speak thus, and condemn that gracious woman, let us make sure that we confess and condemn the same tendency in ourselves. Have we not also dreamed that we might do evil that good might come? Have we not followed policy where we ought to have sternly adhered to principle, and all this because we thought it necessary, and feared that otherwise evil would triumph? Has not our judgment been bewildered by strange providences, and been led to sanction irregular procedures, or at least to think less severely of them? Under the influence of blind unbelief, have we not been ready, like Uzzah, to lay our hand upon the ark of the Lord to steady it, for fear it should fall, as if God's ark could not take care of itself without our sinful hand being laid thereon? That lesson learned by Israel at the Red Sea is still a hard one to us: we cannot stand still and see the salvation of God. Because we do not believe in the Almighty God we are eager to make haste, we hurry, worry, fret, fuss and sin! Fear drives us, and self-sufficiency draws us, and the noble quietude of faith in God is lost. O could we but rest in omnipotent love, could we but know the Lord, and wait patiently for him, how much sin and sorrow we should be spared!

> " With feeble light and half obscure,
> Poor mortals Thy arrangements view;
> Not knowing that the least are sure,
> And the mysterious just and true.
>
> My favour'd soul shall meekly learn
> To lay her reason at Thy throne;
> Too weak Thy secrets to discern,
> I'll trust Thee for my guide alone."

Here is the fit place to set in contrast the conduct of David. He knew that in God's decree it was ordained that he should be king over Israel, yet he took no means to secure the crown. He would not lift his hand to smite Saul, nay, he spared him when he was entirely in his power. He did not unbelievingly interfere to make a providence for himself, but left the course of events in the Lord's hands; and, in con-sequence, when he came to the throne he had an easy conscience and no innocent blood upon his hands. May our faith teach us the same patient waiting, and confident repose of soul. May we believe, to see the glory of the Lord. The Lord All-sufficient will in the end clear the darkest providences from all question, and our souls shall know how happy are those who put their trust in the Lord alone.

This blessed text, "I am God All-sufficient," may apply to us in times when we are inclined to shirk any service for God. Have you never felt on certain seasons that God's choice of you for a special labour could not be a wise one, for you were so unfit for it? Have you never felt in your own hearts—" I cannot do that; I think the Lord would have me do it, but I cannot. I have not the qualification. I believe I am called to it, but it is too difficult for me. I shall not be able to achieve it"? Have you never had the disposition, like Jonah, to flee to Tarshish, or somewhere else, and to escape from Nineveh and its trials? Have you never pleaded, like Jeremiah, "But I am a child?" Have you never cried, like Moses, "I am slow of speech, send by whomsoever thou wilt send, but not by me"? Now, at such a time the Lord may well remind us, "I am God All-sufficient, cannot I strengthen thee? Weak as thou art, cannot I make thee strong? Worm of the dust, cannot I make thee thresh the mountains? Why dost thou fear? Thou art feeble, but I am not. Thou art foolish, but I am wise. Give thyself up to my guidance; trust thyself in my hands, and thou shalt achieve marvels; and exceeding great wonders shalt thou accomplish by my power and grace." It will be sadly sinful if we arrogate to ourselves the right to arrange our own place, and alter heaven's appointments. We are not where we are by chance, or by a freak of fate: as God's servants, our work is allotted us wisely and authoritatively. Dare we be wiser than the Lord? Are we also of Jehovah's council? His choice of instruments is wise, even when he chooses the weak things of the world to work his purposes. Their insufficiency is of no consequence, for their sufficiency is of God. For them to attempt to shun their duty because of conscious feebleness, would be a daring sin against the prerogatives of the King of kings, an impious censure upon the infallible appointments of Infinite wisdom. May not this be a word in season to some brother or sister here, who may happen to be under that temptation? If it be, may the Lord speak it home by his Spirit, and a blessing will come of it! Work on, dear friend, and wait on, for it is no business of yours to correct your Maker's arrangements. He who placed you where you now are, knew what he was at. Look at your infirmities with another eye. No longer allow them to distress you; but the rather glory in them because they afford room and space for the divine power to rest in you and work by you. Listen no more to the wailings of your trembling flesh, which cries, "Alas, I am weak," but hear the voice of him who saith "I am God Almighty."

This word may also be useful to those who are trembling under some present temporal trial and affliction. They are dreading what may yet happen. Forebodings of what may soon come are upon them. Sometimes we have before us a gloomy prospect: we know the trial must come; we are afraid of it; and though we have the promise, "In six troubles I will be with thee, and in seven there shall no evil touch thee," yet we stand trembling. "I am God All-sufficient"—will not that brace your nerves and enable you to press on, though it were through a valley as dark as death-shade itself? Is it poverty? God is All-sufficient to supply your needs. Is it physical pain?—and some of us dread that beyond anything else,—the All-sufficient God can put under your aching head such a peace-creating pillow, that in the sweetness of celestial love you shall forget the smarts of the flesh, and your soul shall be comforted when your body is full of agony. Why, what is it that thou fearest, O child of God? There can be no lack which he cannot supply, no enemy that he cannot subdue. Slander's cruel tooth, doth that dismay thee! Is not the Lord sufficient for this also? "No weapon that is formed against thee shall prosper." Hast thou not his own word for it? "Every tongue that rises against thee in judgment thou shalt condemn." Hath not he declared it? and doth not he know how to accomplish his own purpose? Therefore, again, I say, cast thy doubts and thy fears to the wind, for God as surely says to thee, O trembling believer, as ever he did to his servant Abram, "I am God, Almighty God." O rest in the Lord, and be not troubled. He shall, he must appear: only put not forth thine hand unto iniquity, and do nothing before the time. Thou hast no feeble Deity to trust in; be not a coward, but play the man.

The same may also be applied to each of us when we are under spiritual depressions. Inward tribulations are frequently more severe than temporal trials; the man of God knows this full well. We look within, and we see grace to be at a low ebb with us—at least we think so ; our corruptions and our natural depravity—these we see clearly enough, and we are troubled with the sight. Neglects of duty, omissions of devotion, forgotten opportunities of usefulness, all come up and accuse us; and then we are ready to doubt whether we ever knew the Lord at all : and, perhaps, Satan at the same time assails us, and we fall under his foot for awhile. O, let us not, even in such terrible times, ever doubt our God, for he is All-sufficient still ! If our salvation depended upon ourselves, it would soon be all over with us ; but if it depend upon that arm, the sinews of which can never break,—if it depend upon that heart which can never change and never cease to beat with love omnipotent, why should we be discouraged ? "I am God Almighty," saith the Lord: "Therefore say thou unto the enemy, 'Rejoice not over me, for though I fall yet shall I rise again.'" And suppose, beloved, you should have temporal troubles and spiritual distresses at the same time? This meeting of two seas is very apt to make the mariner expect immediate ship-wreck; but, behold, walking on the waters comes thy God to thee, and saying, "I am God All-sufficient even for thee." Was there ever a storm that was not of his brewing ? Therefore cannot he control it ? Was there ever spirit that came up out of the deeps of hell that was not of his loosing ?—and can he not hold him in as with a chain and restrain his malignant power ? Behold, Jehovah rides upon the wings of the wind, and the storm-cloud is his car, fear not therefore the rattling of the wheels on which thy heavenly Father rides. In the midst of the tempest he reigns supreme, fear not the darkness which is his canopy, or the lightning which is but the glance of his eye. Trust thou him at all times, and let no fear cast thee down or hurry thee into an unbelieving and restless course of action, which would defile thee and bring dishonour upon his blessed name. Yea, if there are signs about thee of approaching departure,—if thy body, weakened by long disease, be like a house that is ready to fall about the tenant's ears, yet God, who is all-sufficient here, will be all-sufficient on yonder dying bed. He who has been almighty in life will be almighty in death. Fear not that solemn flight through tracks unknown, or the awful appearance at the eternal throne. The God of grace is all-sufficient for all the mysteries of eternity; all-sufficient for the thunders of judgment, the terrors of vengeance, and the dread of hell. Fear not the crash of worlds, when he shall bid them all dissolve; the ever-living Redeemer, able to save unto the uttermost, is all-sufficient to support thy spirit—when all created things shall pass away and the elements shall melt with fervent heat. There exists not a conceivable ground of fear to the man who puts his trust in God Almighty! O beloved, set this as a seal upon thine arm to strengthen thee, and roll it as a stone upon the sepulchre of thy doubts. Never let them rise again. Didst thou trust a puny man, thou mightest doubt; but resting upon God, how canst thou be disquieted? Didst thou rely upon changing humanity,—didst thou place thy confidence in a creature that might love to-day and hate to-morrow, then, indeed, wert thou unhappy; but his love is everlasting and his power endureth for ever; why, then, art thou cast down? Thou hast built thy soul's hope upon the immoveable rock of All-sufficiency, and thou shalt prove the truth of that inspired assurance. " Because he hath set his love upon me, therefore will I deliver him: I will set him on high because he hath known my name. He shall call upon me and I will answer him: I will be with him in trouble: I will deliver him and honour him." Why art thou cast down, O my soul? and why art thou disquieted in me? hope thou in God: and cease thou from man whose breath is in his nostrils; then shall thy light shine forth as the morning, and a dew from heaven shall cause thee to bud and blossom with joy and rejoicing. Be glad in the Lord ye righteous, and shout for joy all ye that are upright in heart, for unto you hath he spoken, and given this for the rock of your confidence,—" I am the Almighty God."

II. Secondly, our text goes on to speak of our RIGHT POSITION. The Lord says, " I am Almighty God," and then he adds, " Walk before me." It is much easier for me to talk about this than it will be to practise it. The meaning is simple—the actual obedience grace alone can work in us. Come, gracious Spirit, and teach us to walk before the Lord in the land of the living. God is an All-sufficient God: then, believer, never go away from him, but abide in him evermore. There is a sense in which we always do walk before God, for " in him we live, and move, and have our being;" and he sees us altogether. But that is not what is intended here. It means this: Abide, O believer, in a constant sense of God's presence. " Walk before me, the All-sufficient God." Do not wander into paths wherein you will be made to feel," I have left my God." Have thy friend at hand:

" Be thou my heart still near my God,
And thou my God still near my heart."

Remember, he is a very present help in time of trouble; and do thou strive to realise this as a daily fact. Thou hast not to send for thy

God on an emergency, but thou art to walk before thy God believing him to be always near thee. Hagar once felt the power of that word, "Thou God seest me," but believers ought to feel it every moment. "Seeing him who is invisible" is not a thing for now and then, but an hourly exercise. It should be the general tenor of the believer's life to live always under the great Father's inspection. A poet puts it—"live ever under the great task-master's eye;" but I confess I do not like the word task-master. To live always as under my Father's eye has all the force of the poet's line, but has much more of sweetness. He is near me whether I journey or abide at home, whether I sorrow or rejoice. If I wake, his eyes pour sunlight on my face; if I sleep, he draws the curtains, and his presence shades me from all ill; if I rest, I sit at his feet in contemplation; if I labour, I work in his vineyard in his name, and for his sake, expecting a gracious reward from him.

"*Walk* before me." Not merely "think before me," and "pray before me," but "*walk* before me." I know many find it easy to cultivate a sense of God's presence in their own study, or in the room where they are accustomed to pray, but this is the point—to feel it in business, and in the details of every-day life. God's eye is upon me when I am weighing out or measuring the goods, when I am engrossed with transactions with my fellow merchants, or when I, as a servant, am sweeping up the hearth or minding the household duties. This you should distinctly recognise and act upon. You are to live in the little things of life, knowing that God is always with you, and always looking at you—doing your work just as will please him. Oh, how we smart ourselves up if there is somebody calling to see us. How we adjust our dress in the presence of those whom we admire. I have sometimes thought I have seen working men proceeding very slowly indeed at their tasks when alone, but when the master comes by they quicken their pace wonderfully. That is all wrong. It is eye-service, the custom of a man-pleaser, but not the habit of one who would please the Lord. We should feel, "God is always looking at me." There is many a word we should not say if we remembered that he would hear it, and many an act we dare not do if we remembered that he would register it. Yes, there is the believer's true place,— my God is God Almighty, and I am always in his presence. A person might do fifty things in a certain place, which he would not think of doing if he were at court and had just presented a petition to the queen; there is a decorousness of manner which we all observe when we are in such conditions; and, therefore, the reasoning is cogent when I ask you before the King of kings what manner of persons ought we to be! We are always in Jehovah's courts, and under his royal gaze: "Walk before me." Live ever as in the court, for remember, O believer, you are not like an ordinary person. If an ordinary person sins, it is only a common subject of the king, but you—why, you are a courtier, a favoured courtier! You are one that he has chosen to tread his courts. Nay, more: the Prince Imperial has espoused you to himself. You are the bride of the ever-blessed Bridegroom, the spouse of Immanuel, and there is always jealousy where there is much love. "The Lord thy God is a jealous God." Whatever he may be to others, he is very jealous of those on whom he has set his everlasting love. "Our God is a consuming fire." Walk before a jealous God, then, with scrupulous regard to his honour and his holiness. Oh, it is a great word this—"walk before me." Its brevity is not so notable as its fulness. Surely it means realise my presence, and then, in general life and ordinary conversation, continue under a sense of it, serious, devout, holy, earnest, trustful, consecrated, Christ-like.

But he meant more than that. "Walk before me." That is, "Delight in my company." True believers find their choicest joy in communion with God; and did we always walk before God in a sense of communing with him, our peace would be like a river, and our righteousness like the waves of the sea. Would it be possible for us to feel any distress of heart if we always enjoyed the Saviour's love? Methinks there are no bitters known that would be able to affect our palate if we always had in our mouth the love of the Saviour in its ineffable, all-conquering sweetness. "Walk before me." Do not interfere with God's purposes: do not, unbelieving, try to help omnipotence and supplement omniscience, but rejoice in the Lord and find satisfaction in him only. Be filled with his fulness, and satiated with his favour. Go and do your part, which is to obey and to commune, and leave God's work to God. Walk before him, and attend to that only. Do not doubt God's power to fulfil his own decrees. Do not doubt that he will keep his word to the letter and to the minute; but do thou cultivate fellowship with God, for this will ennoble thee and help thee to give glory to his name.

"Walk before me." Does not it mean just this, in a word, "Do not act as seeing anybody else except me. Walk before me." Now, Abram had walked before Sarah: he had listened to her, and much mischief had come of his so doing at different times. The dearest friends we have are often those who will lead us most astray when we take counsel with flesh and blood. She was peculiarly qualified from her very excellence of character to influence Abram, and, in her unbelieving moods, to lead him away from the glorious absoluteness of his faith. She meant well enough, but she was too politic in her suggestion as to her handmaid. In the present case the Lord seems to say to him, "Do not suffer Sarah to affect you in these things. Walk before me." Beloved, mind you keep clear of the unbelieving advice of good people, and then you will have the less to fear from bad ones. And there was Hagar: Abram had been a great deal distressed about her, and it was but right that he should feel much interest in her welfare. And there was her son Ishmael whom he loved, and whom he would have to send, in future time, away with deep regret from the household. God says to Abram, "Do not allow your course to be shaped by regarding Hagar, or regarding Ishmael, or regarding Sarah, or anybody else. "Walk before me." I am persuaded that a regard for God, a sense of duty, a straightforward following out of convictions, is the only true style of living, for if you begin to notice the whims and wishes of one, then you will have to do the same with another; and if your course of conduct is to be shaped to please men, you will become man's slave and nothing better; and no child of God ought to come into that condition. If I felt I came into this pulpit to please any of you, I should feel mean, utterly mean, and unfit to preach to you; and you would soon know it and find out that God was not blessing me to your souls. And if any of you, in your course of business, are always trying to catch the eye of this person, or cringing and fawning to this other nobleman, or squire, or gentleman, why, you are mean too. But the man who says, " I do the right in God's sight : I have not swerved from a sense of conscious rectitude, as before the living God,"—why, sir, you have got all the freedom of soul that you can desire this side heaven. To walk before *God*, that is the point ; to fear the Lord, and no one else, that is the state of mind to aim at. Make this the master passion of your soul, " For me to live is Christ "; make the honour of God your chief motive, and the law of God your rule. Walk before the Lord in the land of the living.

III. But we must pass on, for there is another point, and that is, as we have considered our sure reliance and our right position, we notice next OUR GLORIOUS AIM : " Be thou perfect."

Now, the connection shows us that the only way to be perfect is to walk before the Lord. If any man desires holiness, he must get it through communion. The way to be transformed into the likeness of God is to live in the company of God. That which thou lookest upon, thou wilt soon be like; and if thine eyes look on God, thy character will become like God. Hence the order of our text is highly suggestive, and should be earnestly noted and practically carried out. First, God must be known as All-sufficient; thus he helps and enables his servant to walk before him, and then, as a consequence, that favoured servant labours to obey the word of command, " BE THOU PERFECT." There could be no walking before the Lord if all-sufficient grace did not work it in us, and the command, " Be thou perfect," would be mere mockery if Almighty love did not stand engaged to work all our works in us. To a man who has learned to rest in Almighty faithfulness, the perfect law is delightful; and with confidence in the energy of the Holy Spirit he is not staggered by its commands. I desire you to note this, for the order of Holy Scripture is always full of reason and weight. Whatever ill-taught divines may do, the Holy Spirit never puts the fruit before the root, and never places the pinnacle where the foundation should be. Begin with God's All-sufficiency, go on to the holy fellowship and obedience, and then aim at scriptural perfection, and so you will take everything in due sequence.

But we must pass on. As you are aware, our margin reads the text thus, " Be thou *sincere*," or " Be thou *upright;*" and either translation would not be incorrect. Now, child of God, you have been saying, " I do not see how God is to fulfil his promise to me." What have you to do with that ? Walk before God, and be you sincere. He will attend to the due performance of all that he has promised. Remember—

> " Though dark be your way, since he is your guide,
> 'Tis yours to obey, 'tis his to provide."

In all things be transparently sincere, never pray a formalistic prayer, or sing a heartless hymn, or prattle out experience you never felt. Shun first and foremost the leaven of the Pharisees, which is hypocrisy. Be what you would seem to be. Be down-right ; intensely real, thorough, and if you are that, you shall never find God less thorough than you are, nor the Lord less true to his word than you shall be. If you are wavering and doubleminded, you must not expect anything of the Lord, but if you are single-hearted he will abundantly reward you. **Mind** this, J pray you, every day you live. This is the age of plausible sham, the era of superficiality ; therefore be unmistakably true before the God of truth. The margin translates the passage by the word "upright; " and it comes to just this. You are fretting about how the Lord will deal with you. Brother, that is no concern of thine. Thy concern is that thou be upright in business. "My trade falls off," says one. Be upright, brother: whatever you do, be upright. "But I have drifted into such difficulties, I am afraid I shall be ruined." Be upright, brother, whatever you do, be upright. "Could not I get away a few of my goods, for instance, which ought to be my creditors' ? " Brother, be upright; be upright. "Ah, but then, surely, I shall hardly have a rag left." Be upright, brother, be upright. "Oh, but I consider my children." "Walk before me," says the Lord, "and be thou upright." "Oh, but a man must take care of himself and his family." Be upright, brother; that is the main thing to take care about. It will not matter how poor you are, if you do not lose your character. Lose everything else and you may yet be happy; but if you lose your peace of mind who can comfort you ? If the worldling can point at you and say, "There is a professor who wronged his creditors," that will be worse than all. No court is so much to be dreaded as the court of conscience—keep all things clear there. Better an honest pauper than a rich rogue. I am sure your fellow Christians will respect you none the less, however low you come, if you come there fairly ; all those whose love is worth the having will cling to you in hearty sympathy, and only false friends, the parasites of the hour, will desert you, and a good riddance will their departure turn out to be. But avoid, I implore you, those tricks so common among traders now-a-days—those rash speculations, those deceptive accommodations, the lying and duping of others, which men fly to as a drowning man catches at a straw—a straw that he ought never to touch. Not losing, but cheating is the mischief ; and the Lord says to you, "I am God All-sufficient: I can take care of you : I can bring you through all this ; but do not touch forbidden things in order to escape from trial, or your trials will multiply and crush you. Walk before me, as under my eye ; and be thou upright."

But our version says, "Be thou perfect," and for my part, I like it as it stands: "Be thou perfect." "Oh," says one, "but how can we be perfect ?" I will ask thee another question: Wouldst thou have God command thee to be less than perfect ? If so, he would be the author of an imperfect law. "The law of the Lord is perfect ;" how could it be otherwise ? I do not find that he bids us partly keep his law, but wholly keep it. And so the Lord holds up this as the standard of a Christian, "Be thou perfect."

And does it not mean, let us be perfect in desiring to have all the round of graces ? Suppose a man should have faith, and should have love, but no hope: he would not be perfect. He would be like a child that had two arms, but only one foot ; it would not be a perfect child. You must have all the graces, if you are to be a perfect man. I think I have known some Christians who have had all the graces except patience, but they never could be patient. "Walk before me," saith the

THE LIFE, WALK, AND TRIUMPH OF FAITH.

Lord, " and be thou perfect in patience." I have known some others who seemed to have almost every grace except the grace of forgiveness ; they could not very readily forget any injury that had been done to them. Dear brother, you must get that grace, the grace of forgiveness, and walk before the Lord with that, or you will remain a mutilated character. A Christian's character is spoilt by the omission of any one virtue. And you must labour in the presence of God to have all these things, that they be in you and abound. Be ye in this sense perfect.

And as we have all the graces, so we should seek to have in our lives exhibited all the virtues, in the fulfilment of all our duties. It is a very sad thing when you hear of a Christian man that he is a very excellent deacon, that he is a very admirable local preacher or Sabbath-school teacher, but that he is a very unkind father. That " but" spoils it all. A saint abroad is no saint if he be a devil at home. We have known men of whom it has been said that out of doors they were all that could be desired, *but* they were bad husbands. That " but,"—how it mars the tale. It is the dead fly which has got into a very good pot of ointment, and made the whole of it stink. Keep the dead flies out, brethren. By God's grace may your character be full-orbed ! May God grant you grace to be at home and to be abroad, to be in the shop and in the chamber, and to be in every department of life, just that which a man should be who walks before the All-sufficient God.

Now, I think I hear somebody saying, " How shall we ever reach such a height ? " My dear brother, you never will do so except you remember the first part of the text—" I am the Almighty God." He can help you. If there be any sin that you cannot overcome yourself, he can overcome it for you. If there be any virtue you have not yet reached, he can lead you up to it. Never despair of the highest degree of grace. What the best of men have been, you also may be. There is no reason why you should not yet be elevated beyond all the sin into which you may have fallen from inadvertence or temptation. Have hope, my brother ; have hope for a higher platform of character. Have hope yet to be conformed unto the image of God's dear Son. Aim at nothing less than perfection.

But I will not detain you longer, except to notice that last word. It is a very sweet word : " I will make my covenant between me and thee." How run the words ? " I will make my covenant between me and thee."

Oh, it is the man that knows an All-sufficient God, and that lives in the presence of God, and that endeavours to be perfect in his life—it is that man that enjoys intercourse and communion with God, such as no one else knows, for " The secret of the Lord is with them that fear him." " There shall be a covenant between me and thee." It sounds so sweetly to me—as if he had said, " I will say nothing to the outside world ; neither wilt thou tell them. It shall be with thee and me. We will strike hands together. Abram, thou shalt be my friend, and I will be thy friend for ever. Thou wilt say, 'My Father,' and I will say 'My son.' Thou wilt put thyself into my hand, and I will carry thee therein. Thou wilt ask to see my glory, and I will make my glory pass before thee. I will tell thee what I mean to do. If I am going to destroy Sodom, I will come and tell Abram my friend. I will let thee speak to me, and I will hear thee. Time after time I will stay whilst thou dost plead for fifty, and for forty-five, and thirty, and twenty, and ten. 'There shall be a covenant between me and thee.' And *I* will make it. It shall not be such a one as thy timorous faith would make. I will make it after the manner of my bounty, my eternity, and my all-sufficiency." When the Lord makes a covenant, it it will stand; it will be sure ; it will be rich; it will be full. And, O, I pray that every one of you may know that covenant and live upon its incomparable blessings. "The secret of the Lord is with them that fear him," and he will show them his covenant. But many a child of God walks frowardly, and the Lord will not fully reveal the covenant to such. Some of his Peters follow afar off, and they get into trouble ; but they do not enjoy the sweets of divine fellowship and peculiar manifestation. But this careful walking, this close walking, this keeping near to an All-sufficient God, this resting solely in him— Oh, this it is that brings the sweetness and the joy which are the antepast of heaven—which are, indeed, a young heaven begun this side the tomb. The Lord bring my dear friends all into holy fellowship with God ; and if any of you have not come to the border of the happy land, I pray you may be led there at once. The way of salvation is, " Believe in the Lord Jesus Christ." Faith is both the road to the highest happiness, and the way to the first safety—faith is both the the highest round of the ladder, and its first step—" Believe in the Lord Jesus Christ, and thou shalt be saved." Have done with the self-righteous working, and come to the trusting. Have done with seeking to save self, and accept Jesus alone as your Redeemer.

The Lord grant you grace so to do; and his shall be the praise for ever and ever ! Amen.

7. A Luther Sermon at the Tabernacle

"But the just shall live by his faith."—Habakkuk ii. 4.

THIS text is three times employed by the apostle Paul as an argument. Read Romans i. 17, Galatians iii. 11, and Hebrews x. 38: in each of these cases it runs, "The just shall live by faith." This is the old original text to which the apostle referred when he said, " As it is written, The just shall live by faith." We are not wrong in making the inspiration of the Old Testament to be as important as that of the New; for the truth of the gospel must stand or fall with that of the prophets of the old dispensation. The Bible is one and indivisible, and you cannot question the first Testament and retain the New. Habakkuk must be inspired, or Paul writes nonsense.

Yesterday, four hundred years ago, there came into this wicked world the son of a miner, or refiner of metals, who was to do no little towards undermining the Papacy and refining the church. The name of that babe was Martin Luther: a hero and a saint. Blessed was that day above all the days of the century which it honoured, for it bestowed a blessing on all succeeding ages, through " the monk that shook the world." His brave spirit overturned the tyranny of error which had so long held nations in bondage. All human history since then has been more or less affected by the birth of that marvellous boy. He was not an absolutely perfect man, we neither endorse all that he said nor admire all that he did; but he was a man upon whose like men's eyes shall seldom rest, a mighty judge in Israel, a kingly servant of the Lord. We ought oftener to pray to God to send us men—men of God, men of power. We should pray that, according to the Lord's infinite goodness, his ascension gifts may be continued and multiplied for the perfecting of his church; for when he ascended up on high he led captivity captive, and received gifts for men, and " he gave some, apostles; and some, prophets : and some, evangelists; and some, pastors and teachers." He continues to bestow these choice gifts according to the church's necessity, and he would scatter them more plentifully, mayhap, if our prayers more earnestly ascended to the Lord of the harvest to thrust forth labourers into his harvest. Even as we believe in the crucified Saviour for our personal salvation, we ought to believe in the ascended Saviour for the perpetual enriching of the church with confessors and evangelists who shall declare the truth of God.

I wish to take my little share in commemorating Luther's birthday, and I think I can do no better than use the key of truth by which Luther unlocked the dungeons of the human mind, and set bondaged hearts at liberty. That golden key lies in the truth briefly contained in the text before us—"The just shall live by his faith."

Are you not a little surprised to find such a clear gospel passage in Habakkuk; to discover in that ancient prophet an explicit statement which Paul can use as a ready argument against the opponents of justification by faith? It shows that the cardinal doctrine of the gospel is no new-fangled notion; assuredly it is not a novel dogma invented by Luther, nor even a truth which was first taught by Paul. This fact has been established in all ages, and, therefore, here we find it among the ancient things, a lamp to cheer the darkness which hung over Israel before the coming of the Lord.

This also proves that there has been no change as to the gospel. The gospel of Habakkuk is the gospel of our Lord Jesus Christ. A clearer light was cast upon the truth by the giving of the Holy Ghost, but the way of salvation has in all ages been one and the same. No man has ever been saved by his good works. The way by which the just have lived has always been the way of faith. There has not been the slightest advance upon this truth; it is established and settled, evermore the same, like the God who uttered it. At all times, and everywhere, the gospel is and must for ever be the same. "Jesus Christ the same yesterday, and to day, and for ever." We read of "the gospel" as of one; but never of two or three gospels, as of many. Heaven and earth shall pass away, but Christ's word shall never pass away.

Noteworthy also is it, not only that this truth should be so old, and should continue so unchanged, but that it should possess such vitality. This one sentence, "The just shall live by his faith," produced the Reformation. Out of this one line, as from the opening of one of the Apocalyptic seals, came forth all that sounding of gospel trumpets, and all that singing of gospel songs, which made in the world a sound like the noise of many waters. This one seed, forgotten and hidden away in the dark mediæval times, was brought forth, dropped into the human heart, made by the Spirit of God to grow, and in the end to produce great results. This handful of corn on the top of the mountains so multiplied that the fruit thereof did shake like Lebanon, and they of the city flourished like grass of the earth. The least bit of truth, thrown anywhere, will live! Certain plants are so full of vitality, that if you only take a fragment of a leaf and place it on the soil, the leaf will take root and grow. It is utterly impossible that such vegetation should become extinct; and so it is with the truth of God—it is living and incorruptible, and therefore there is no destroying it. As long as one Bible remains, the religion of free grace will live; nay, if they could burn all printed Scriptures, as long as there remained a child who remembered a single text of the word, the truth would rise again. Even in the ashes of truth the fire is still living, and when the breath of the Lord bloweth upon it, the flame will burst forth gloriously. Because of this, let us be comforted in this day of blasphemy and of rebuke,—comforted because though "the grass withereth, and the flower thereof falleth away: but the word of the Lord endureth for ever. And this is the word which by the gospel is preached unto you."

Let us now examine this text, which was the means of enlightening the heart of Luther, as I shall tell you by-and-by.

I. I shall in the outset make a brief observation upon it: A MAN WHO HAS FAITH IN GOD IS JUST. "The just shall live by his faith;" the man who possesses faith in God is a just man: his faith is his life as a just man.

He is "just" in the gospel sense, namely, that having the faith which God prescribes as the way of salvation, he is by his faith justified in the sight of God. In the Old Testament (Gen. xv. 6) we are told concerning Abraham that "he believed in the Lord; and he counted it to him for righteousness." This is the universal plan of justification. Faith lays hold upon the righteousness of God, by accepting God's plan of justifying sinners through the sacrifice of Jesus Christ, and thus she makes the sinner just. Faith accepts and appropriates for itself the whole system of divine righteousness which is unfolded in the person and work of the Lord Jesus. Faith rejoices to see him coming into the world in our nature, and in that nature obeying the law in every jot and tittle, though not himself under that law until he chose to put himself there on our behalf; faith is further pleased when she sees the Lord, who had come under the law, offering up himself as a perfect atonement, and making a complete vindication of divine justice by his sufferings and death. Faith lays hold upon the person, life, and death of the Lord Jesus as her sole hope, and in the righteousness of Christ she arrays herself. She cries, "The chastisement of my peace was upon him, and by his stripes I am healed." Now, the man who believes in God's method of making men righteous through the righteousness of Jesus, and accepts Jesus and leans upon him, is a just man. He who makes the life and death of God's great propitiation to be his sole reliance and confidence is justified in the sight of God, and is written down among the just by the Lord himself. His faith is imputed to him for righteousness, because his faith grasps the righteousness of God in Christ Jesus. "All that believe are justified from all things, from which ye could not be justified by the law of Moses." This is the testimony of the inspired word, and who shall gainsay it?

But the believer is also just in another sense, which the outside world better appreciates, though it is not more valuable than the former. The man who believes in God becomes by that faith moved to everything that is right, and good, and true. His faith in God rectifies his mind, and makes him just. In judgment, in desire, in aspiration, in heart, he is just. His sin has been forgiven him freely, and now, in the hour of temptation, he cries, "How then can I do this great wickedness, and sin against God?" He believes in the blood-shedding which God has provided for the cleansing of sin, and, being washed therein, he cannot choose to defile himself again. The love of Christ constraineth him to seek after that which is true, and right, and good, and loving, and honourable in the sight of God. Having received by faith the privilege of adoption, he strives to live as a child of God. Having obtained by faith a new life, he walks in newness of life. "Immortal principles forbid the child of God to sin." If any man live in sin and love it, he has not the faith of God's elect; for true faith purifies the soul. The faith which is wrought in us by the Holy Ghost is the greatest sin-killer under heaven. By the grace of God it affects the inmost heart, changes the desires and the affections, and makes the man a new creature in Christ Jesus. If there be on earth any who can truly be called just, they are those who are made so by faith in God through Jesus Christ our Lord. Indeed, no other men are "just" save those to whom the holy God gives the title, and of these the text says that they live by faith. Faith trusts God, and therefore loves him, and therefore obeys him, and therefore grows like him. It is the root of holiness, the spring of righteousness, the life of the just.

II. Upon that observation, which is vital to the text, I dwell no longer, but advance to another which is the converse of it, namely, that A MAN WHO IS JUST HAS FAITH IN GOD. Else, let me say, he were not just; for God deserves faith, and he who robs him of it is not just. God is so true that to doubt him is an injustice: he is so faithful that to distrust him is to wrong him—and he who does the Lord such an injustice is not a just man. A just man must first be just with the greatest of all beings. It would be idle for him to be just to his fellow-creatures only; if he did a wilful injustice to God, I say he would be unworthy of the name of just. Faith is what the Lord justly deserves to receive from his creatures: it is his due that we believe in what he says, and specially in reference to the gospel. When the great love of God in Christ Jesus is set forth plainly it will be believed by the pure in heart. If the great love of Christ in dying for us is fully understood it must be believed by every honest mind. To doubt the witness of God concerning his Son is to do the sorest injustice to infinite love. He that believeth not has rejected God's witness to the gift unspeakable and put from him that which deserves man's adoring gratitude, since it alone can satisfy the justice of God, and give peace to the conscience of man. A truly just man must, in order to the completeness of his justness, believe in God, and in all that he has revealed.

Some dream that this matter of justness only concerns the outer life, and does not touch man's belief. I say not so; righteousness concerns the inner parts of a man, the central region of his manhood; and truly just men desire to be made clean in the secret parts, and in the hidden parts they would know wisdom. Is it not so? We hear it continually asserted that the understanding and the belief constitute a province exempt from the jurisdiction of God. Is it indeed true that I may believe what I like without being accountable to God for my belief? No, my brethren; no single part of our manhood is beyond the range of the divine law. Our whole capacity as men lies under the sovereignty of him that created us, and we are as much bound to believe aright as we are bound to act aright: in fact, our actions and our thinkings are so intertwisted and entangled that there is no dividing the one from the other. To say that the rightness of the outward life sufficeth is to go clean contrary to the whole tenor of the word of God. I am as much bound to serve God with my mind as with my heart. I am as much bound to believe what God reveals as I am to do what God enjoins.

Errors of judgment are as truly sins as errors of life. It is a part of our allegiance to our great Sovereign and Lord that we do yield up our understanding, our thought, and our belief to his supreme control. No man is right until he is a right believer. A just man must be just towards God by believing in God, and trusting him in all that he is, and says, and does.

I see not also, my dear friends, what reason there is for a man to be just towards his fellow-men when he has given up his belief in God. If it comes to a pinch, and a man can deliver himself by a piece of dishonesty, why should he not be dishonest if there be no higher law than that which his fellow-men have made, no judgment-seat, no Judge, and no hereafter? A few weeks ago a man deliberately killed his employer, who had offended him, and as he gave himself up to the police, he said that he was not in the least degree afraid nor ashamed of what he had done. He admitted the murder, and owned that he knew the consequences very well; he expected to suffer about half-a-minute's pain upon the gallows, and then there would be an end of him, and he was quite prepared for that. He spoke and acted in consistency with his belief or his non-belief; and truly there is no form of crime but what becomes logical and legitimate if you take away from man faith in God and the hereafter. That gone, break up your commonwealth; there is nothing to hold humanity together; for without a God the moral government of the universe has ceased, and anarchy is the natural state of things. If there be no God, and no judgment to come, let us eat and drink, for to-morrow we die. If necessary, let us thieve, lie, and kill. Why not? if there be no law, no judgment, and no punishment for sin. I forget —nothing can be sinful; for if there be no lawgiver, there is no law; and if there be no law, then there can be no transgression. To what a chaos must all things come if faith in God be renounced. Where will the just be found when faith is banished? The logically just man is a believer in some measure or other; and he that is worthy to be called "just" in the scriptural sense, is a believer in the Lord Jesus Christ, who is made of God unto us righteousness.

III. But now I come to the point upon which I mean to dwell. Thirdly, BY THIS FAITH THE JUST MAN SHALL LIVE.

This is at the outset *a narrow statement;* it cuts off many pretended ways of living by saying, "The just shall live *by faith.*" This sentence savours of the strait gate which standeth at the head of the way—the narrow way which leadeth into life eternal. At one blow this ends all claims of righteousness apart from one mode of life. The best men in the world can only live by faith, there is no other way of being just in the sight of God. We cannot live in righteousness by self. If we are going to trust to ourselves, or anything that cometh of ourselves, we are dead while we so trust; we have not known the life of God according to the teaching of Holy Writ. You must come right out from confidence in everything that you are or hope to be. You must tear off the leprous garment of legal righteousness, and part with self in any and every form. Self-reliance as to the things of religion will be found to be self-destruction; you must rest in God as he is revealed in his Son Jesus Christ, and there alone. The just shall live by faith; but those who look to the works of the law are under the curse, and cannot live before God. The same is also true of those who endeavour to live by sense or feeling. They judge God by what they see : if he is bountiful to them in providence, he is a good God ; if they are poor, they have nothing good to say of him, for they measure him by what they feel, and taste, and see. If God works steadily to a purpose, and they can see his purpose, they commend his wisdom ; but when they either cannot see the purpose, or cannot understand the way by which the Lord is working unto it, straightway they judge him to be unwise. Living by sense turns out to be a senseless mode of life, bringing death to all comfort and hope.

> "Judge not the Lord by feeble sense,
> But trust him for his grace,"

for only by such trust can a just man live.

The text also cuts off all idea of living by mere intellect. Too many say, " I am my own guide, I shall make doctrines for myself, and I shall shift them and shape them according to my own devices." Such a way is death to the spirit. To be abreast of the times is to be an enemy to God. The way of life is to believe what God has taught, especially to believe in him whom God has set forth to be a propitiation for sin ; for that is making God to be everything and ourselves nothing. Resting on an infallible revelation, and trusting in an omnipotent Redeemer, we have rest and peace ; but on the other unsettled principle we become wandering stars, for whom is appointed the blackness of darkness for ever. By faith the soul can live, in all other ways we have a name to live and are dead.

The same is equally true of fancy. We often meet with a fanciful religion in which people trust to impulses, to dreams, to noises, and mystic things which they imagine they have seen : fiddle-faddle all of it, and yet they are quite wrapt up in it. I pray that you may cast out this chaffy stuff, there is no food for the spirit in it. The life of my soul lies not in what I think, or what I fancy, or what I imagine, or what I enjoy of fine feeling, but only in that which faith apprehends to be the word of God. We live before God by trusting a promise, depending on a person, accepting a sacrifice, wearing a righteousness, and surrending ourselves up to God—Father, Son, and Holy Ghost. Implicit trust in Jesus, our Lord, is the way of life, and every other way leads down to death. It is a narrowing statement, let those who call it intolerance say what they please ; it will be true when they have execrated it as much as it is now.

But, secondly, this is *a very broad statement*. Much is comprehended in the saying—"the just shall live by his faith." It does not say what part of his life hangs on his believing, or what phase of his life best proves his believing : it comprehends the beginning, continuance, increase, and perfecting of spiritual life as being all by faith. Observe that the text means that the moment a man believes he begins to live in the sight of God : he trusts his God, he accepts God's revelation of himself, he confides, reposes, leans upon his Saviour, and that moment he becomes a spiritually living man, quickened with spiritual life by God the Holy Ghost. All his existence before that belief was but a form of death : when he comes to trust in God he enters upon eternal life, and is born from above. Yes, but that is not all, nor half; for if that man is to continue living before God, if he is to hold on his way in holiness, his perseverance must be the result of continued faith. The faith which saves is not one single act done and ended on a certain day: it is an act continued and persevered in throughout the entire life of man. The just not only commences to live by his faith, but he continues to live by his faith: he does not begin in the spirit and end in the flesh, nor go so far by grace, and the rest of the way by the works of the law. "The just shall live by faith," says the text in the Hebrews, "but if any man draw back, my soul shall have no pleasure in him. But we are not of them who draw back unto perdition; but of them that believe to the saving of the soul." Faith is essential all along; every day and all the day, in all things. Our natural life begins by breathing, and it must be continued by breathing: what the breath is to the body, that is faith to the soul.

Brethren, if we are to make advance and increase in the divine life, it must still be in the same way. Our root is faith, and only through the root comes growth. Progress in grace comes not of carnal wisdom, or legal effort, or unbelief; nay, the flesh bringeth no growth unto the spiritual life, and efforts made in unbelief rather dwarf the inner life than cause it to grow. We become no stronger by mortifications, mournings, workings, or strivings, if these are apart from simple faith in God's grace; for by this one sole channel can nourishment come into the life of our spirit. The same door by which life came in at the first is that by which life continues to enter. If any man saith to me, "I once lived by believing in Christ; but I have now become spiritual and sanctified, and therefore I have no longer any need to look as a sinner to the blood and righteousness of Christ:" I tell that man that he has need to learn the first principles of the faith. I warn him that he has drawn back from the faith; for he who is justified by the law, or in any other way beside the righteousness of Christ, has fallen from grace, and left the only ground upon which a soul can be accepted with God. Ay, up to heaven's gate there is no staff for us to lean upon but faith in the ever-blessed Saviour and his divine atonement. Between this place and glory we shall never be able to live by merits, or live by fancies, or live by intellect; we shall still have to be as children taught of God, as Israel in the desert depending wholly on the great Invisible One. Ours it is for ever to look out of self, and to look above all things that are seen; for "the just shall live by his faith." It is a very broad sentence, a circle which encompasses the whole of our life which is worthy of the name. If there be any virtue, if there be any praise, if there be aught that is lovely or of good repute, we must receive it, exhibit it, and perfect it by the exercise of faith. Life in the Father's house, life in the church, life in private, life in the world, must all be in the power of faith if we are righteous men. That which is without faith is without life; dead works cannot gratify the living God; without faith it is impossible to please God.

I beg you to notice, in the third place, what *a very unqualified state-ment* it is. "The just shall live by his faith." Then, if a man have but a little faith, he shall live; and if he be greatly just, he shall still live by faith. Many a just man has come no further than striving after holiness, but he is justified by his faith : his faith is trembling and struggling, and his frequent prayer is, " Lord, I believe ; help thou mine unbelief ; " yet his faith has made him a just man. Sometimes he is afraid that he has no faith at all ; and when he has deep depression of spirits, it is as much as he can do to keep his head above water ; but even then his faith justifies him. He is like a barque upon a stormy sea : sometimes he is lifted up to heaven by flashing waves of mercy, and anon he sinks into the abyss among billows of affliction. What, then, is he a dead man ? I answer, Does that man truly believe God ? Does he accept the record concerning the Son of God ? Can he truly say, " I believe in the forgiveness of sins," and with such faith as he has does he cling alone to Christ and to none beside ? Then that man shall live, he shall live by his faith. If the littleness of our faith could destroy us how few would be numbered with the living ? " When the Son of man cometh, shall he find faith on the earth ? " Only here and there, and now and then, a Luther appears who really does believe with all his heart. The most of us are not so big as Luther's little finger : we have not so much faith in our whole souls as he had in one hair of his head : but yet even that little faith makes us live. I do not say that little faith will give us the strong, and vigorous, and lion-like life which Luther had ; but we shall live. The statement makes no distinction between this and that degree of faith, but lays it down still as an unquestionable truth, " the just shall live by faith." Blessed be God, then, I shall live, for I do believe in the Lord Jesus as my Saviour and my all. Do you not also believe in him ?

Ay, and is it not singular that this unqualified statement should not mention any other grace, as helping to make up the ground on which a just men lives ? " The just shall live by his faith :" but has he not love, has he not zeal, has he not patience, has he not hope, has he not humility, has he not holiness ? Oh, yes, he has all these, and he lives *in* them, but he does not live *by* them, because none of these so intimately connects him with Christ as does his faith. I will venture to use a very homely figure, because it is the best I can think of. Here is a little child, a suckling. It has many necessary members, such as its eyes, its ears, its legs, its arms, its heart, and so forth, and all these are necessary to it ; but the one organ by which the tiny babe lives is its mouth, by which it sucks from its mother all its nourishment. Our faith is that mouth by which we suck in fresh life from the promise of the ever-blessed God. Thus faith is that which we live by. Other graces are needful, but faith is the life of them all. We do not undervalue love, or patience, or penitence, or humility, any more than we depreciate the eyes or the feet of the babe. Still, the means of the life of the spiritual man is that mouth by which he receives divine food from the truth revealed by the Holy Ghost in sacred Scripture. Other graces produce results from that which faith receives, but faith is the Receiver-General for the whole isle of man.

This, dear friends, to proceed a little further, is *a very suggestive statement*,—" The just shall live by his faith ;" because it wears so many meanings. First, the righteous man is even to exist by his faith, that is to say, the lowest form of grace in a righteous character is dependent upon faith. But, brother, I hope you will not be so foolish as to say,—

"If I am but a living child of God, it is all I want : " no, we wish not only to have life, but to have it more abundantly. See yonder man rescued from drowning ; he is yet alive, but the only evidence of it is the fact that a mirror is somewhat bedewed by his breath: you would not be content to be alive for years in that poor fashion, would you? You ought to be grateful if you are spiritually alive even in that feeble way; but still we do not want to remain in a swooning state, we wish to be active and vigorous. Yet even for that lowest life you must have faith. For the feeblest kind of spiritual existence that can be called life at all, faith is needful. The just who barely live, who are feeble in mind, who are scarcely saved, are nevertheless delivered by faith. Without faith there is no heavenly life whatever.

Take the word "life" in a better sense, and the same will apply; "The just shall live by his faith." We sometimes meet with very poor persons who say to us in a pitiful tone, " Our wages are dreadfully scant." We say to them, " Do you really live upon so small a sum ? " They answer, " Well, Sir, you can hardly call it living; but we exist somehow." None of us would wish to live in that style if we could help it. We mean, then, by "life," some measure of enjoyment, happiness, and satisfaction. The just, when they have comfort, and joy, and peace, have them by faith. Thank God, peace of heart is our normal state, because faith is an abiding grace. We sing for joy of heart and rejoice in the Lord, and blessed be the Lord this is no novelty to us; but we have known this bliss, and still know it by faith alone. The moment faith comes in the music strikes up: if it were gone the owls would hoot. Luther can sing a psalm in spite of the devil; but he could not have done so if he had not been a man of faith. He could defy emperors, and kings, and popes, and bishops while he took firm hold upon the strength of God, but only then. Faith is the life of life, and makes life worth living. It puts joy into the soul to believe in the great Father and his everlasting love, and in the efficacious atonement of the Son, and in the indwelling of the Spirit, in resurrection, and eternal glory : without these we were of all men most miserable. To believe these glorious truths is to live—" The just shall live by his faith."

Life also means strength. We say of a certain man, What life he has in him: he is full of life, he seems all alive. Yes, the just obtain energy, force, vivacity, vigour, power, might, life—by faith. Faith bestows on believers a royal majesty. The more they can believe, the more mighty they become. This is the head that wears a crown; this is the hand that wields a sceptre; this is the foot whose royal tread doth shake the nations; faith in God links us with the King, the Lord God Omnipotent.

By faith the just live on when others die. They are not overcome by prevalent sin, or fashionable heresy, or cruel persecution, or fierce affliction : nothing can kill spiritual life while faith abides—"The just shall live by faith." Continuance and perseverance come this way. The righteous man when he is put back a while is not baffled; and when he is wounded by enemies, he is not slain. Where another man is drowned, he swims; where another man is trampled under foot, he rises and shouts victoriously,—" Rejoice not over me, O mine enemy. If I fall, yet shall I rise again !" In the fiery furnace of affliction he walks unharmed through faith. Ay, and when his turn comes to die, and, with many tears his brethren carry his ashes to the tomb, "he being dead yet speaketh." The blood of righteous Abel cried from the ground to the Lord, and it is still crying adown the ages, even to this hour. Luther's voice through four hundred years still sounds in the ears of men, and quickens our pulses like the beat of drum in martial music: he lives, he lives because he was a man of faith.

I would sum up and illustrate this teaching by mentioning certain incidents of Luther's life. Upon the great Reformer gospel light broke : y slow degrees. It was in the monastery that, in turning over the old Bible that was chained to a pillar, he came upon this passage —"The just shall live by his faith." This heavenly sentence stuck to him ; but he hardly understood all its bearings. He could not, however, find peace in his religious profession and monastic habit. Knowing no better, he persevered in penances so many, and mortifications so arduous, that sometimes he was found fainting through exhaustion. He brought himself to death's door. He must make a journey to Rome, for in Rome there is a fresh church for every day, and you may be sure to win the pardon of sins and all sorts of benedictions in these holy shrines. He dreamed of entering a city of holiness; but he found it to be a haunt of hypocrites and a den of iniquity. To his horror he heard men say that if there was a hell Rome was built on the top of it, for it was the nearest approach to it that could be found in this world; but still he believed in its Pope and he went on with his penances, seeking rest, but finding none. One day he was climbing upon his knees the Sancta Scala which still stands in Rome. I have stood amazed at the bottom of this staircase to see poor creatures go up and down on their knees in the belief that it is the very staircase that our Lord descended when he left Pilate's house, and certain steps are said to be marked with drops of blood; these the poor souls kiss most devoutly. Well, Luther was crawling up these steps one day when that same text which he had met with before in the monastery, sounded like a clap of thunder in his ears, "The just shall live by his faith." He rose from his prostration, and went down the steps never to grovel upon them again. At that time the Lord wrought him a full deliverance from superstition, and he saw that not by priests, nor priestcraft, nor penances, nor by anything that he could do, was he to live, but that he must live by his faith. Our text of this morning had set the monk at liberty, and set his soul on fire.

No sooner did he believe this than he began to live in the sense of being active. A gentleman, named Tetzel, was going about all over Germany selling the forgiveness of sins for so much ready cash. No matter what your offence, as soon as your money touched the bottom of the box your sins were gone. Luther heard of this, grew indignant, and exclaimed, " I will make a hole in his drum," which assuredly he did, and in several other drums. The nailing up of his theses on the church door was a sure way of silencing the indulgence music. Luther proclaimed pardon of sin by faith in Christ without money and without price, and the Pope's indulgences were soon objects of derision. Luther lived by his faith and therefore he who otherwise might have been quiet, denounced error as furiously as a lion roars upon his prey. The faith that was in him filled him with intense life, and he plunged into war with the enemy. After a while they summoned him to Augsburg, and to Augsburg he went, though his friends advised him not to go. They summoned him, as a heretic, to answer for himself at the Diet of Worms, and everybody bade him stay away, for he would be sure to be burned; but he felt it necessary that the testimony should be borne, and so in a wagon he went from village to village and town to town, preaching as he went, the poor people coming out to shake hands with the man who was standing up for Christ and the gospel at the risk of his life. You remember how he stood before that august assembly, and though he knew as far as human power went that his defence would cost him his life, for he would, probably, be committed to the flames like John Huss, yet he played the man for the Lord his God. That day in the German Diet Luther did a work for which ten thousand times ten thousand mothers' children have blessed his name, and blessed yet more the name of the Lord his God.

To put him out of harm's way for a while a prudent friend took him prisoner, and kept him out of the strife in the castle of Wartburg. There he had a good time of it, resting, studying, translating, making music, and preparing himself for the future which was to be so eventful. He did all that a man can do who is outside of the fray; but "the just shall live by his faith," and Luther could not be buried alive in ease, he must be getting on with his life-work. He sends word to his friends that he who was coming would soon be with them, and on a sudden he appeared at Wittenberg. The prince meant to have kept him in retirement somewhat longer, but Luther must live; and when the Elector feared that he could not protect him, Luther wrote him, "I come under far higher protection than yours; nay, I hold that I am more likely to protect your Grace than your Grace to protect me. He who has the strongest faith is the best Protector." Luther had learned to be independent of all men, for he cast himself upon his God. He had all the world against him, and yet he lived right merrily : if the Pope excommunicated him he burned the bull; if the Emperor threatened him he rejoiced, because he remembered the word of the Lord, "The kings of the earth set themselves, and the rulers take counsel together. He that sitteth in the heavens shall laugh." When they said to him, "Where will you find shelter if the Elector does not protect you?" he answered, "Under the broad shield of God."

Luther could not be still; he must speak, and write and thunder; and oh! with what confidence he spoke! Doubts about God and Scripture he abhorred. Melancthon says he was not dogmatical; I rather differ from Melancthon there, and reckon Luther to be the chief of dogmatists. He called Melancthon the "soft treader," and I wonder what we should have done if Luther had been Melancthon, and had trodden softly, too. The times needed a firmly assured leader, and faith made Luther all that for years, notwithstanding his many sorrows and infirmities. He was a Titan, a giant, a man of splendid mental calibre and strong physique; but yet his main life and force lay in his faith. He suffered much in exercises of the mind and through diseases of body, and these might well have occasioned a display of weakness; but that weakness did not appear; for when he believed, he was as sure of what he believed as of his own existence, and hence he was strong. If every angel in heaven had passed before him and each one had assured him of the truth of God, he would not have thanked them for their testimony, for he believed God without the witness of either angels or men : he thought the word of divine testimony to be more sure than aught that seraphim could say.

This man was forced to live by his faith, for he was a man of stormy soul, and only faith could speak peace to him. Those stirring excitements of his brought on him afterwards fearful depressions of spirit, and then he needed faith in God. If you read a spiritual life of him you will find that it was hard work sometimes for him to keep his soul alive. Being a man of like passions with us, and full of imperfections, he was at times as desponding and despairing as the weakest among us ; and the swelling grief within him threatened to burst his mighty heart. But both he and John Calvin frequently sighed for the rest of heaven, for they loved not the strife in which they dwelt, but would have been glad peacefully to feed the flock of God on earth, and then to enter into rest. These men dwelt with God in holy boldness of believing prayer, or they could not have lived at all.

Luther's faith laid hold upon the cross of our Lord, and would not be stirred from it. He believed in the forgiveness of sins, and could not afford to doubt it. He cast anchor upon Holy Scripture, and rejected all the inventions of clerics and all the traditions of the fathers. He was assured of the truth of the gospel, and never doubted but what it would prevail though earth and hell were leagued against it. When he came to die his old enemy assailed him fiercely, but when they asked him if he held the same faith his " Yes " was positive enough. They needed not to have asked him, they might have been sure of that. And now to-day the truth proclaimed by Luther continues to be preached, and will be till our Lord himself shall come. Then the holy city shall need no candle, neither light of the sun, because the Lord himself shall be the light of his people ; but till then we must shine with gospel light to our utmost. Brethren, let us stand to it that as Luther lived by faith even so will we ; and may God the Holy Ghost work in us more of that faith. Amen and Amen.

8. The Search for Faith

"Nevertheless when the Son of man cometh, shall he find faith on the earth?"—Luke xviii. 8.

IT is absolutely certain that God will hear the prayers of his people. From beneath the altar souls cry unto him day and night to vindicate the cause of Christ, the cause of truth and righteousness, and to cast down his adversary : these shall be answered speedily. Here on earth, scant though the supplication may be, yet there is a remnant according to the election of grace, who cease not to importune the Almighty God to make bare his arm, and display the majesty of his Word. Though for wise and gracious purposes the answer to those prayers may be delayed, yet it is absolutely certain. Shall not God avenge his own elect, which cry day and night unto him, though he keep their case long in hand ? Assuredly he will ; for those prayers are inspired by the Spirit, who knows the mind of God ; they are for the glory of God and of his Christ, and they are presented by our great High Priest. Longsuffering keeps back the advent and the judgment for a while ; for the Lord is not willing that any should perish, but that all should come to repentance ; but he will not for ever delay the long-expected end. The Lord Jesus himself gives us this personal assurance, "I tell you that he will avenge them speedily." No doubt remains when Jesus says, "I tell you." The Lord will come, and, according to his own reckoning, he will come *quickly*. His reckoning is according to the chronology of heaven, and this the heirs of heaven ought gladly to accept : it is meet that we keep celestial time even now.

Brethren, let not your hearts fail you as to the ultimate issue of the present conflict. "The Lord shall reign for ever and ever. Hallelujah." The idols he shall utterly abolish. Antichrist shall be overthrown ; like a millstone cast into the sea, it shall fall and be no more. The heathen shall be our Lord's inheritance, and the uttermost parts of the earth shall be his possession. He must reign until all enemies shall be put under his feet. If the present contest should be continued century after century, be not weary. It is only long to your impatience ; it is a short work unto God. So grand a volume of the book as this, which contains the history of redemption, may well

89

require a long time for its unrolling, and to such poor readers as we are the spelling of it out word by word may seem an endless task; but we shall yet come to its close, and then we shall find that, like the Book of Psalms, it ends in hallelujahs.

The matter to be questioned is not what God will do, but what men will do. Faithfulness is established in the very heavens: but what of faithfulness upon the earth? The part that God allots to us is that we believe his word, for so shall we be established: it is the child's part to trust his father, it is the disciple's part to accept the teaching of his Master. Alas! how little there is of it at this moment! Knowing the feebleness of the faith of those around him, and foreseeing that future generations would partake of the same folly, the Saviour gave utterance to this memorable question, "When the Son of man cometh, shall he find faith on the earth?" God is faithful; but are men faithful? God is true; but do we believe him? This is the point: and it is upon this that I shall speak this morning as the Holy Ghost shall help me.

I. I notice with regard to our text, first, that IT IS REMARKABLE IF WE CONSIDER THE PERSON MENTIONED AS SEARCHING FOR FAITH: "When the Son of man cometh, shall he find faith on the earth?"

When Jesus comes he will look for precious faith. He has more regard for faith than for all else that earth can yield him. Our returning Lord will care nothing for the treasures of the rich or the honours of the great. He will not look for the abilities we have manifested, nor the influence we have acquired; but he will look for our faith. It is his glory that he is "believed on in the world," and to that he will have respect. This is the jewel for which he is searching. This heavenly merchantman counts faith to be the pearl of great price—faith is precious to Jesus as well as to us. The last day will be occupied with a great scrutiny, and that scrutiny will be made upon the essential point—where is there faith, and where is there no faith? He that believeth is saved; he that believeth not is condemned. A search-warrant will be issued for our houses and our hearts, and the enquiry will be: Where is your faith? Did you honour Christ by trusting his word and his blood, or did you not? Did you glorify God by believing his revelation and depending upon his promise, or did you not? The fact that our Lord, at his coming, will seek for faith should cause us to think very highly of faith. It is no mere act of the intellect; it is a grace of the Holy Spirit which brings glory to God and produces obedience in the heart. Jesus looks for it because he is the proper object of it, and it is by means of it that his great end in his first advent is carried out. Dear hearers, conceive for a minute that our Saviour is searching for faith now. "His eyes behold, his eyelids try, the children of men." This is the gold he seeks after amid the quartz of our humanity. This is the object of his royal quest—Dost thou believe in the Lord Jesus Christ?"

When our Lord comes and looks for faith, *he will do so in his most sympathetic character.* Our text saith not, When the Son of *God* cometh, but "When *the Son of man* cometh, will he find faith on the earth?" It is peculiarly as the Son of man that Jesus will sit as a refiner, to discover whether we have true faith or not. He also as the Son of man displayed faith in God. In the Epistle to the Hebrews it is mentioned as one of the points in which he is made like unto his brethren, that he said, "I will put my trust in him." The life of Jesus was a life of faith—faith which cried, "My God, my God," even when he was forsaken. His was, on a grander scale than ours, the battle of faith in the great Father, waged against all the rebellious influences which were in array against him. He knows what fierce temptations men experience, for he has felt the same. He knows how want tries the faithful, and what faith is needed to be able to say, " Man shall not live by bread alone, but by every word that proceedeth out of the mouth of God shall man live." He knows how elevation tests the soul; for he once stood on the pinnacle of the temple, and heard the infernal whisper, "Cast thyself down: for he shall give his angels charge over thee." He knows what faith means in contradistinction to a false confidence which misreads the promise, and forgets the precept altogether. He will not err in judgment, and accept brass for gold. He knows what it is to be tempted with the proffer of honour and gain: " All these things will I give thee," said the fiend, " if thou wilt fall down and worship me." He knows how faith puts all the glory of the world away with its one brave and prompt utterance, "Get thee hence, Satan: for it is written, Thou shalt worship the Lord thy God, and him only shalt thou serve." Beloved, when Jesus comes as the Son of man he will recognize our weaknesses, he will remember our trials; he will know the struggle of our hearts, and the sorrow which an honest faith has cost us. He is best qualified to put the true price upon tried faith, self-denying faith, long-enduring faith. He will discern between the men who presume and the men who believe; the men who dote upon vain delusions, and those who follow the plain path of God's own word.

Further, I would have you note well that *the Son of man is the most likely person to discover faith if it is to be found*. Not a grain of faith exists in all the world except that which he has himself created. If thou hast faith, my brother, the Lord has dealt with thee; this is the mark of his hand upon thee. By faith he has brought thee out of thy death in sin, and the natural darkness of thy mind. " Thy faith hath saved thee," for it is the candlestick which holds the candle by which the chamber of thy heart is enlightened. Thy God and Saviour has put this faith in thee. Now, if faith in every instance is our Lord's gift, he knows where he has given it. If it is the work of God, he knows where he has produced it; for he never forsakes the work of his own hands. If that faith be only as a grain of mustard seed, and if it be hidden away in the obscurest corner of the earth, yet the loving Jesus spies it out, for he has an intimate concern in it, since he is its author and finisher. Our Lord is also the sustainer of faith; for faith is never independent of him upon whom it relies. The greatest believer would not believe for another moment unless grace were constantly given him to keep the flame of faith burning. Beloved friend, if thou hast had any experience of the inner life at all, thou knowest that he that first made thee live, must keep thee alive, or else thou wilt go back to thy natural death. Since faith from day to day feeds at the table of Jesus, then *he* knows where it is. It is well for us that we have one looking for faith who, on account of his having created and sustained it, will be at no loss to discern it.

Besides, *faith always looks to Christ.* There is no faith in the world worth having, but what looks to him, and through him to God, for everything. On the other hand, Christ always looks to faith; there never yet was an eye of faith but what it met the eye of Christ. He delights in faith: it is his joy to be trusted: it is a great part of the reward of his death that the sons of men should come and shelter in him. If faith looks to Christ, and Christ looks to faith, he is sure to find it out when he comes, and that makes the text so very striking: " When the Son of man cometh, shall *he* find faith on the earth ? "

The Son of man will give a wise and generous judgment in the matter. Some brethren judge so harshly that they would tread out the sparks of faith; but it is never so with our gracious Lord; he does not quench the smoking flax, nor despise the most trembling faith. The question becomes most emphatic when it is put thus. The tender and gentle Saviour, who never judges too severely, when he comes, shall even he find faith on the earth ? What a sad and humbling question it is! He who is no morose critic but a kind interpreter of character, he who makes great allowances for feebleness, he that carrieth the lambs of faith in his bosom and gently leads the weak ones—when even he shall come to make a kindly search, will he be able to find faith on the earth? Unbelief is rampant indeed, when he who is omniscient can scarce find a grain of faith amid the mass of doubt and denial! Ah me! that ever I should have to explain the question, " When the Son of man cometh, shall he find faith on the earth ? "

Once more: I want to put this question into a striking light by dwelling on *the time of the scrutiny.* " When the Son of man cometh, shall he find faith on the earth ? " Look ye, brethren, the ages are accumulating proofs of the truth of Christianity, and the search takes place when this process has reached its climax. Whatever may be said about the present torrent of doubt, which no doubt is exceedingly strong, yet the reason for doubt grows weaker and weaker every year. Every mound of earth in the East contributes a fresh testimony to the accuracy of the Word of God. Stones are crying out against the incredulity of sceptics. Moreover, all the experiences of all the saints, year after year, are swelling the stream of testimony to the faithfulness of God. You that are growing grey in his service know how every year confirms your confidence in the eternal verities of your God and Saviour. I know not how long this dispensation of longsuffering will last; but certainly the longer it continues the more wantonly wicked does unbelief become. The more God reveals himself to man in ways of providence, the more base is it on man's part to belie his solemn witness. But yet, my brethren, at the winding-up of all things, when revelation shall have received its utmost confirmation, even then faith will be such a rarity on the earth that it is a question if the Lord himself will find it. You have, perhaps, a notion that faith will go on increasing in the world; that the church will grow purer and brighter, and that there will be a wonderful degree of faith among men in the day of our Lord's appearing. Our Saviour does not tell us so; but he puts the question of our text about it. Even concerning the dawn of the golden age he asks, " When the Son of man cometh, shall he find faith on the earth ? "

I want you to notice *the breadth of the region of search.* He does not say, shall he find faith among philosophers ? When had they any ? He does not confine his scrutiny to an ordained ministry or a visible church; but he takes a wider sweep—"Shall he find faith *on the earth ?* " As if he would search from throne to cottage, among the learned and among the ignorant, among public men and obscure individuals : and, after all, it would be a question whether among them all, from the pole to the equator, and again from the equator to the other pole, he would find faith at all. Alas, poor earth, to be so void of faith ! Is there none in her vast continents, or on the lone islets of the sea? May it not be found in some of the countless ships upon the deep ? What! not upon the earth ? Not with Jesus himself to look for it ?

I have tried to set forth the question as distinctly as I can, that it may have due effect upon your minds. It sounds through the chambers of my soul like the knell of many a gay hope and pleasant imagination. Lord, what is man, that centuries of mercy can scarce produce a single fruit of faith among a whole world of the sons of Adam ? When thousands of summers and autumns have come and gone, shall there be no harvest of faith upon the earth, except a few ears of corn, thin and withered by the east wind ?

II. Let us somewhat change the run of our thoughts : having introduced the question as a remarkable one, we will next notice that IT IS EXCEEDINGLY INSTRUCTIVE IN CONNECTION WITH THE PARABLE OF WHICH IT IS PART. It is wrong to use the Bible as if it were a box full of separate links, and not a chain of connected truth. Some pick sentences out of it as a crow picks worms out of a ploughed field. If you tear words from their connection, they may not express the mind of the Spirit at all. No book, whether written by God or man, will bear to be torn limb from limb without being horribly mutilated. Public speakers know the unfairness of this to themselves, and Holy Scripture suffers even more. The connection settles the drift and directs us to the true meaning—a meaning which may be very different from that which it seems to bear when rent from its surroundings. Let us carefully note that this passage occurs in connection with the parable of the importunate widow pleading with the unjust judge; for it is to be interpreted in connection with it.

Hence, it means, first of all : When the Son of man cometh, shall he find upon the earth *the faith which prays importunately,* as this widow did ? Now, the meaning is dawning upon us. We have many upon the earth who pray; but where are those whose continual coming is sure to prevail ? I thank God that the prayer-meetings of this church are well sustained by praying men and women ; but where are the Jacob-like wrestlers ? I am afraid it cannot even be said of many churches that their prayer-meetings are at all what they should be ; for among many the gathering for prayer is despised, and men say, " It is only a prayer-meeting ! " As if that were not the very crown and queen of all the assemblies of the church, with the sole exception of that for the breaking of bread. Brethren, I will not judge with severity, but where are those who offer effectual, fervent, much-prevailing prayer ? I know that there are many here who do not neglect private and family devotion, and who pray constantly for the prosperity of the Church of Jesus Christ, and for the salvation of souls. But even to you I put the question: If the Son of man were now to come, how many would he find among us that pray with a distinct, vehement, irresistible importunity of faith? In the olden days, there was a John Knox, whose prayers were more terrible to the adversary than whole armies, because he pleaded in faith; but where shall we find a Knox at this hour? Every age of revival has had its men mighty in prayer—where are ours? Where is the Elias on the top of Carmel who will bring down the rain upon these parched fields? Where is the church that will pray down a Pentecost? I will not decry my brethren in the ministry, nor speak little of deacons and elders, and other distinguished servants of my Lord; but still, my brothers and sisters, taking us all round, how few of us know what it is to pray the heaven-overcoming prayer which is needful for this crisis! How few of us go again, and again, and again to God, with tears, and cries, and heart-break, pleading as for our own lives for the increase of Zion, and the saving of the ungodly! If the Son of man cometh, will he find much of such praying faith among our own churches? Ah me! that I should have to ask such a question; but I do ask it, hanging my head for shame.

The importunate widow waited with strong resolve, and never ceased through sullen doubt. If the judge had not yet heard her, she was sure he must hear her, for she had made up her mind that she would plead until he did. A waiting faith is rare. Men can believe for a time, but to hold out through the long darkness is another matter. Some soldiers are good at a rush, but they cannot form a square, and stand fast hour after hour. When the Son of man cometh, will he find many who can believe in a delaying God, and plead a long-dated promise—waiting, but never wearying? When we have a revival, and everybody is crying "Hosannah!" certain eager folk are sure to be in the front; but when the popular voice growls out its "Crucify him!" where are they? Where are even Peter, and John, and the rest of the disciples? Go, learn to plead on when no answer comes, and to press on when repulsed: this is the test of faith. It is so easy to be a believer when everybody believes; but to be a believer when nobody believes, and to be none the less a firm believer because nobody believes with you, this is the mark of the man valiant for truth, and loyal to Jesus. Brethren, is it, after all, a matter of counting heads? Can you not dare to be in the right with two or three? Can you not be like rocks which defy the raging waves? Can you not let the billows of popular misbelief wash over you, and break and crash, and break and crash in vain? If these things move you, where is your faith? When the Son of man cometh, how many will he find on the earth whose faith stands not in men, but in the witness of God?

The widow staked her all upon the result of her pleading with the judge. She had not two strings to her bow, she had but one resort in her trouble: the judge must hear her. She would lose her little property, and her children would die of starvation, if he did not hear her. He must hear her; about that she had no two opinions. What we want at the present moment is the man that believes God, and believes the gospel, and believes Christ, and does not care two pins about anything else. We need those who will stake reputation, hope, and life itself upon the veracity of God and the certainty of the everlasting gospel. To such the revelation of God is not one among many truths : it is the one and only saving truth. Alas! we have nowadays to deal with foxes with holes to run to in case they are too closely hunted. Oh, to have done with all glory but glorying in the cross! For my part, I am content to be a fool if the old gospel be folly. What is more, I am content to be lost if faith in the atoning sacrifice will not bring salvation. I am so sure about the whole matter, that if I were left alone in the world as the last believer in the doctrines of grace, I would not think of abandoning them, nor even toning them down to win a convert. My all is staked on the veracity of God: "Let God be true, but every man a liar."

"When the Son of man cometh, shall he find faith on the earth," such as he deserves at our hands ? Do we believe in Jesus practically, in matter-of-fact style ? Is our faith fact, and not fiction ? If we have the truth of faith, have we the degree of faith which we might have ? Just think of this : "If ye have faith as a grain of mustard seed, ye shall say unto this mountain, Remove hence to yonder place, and it shall remove." What does this mean ? Brethren, are we not off the rails ? Do we even know what faith means ? I begin sometimes to question whether we believe at all. What signs follow our believing ? When we think what wonders faith could have done ; when we consider what marvels our Lord might have wrought among us if it had not been for our unbelief; are we not humiliated ? Have we ever cut ourselves clear of the hamper of self-trustfulness ? Have we ever launched out into the deep in clear reliance upon the eternal God ? Have we ever quitted the visible for the invisible ? Have we clung to the naked promise of God and rested upon the bare arm of omnipotence, which in and of itself is more than sufficient for the fulfilment of every promise ? O Lord, where are we ? Where shall we find an oasis of faith amid this wilderness of doubt ? Where shall we find an Abraham ? Is not the question an instructive one when set in connection with the parable which teaches us the power of importunate prayer ?

III. In the next place, our text seems to me to be SUGGESTIVE IN VIEW OF ITS VERY FORM. It is put as a question : "When the Son of man cometh, shall he find faith on the earth ?" I think it warns us *not to dogmatize about what the latter days will be.* Jesus puts it as a question. Shall he find faith on the earth ? If you say, "No," my dear friend, I shall be very much inclined to take the other side, and warmly plead the affirmative. I remember how Elias said that he only was left, and yet the Lord had reserved unto himself seven thousand men that had not bowed the knee to Baal. Nations that know not Christ shall run unto him, and the kings of Sheba and Seba shall offer gifts. I venture to hope that when the Son of man comes he will find faith on the earth : but if you vehemently assert that it will be so, I shall be driven to advance the negative side with much apprehension that it may prove true. When our Lord was here before, he found little enough of faith ; and he has distinctly told us that when he shall come the second time, men will be as they were in the days of Noah : " they did eat, they drank, they married wives, they were given in marriage, until the day that Noe entered into the ark." I am inclined to take neither side. Let it remain a question, as our Lord has put it.

This question leads us to much holy fear as to the matter of faith. If our gracious Lord raises the question, the question ought to be raised. They say that some of us are old fogies, because we are jealous for the Lord of hosts. They say that we are nervous and fidgety, and that our fears are the result of advancing age. Yes, at fifty-three I am supposed to be semi-imbecile with years. If I were of their way of thinking, I do not suppose that this would occur to them. We fall into a pessimism—I think that is the word they use : I do not know much about such terms. Surely the Saviour was not nervous. None will dare to accuse him of foolish anxiety ; but yet he puts it, " When the Son of man cometh, shall he find faith on the earth ?" As far as my observation goes, it is a question which might suggest itself to the most hopeful persons at this time ; for *many processes are in vigorous action which tend to destroy faith.* The Scriptures are being criticized with a familiarity which shocks all reverence, and their very foundation is being assailed by persons who call themselves Christians. A chilling criticism has taken the place of a warm, childlike, loving confidence. As one has truly said, " We have now a temple without a sanctuary." Mystery is discarded that reason may reign. Men have eaten of the fruit of the tree of knowledge of good and evil till they think themselves gods. Revealed truth is not now a doctrine to be believed, but a proposition to be discussed. The loving woman at Jesus' feet is cast out to make room for the traitor kissing Christ's cheek. Like Belshazzar, our men of modern thought are drinking out of the vessels of Jehovah's sanctuary in honour of their own deities. The idea of child-like faith is scouted, and he is regarded as the most honest man that can doubt the most, and pour most contempt upon the authority of the divine word. If this continues we may well say, " When the Son of man cometh, shall he find faith on the earth?" In some places the greatest fountain of infidelity is the Christian pulpit. If this is the case—and I am sure it is so—what must become of the churches, and what must come to the outlying world ? Will Jesus find faith in the earth when he comes ?

In addition to many processes which are in action to exterminate faith, *are there not influences which dwarf and stunt it?* Where do you find great faith ? Where is the preaching or the teaching that is done in full faith in what is preached and taught ? It is no use flogging other people ; let us come home to ourselves. My brothers and sisters, where is our own faith ? It seemed almost a novelty in the church when it was stated long ago that Mr. George Müller walked by faith in regard to temporal things. To feed children by faith in God was looked upon as a pious freak. We have come to a pretty pass, have we not, when God is not to be trusted about common things ? Abraham walked with God about daily life ; but, nowadays, if you meet with a man who walks with God as to his business, trusts God as to every item and detail of his domestic affairs, persons look at him with a degree of suspicious wonder. They think he has grace in his heart, but they also suspect that he has a bee in his bonnet, or he would not act in that sort of way. Oh yes, we have a fancied faith; but when it comes to the stern realities of life where is our faith?

My brethren, why are you so full of worldly care? Why are you so anxious, if you have faith in God? Why do you display in worldly things almost as much distrust as worldly men? Whence this fear? this murmuring? this worry? O my Saviour, if thou wert to come, we could not defend ourselves for our wretched mistrust, our foolish apprehension, our want of loving reliance upon thee. We do not trust thee as thou oughtest to be trusted; and if this be the case among those who are such great debtors to thy loving faithfulness, where wilt thou find faith on earth? Where is that unstaggering faith which betakes itself to prevailing prayer, and so rises above the petty miseries of the hour, and the fears of a threatening future?

Do you not think that this, put in a question as it is, *invites us to intense watchfulness over ourselves?* Do you not think it should set us scrutinizing ourselves as our Lord will scrutinize us when he comes? You have been looking for a great many things in yourself, my brother; let me entreat you to look to your faith. What if love grow cold! I am sorry for it; but, after all, the frost must have begun in your faith. You are not so active as you used to be; that is to be greatly regretted; but the streams run low because the well-head is not so full as it was wont to be; your faith is failing. Oh that your soul were fed upon divine realities! Oh that you had a vivid consciousness of the certainty of God's presence and power! When faith is strong, all the other graces are vigorous. The branches flourish when the root sucks up abundant nutriment; and when faith is in a healthy state, all the rest of the spiritual man will be vigorous also. Brethren, guard well your faith. My fear is that when Christ comes, if he delays much longer, he will find many of us faint because of our long waiting, and because of the disappointments which arise out of the slow spread of the gospel. The nations continue in unbelief. O Lord, how long! Because we have not accomplished all that we hoped to have done, we are apt to grow weary. Or perhaps when he comes he will find us sleeping for sorrow, like the disciples in the garden when he came to them thrice and found them very heavy. We may get to feel so sad that the gospel does not conquer all mankind, that we may fall into a swoon of sadness, a torpor of despair, and so be asleep when the Bridegroom cometh. I fear, most of all, that when Jesus comes he may find that the love of many has waxed cold because iniquity abounds. Warm-hearted saints keep each other warm, but cold also is contagious. When sin abounds saints may be able to stand against it; and yet it has a sad tendency to chill their faith. If the Master comes and finds us lukewarm, it will be a calamity indeed. The question stirs a bitter anguish in my soul. I trust it moves you also.

It is a question. I cannot answer it, but I open wide the doors of my heart to let it enter and try me. It acts like a fan in the Lord's hand to purge the floor. It sweeps away my self-confidence and leads me to watch and pray, that I enter not into the temptation of giving up my faith. I pray that we may stand fast when others slide, so that when the Lord cometh we may be found accepted of him.

97

IV. I will close with this remark: my text is very IMPRESSIVE IN RESPECT TO PERSONAL DUTY. "When the Son of man cometh, shall he find faith on the earth." Let faith have a home in *our* hearts, if it is denied a lodging everywhere else. If *we* do not trust our Lord, and trust him much more than we have ever done, we shall deserve his gravest displeasure. It will be a superfluity of naughtiness for us to doubt; for to some of us conversion was a clear, sharp, and distinct fact. The change made in our characters was so manifest that the devil himself could not make us doubt it. We know that the misery we suffered under a sense of sin was no fiction, and that the peace we received through faith in Jesus was no dream. Wherefore do we doubt? Since conversion some of us have been led in a strange way, and every step of it has shown us that the Lord is good and true, and ought to be trusted without stint. We have been sore sick, and full of pain, and anguish, and depression of spirit, and yet we have been upheld, and sustained, and brought through. In great labours we have been strengthened, in great undertakings we have been supported. Some of you have been very poor, or your business has been declining, and emergencies have been frequent, and yet all these have proved the truth of God. Do not these things make it the more incumbent upon you to trust him? Others of you have suffered sad bereavements: you have lost, one after another, the props of your comfort; but when you have gone to God he has heard your prayers, and been better to you than father, husband, or friend. It is down in your diary in black and white that his mercy endureth for ever; and you have said to yourself many times, "I shall never doubt again after this." Brethren, it ought to us to be impossible to mistrust, and natural to confide; and yet I fear it is not so. If after all this watering we grow so little faith, we may not wonder that our Lord said, "When the Son of man cometh, shall he find faith on the earth?"

Some of us have been so familiar with dying beds, we have seen so many pass away in holy calm, and even with transporting triumph, that for us to doubt is disrespect to the memories of the saints. For us to doubt would be treachery to the Lord who has favoured ourselves also with visits of his love. We may doubt the dearest ones we have, and that would be cruel; but we had better do that than cast any suspicion upon him who has manifested himself to us as he does not to the world. I speak not to you all, but I speak to those whom the Lord has specially favoured, to whom he has revealed his secrets, and made known his covenant; for these to question his faithfulness is wickedness. What shall I say of his own elect, if they do not believe him? If it were possible for you to quit your faith, you would crucify your Lord afresh. He must not be thus wounded in the house of his friends. No, go where thou wilt, O unbelief, thou shalt not find willing lodgment in my heart. From my spirit thou shalt be banished as a detested traitor; for my Beloved is true, and I will lean upon him.

I think I hear you say, "We are resolved upon it; we are called to have faith in our Lord, even if none else believe him." Then look to it that you do not fail in these evil times. If you would keep your faith, settle it in your minds that the Holy Scriptures are inspired of the Holy Ghost, and so are our infallible rule of faith. If you give up that foundation you cannot exhibit faith worthy of the name. It is as clear as the sun in the heavens that a childlike faith in God as he is revealed is not possible to the man who doubts the revelation. You must accept the revelation as infallible, or you cannot unquestioningly believe in the God therein revealed. If you once give up inspiration, the foundations are removed, and all building is laborious trifling. How are the promises the support of faith if they are themselves questionable? God can only be known by his own light, and if we cannot trust the light, where are we? Next, settle it in your soul as to the Holy Spirit's dealings with yourself. He has renewed you in the spirit of your mind. At least, I ask the question—Has he or has he not? You were converted by a divine agency from your lost estate of sin, and brought by the same divine agency into newness of life: were you or were you not? Unless you are quite certain about this, it is not possible for you to rise to any height of faith. You must know that God has come into contact with your soul, or else what have you to believe? Next to that belief, you must know your full pardon and sure justification through the blood and righteousness of Jesus Christ your Lord. Believe in the precious blood: whatever else you doubt, believe in the merit of the great sacrifice of Calvary. Rejoice in your own acceptance through the sacrifice, seeing your whole faith rests therein. O brothers, our eternal hopes cannot be built on speculation; we need revelation. We cannot fight the battles of life with probabilities; we need certainties for such a conflict. If God has not revealed fixed truth, you may go and think and dream; but if he has given us a clear revelation, let us believe it, and cease to imagine and invent. O sirs, if you must speculate, risk your silver and your gold; but I beseech you to lay aside all idea of speculating in reference to your souls. I want absolute certainties and unquestionable verities to bear me up when death's cold flood is rising up to my loins. Divine truths, as they are written in the Book, and brought home to the heart by the Holy Ghost, are sure standing ground for that faith which Jesus looks for. He looks for it in vain when men no longer accept his work as undoubted fact. Again, if you would have strong faith, never relax your confidence in the efficacy of prayer. This is essential to my text; for the widow used no other weapon than prayer in her importunity with the judge. She would not have persevered as she did in her pleadings if she had not felt morally certain that in the long run she would prevail. Brethren, believe that God hears your prayers, and that he will answer them. As for me, I do not want any argument to prove the influence of prayer with God. I have tried it, and do try it, till it is no longer an experiment. The man that habitually eats bread knows that he is nourished by it: the man that habitually lives by prayer to God knows that God hears him. It would be absurd to offer him evidence for or against the statement. If a person were to argue with me that there was no sun in the heavens, I am afraid I should laugh outright. If anyone said that he did not believe me to be alive, I do not know in what way I could prove it to him. Would it be lawful to kick him, by way of argument? When a man says, "I do not believe in prayer," I answer, "What if you do not? You are the only loser." That God answers prayer is a living certainty to me, and I can say no more and no less. If you do not believe in prayer, assuredly the Lord will not find in you the faith of which our text speaks. If you regard it as a pious exercise which refreshes the devout but has no power whatever with God—well then, if all are of your mind, the Son of man will find no faith on the earth. Do not talk about believing, you know nothing of the matter.

If you do believe, believe up to the hilt. Plunge into this sea of holy confidence in God, and you shall find waters to swim in. He that believes what he believes shall see what he shall see. No man was ever yet found guilty of believing in God too much. Among the high intelligences of heaven no creature was ever censured for being too credulous when dealing with the word of the Most High. Let us believe implicitly and explicitly. Let us believe without measure and without reserve. Let us hang our all upon the truth of God. Let us aspire also to walk with God in the heavenlies, and become the King's Remembrancers. Let us seek grace to become importunate pleaders of a sort that cannot be denied, since their faith overcomes heaven by prayer. Oh, that I might have in my church many a prevailing Israel! Some here know what it is to be up early in the morning to besiege the throne of grace with all the power of believing prayer. How much I owe to these dear ones, eternity alone will declare! Oh, that we had many more intercessors, who would bear sinners on their hearts day and night, before the Lord, and, like their Saviour, would never rest till the Lord built up his church! Alas, for the rarity of such conquering faith! I question whether there are not Christian people here who have never heard a certain text which I am about to quote; and I am sure there are others who will shudder when they hear it. "Thus saith the Lord, concerning the work of my hands command ye me." "Surely that cannot be Scripture!" cries one. But it is so. Turn to Isaiah xlv. 11, and read it both in the Authorized and the Revised Versions. Can a man command the Lord? Yes, to believing men he puts himself at their call; he bids them command his help, and use it as they will. Oh that we could rise to this! Is there such faith among us? If there be not, may our Lord Jesus, by his Spirit, work it in us for his own glory! Amen.

9. Faith Essential to Pleasing God

" But without faith it is impossible to please him : for he that cometh to God must believe that he is, and that he is a rewarder of them that diligently seek him."— Hebrews xi. 6.

MEN have lived who have pleased God : Enoch was one of them, but he was not the only one. In all ages certain persons have been well-pleasing to God, and their walk in life has been such as was his delight. It should be the aim of every one of us to please God. The thing is possible, notwithstanding all our imperfections and infirmities : let us aim at it in the power of the Holy Ghost. What has been wrought in one man may be wrought in another. We, too, may be well-pleasing unto God ; therefore let us seek after it with hopefulness. If we so live as to please the Lord, we shall only be acting as we ought to act ; for we ought to please him who made us and sustains us in being. He is our God and Lord, and obedience to him is the highest law of our being. Moreover, the glorious Jehovah is so perfectly good, so supremely holy, that the conduct which pleases him must be of the best and noblest sort, and therefore we should seek after it. Should we not aspire to that character upon which God himself can smile? The approbation of our fellow-men is pleasant in its way ; but they are always imperfect, and often mistaken ; and so we may be well-pleasing to them, and yet may be far removed from righteousness. It may be a calamity to be commended in error, for it may prevent our becoming really commendable. But God makes no mistake ; the Infinitely Holy knows no imperfection ; and if it be possible for us to be pleasing to him, it should be our one object to reach that condition. As Enoch, in a darker age, was pleasing to him, why should not we, upon whom the gospel day has dawned? God grant us to find grace in his sight !

If we please God, we shall have realized the object of our being. It is written concerning all things, " For his pleasure they are and were created " ; and we miss the end of creation if we are not pleasing to the Lord. To fulfil God's end in our creation is to obtain the highest joy. If we are pleasing to God, although we shall not escape

101

trial, for even the highest qualities must be tested, yet we shall find great peace and special happiness. He is not an unhappy man who is pleasing to God : God hath blessed him, yea, and he shall be blessed. By pleasing God we shall become the means of good to others : our example will rebuke and stimulate ; our peace will convince and invite. Being himself well-pleasing to God, the godly man will teach transgressors God's way, and sinners shall be converted unto him. I therefore, without the slightest hesitancy, set it before you as a thing to be desired by us all, that we should win this testimony—that we are pleasing unto God.

Here the apostle comes in with a needful instruction. *He asserts that faith is absolutely needful, if we would please God.* Then, to help us still further, *he mentions two essential points of faith :* " He that cometh to God must believe that he is, and that he is a rewarder of them that diligently seek him." When I have spoken on these two points, I shall close, as God shall help me, by showing that *he then teaches us many valuable lessons.*

I. First, then, THE APOSTLE ASSERTS THAT FAITH IS ABSOLUTELY ESSENTIAL TO THE PLEASING OF GOD. Take, as a key-word, the strong word *"impossible."* " Without faith it is impossible to please God." He does not say it is difficult, or so needful that without it success is barely possible ; but, point-blank, he declares it to be *" impossible."* When the Holy Spirit says that a thing is impossible, it is so in a very absolute sense. Let us not attempt the impossible. To attempt a difficulty may be laudable, but to rush upon an impossibility is madness. We must not, therefore, hope to please God by any invention of our own, however clever, nor by any labour of our own, however ardent; since infallible inspiration declares that, " without faith it is impossible to please God."

We are bound to believe this statement, because we have it in the sacred volume, stated upon divine authority; but, for your help, I would invite you to think of some few matters which may show you how impossible it is to please God without faith in him.

For, first, *without faith there is no capacity for communion with God at all.* The things of God are spiritual and invisible : without faith we cannot recognize such things, but must be dead to them. Faith is the eye which sees ; but without that eye we are blind, and can have no fellowship with God in those sacred truths which only faith can perceive. Faith is the hand of the soul, and without it we have no grasp of eternal things. If I were to mention all the images by which faith is set forth, each one would help you to see that you must have faith in order to know God and enter into converse with him. It is only by faith that we can recognize God, approach him, speak to him, hear him, feel his presence, and be delighted with his perfections. He that has not faith is toward God as one dead ; and Jehovah is not the God of the dead, but of the living. The communion of the living God goes not forth toward death and corruption ; his fellowship is with those who have spiritual life, a life akin to his own. Where there is no faith, there has been no quickening of the Holy Spirit, for faith is of the very essence of spiritual life ; and so the man who has no faith can no more commune with the living God, and give him pleasure, than can a stock or a stone, a horse or an ox, hold converse with the human mind.

Again, *without faith the man himself is not pleasing to God.* We read, " Without faith it is impossible to please God "; but the Revision has it better: " Without faith it is impossible to be well-pleasing unto God." The way of acceptance described in Scripture is, first, the man is accepted, and then what that man does is accepted. It is written : " And he shall purify the sons of Levi, that they may offer unto the Lord an offering in righteousness." First, God is pleased with the person, and then with the gift, or the work. The unaccepted person offers of necessity an unacceptable sacrifice. If a man be your enemy, you will not value a present which he sends you. If you know that he has no confidence in you, but counts you a liar, his praises are lost upon you; they are empty, deceptive things which cannot possibly please you. O my hearers, in your natural state you are so sinful that God cannot look upon you with complacency! Concerning our race it is written : " It repented the Lord that he had made man on the earth, and it grieved him at his heart." Concerning many God has said, " My soul lothed them, and their soul also abhorred me." Is this true of us ? " Ye must be born again," or ye cannot be pleasing to the Lord. Ye must believe in Jesus; for only to as many as receive him does he give power to become the sons of God. When we believe in the Lord Jesus, the Lord God accepts us for his Beloved's sake, and in him we are made kings and priests, and permitted to bring an offering which pleases God. As the man is, such is his work. The stream is of the nature of the spring from which it flows. He who is a rebel, outlawed and proclaimed, cannot gratify his prince by any fashion of service; he must first submit himself to the law. All the actions of rebels are acts done in rebellion. We must first be reconciled to God, or it is a mockery to bring an offering to his altar. Reconciliation can only be effected through the death of the Lord Jesus, and if we have no faith in that way of reconciliation we cannot please God. Faith in Christ makes a total change in our position towards God—we who were enemies are reconciled; and from this comes towards God a distinct change in the nature of all our actions : imperfect though they be, they spring from a loyal heart, and they are pleasing to God.

Remember, that, *in human associations, want of confidence would prevent a man's being well-pleasing to another.* If a man has no confidence in you, you can have no pleasure in him. If you had a child, and he had no trust in his father, no belief in his father's kindness, no reliance on his father's word—it would be most painful, and it would be quite impossible that you should take any pleasure in such a child. If you had a servant in your house who always suspected your every action, and believed in nothing that you said or did, but put a wrong construction upon everything, it would make the house very miserable, and you would be well rid of such an inmate. How can I take pleasure in a man who associates with me, and pretends to serve me, but all the while thinks me a sheer impostor, and gives me no credit for truthfulness ? Such a person would be an eye-sore to me. It is clear that want of confidence would destroy any pleasure which one man might have in another. When the creature dares to doubt his Creator, how can the Creator be pleased? When the word which wrought creation is not enough for a man to rest upon, he may pretend what he will of righteousness and obedience, but the whole affair is rotten at the core, and God can take no pleasure in it.

Note again: *unbelief takes away the common ground upon which God and man can meet.* Two persons who are pleasant to one another, must have certain common views and objects. God's great object is the glorification of his Son; and how can we be pleasing to him if we dishonour that Son? The Father delights in Jesus: the very thought of him is a pleasure to God. He said, as if to himself only, "This is my beloved Son, in whom I am well pleased." This he said, afterwards, to others, that they might regard it—"This is my beloved Son; hear ye him." He delights in what his Son has done: he smells a sweet savour of rest in his glorious sacrifice. If you and I believe in God's plan of salvation through Jesus Christ, we have a common ground of sympathy with God; but if not, we are not in harmony. How can two walk together except they be agreed? If we have thoughts of Jesus such as the Father has, we can live together and work together; but if we are opposed to him on a point which is as the apple of his eye, we cannot be well-pleasing to him. If Jesus be despised, rejected, distrusted, or even neglected, it is not possible for us to be pleasing to God. According to the well-worn fable, two persons who are totally different in their pursuits cannot well live together: the fuller and the charcoal-burner were obliged to part; for whatever the fuller had made white, the collier blackened with his finger. If differing pursuits divide, much more will differing feelings upon a vital point. It is Jesus whom Jehovah delights to honour; and if you will not even trust Jesus with your soul's salvation, you grieve the heart of God, and he can have no pleasure in you. Unbelief deprives the soul of the divinely-appointed meeting-place at the mercy-seat, which is the person of the Lord Jesus, where God and man unite in one Mediator, and the Lord shines forth on the suppliant.

Assuredly, again, *want of faith destroys all prospect of love.* Although we may not perhaps see it, there lies at the bottom of all love a belief in the object loved, as to its loveliness, its merit, or its capacity to make us happy. If I do not believe in a person, I cannot love him. If I cannot trust God, I cannot love him. If I do not believe that he loves me, I shall feel but slight emotions of love to him. If I refuse to see anything in the greatest display of his love, if I do not value the gift of his dear Son, then I cannot love him. We love him because he first loved us; but if we will not believe in his love, the motive power is gone. If we reject the word which saith, "God so loved the world, that he gave his only begotten Son, that whosoever believeth in him should not perish, but have everlasting life," then we have put from out of the heart the grand incentive to love. But love on our part is essential to our pleasing God: how can he be pleased with an unloving heart? Is not the Lord's chief demand of men that we love him with all our heart, with all our soul, with all our mind, and with all our strength? Without faith love is impossible, and God's pleasure in us must be impossible.

Again, dear friends, *want of faith will create positive variance* on many points. Note a few. If I trust God, and believe in him, I shall submit myself to his will; even when it becomes very painful to me I shall say, "It is the Lord: let him do what seemeth him good." But if I do not believe that he is God, and that he is aiming at my good, then I shall resent his chastisements, and shall kick against his will. What he wills me to suffer, I shall not be willing to suffer; but I shall rebel, and murmur, and proudly accuse my Maker of injustice, or want of love. I shall be in a rebellious state towards him, and then he cannot have pleasure in me. "The Lord taketh pleasure in them that fear him, in those that hope in his mercy"; but he will walk contrary to us, if we walk contrary to him by refusing to bow ourselves before his hand.

Without faith, moreover, I get to be at variance with God in another way; for inasmuch as I desire to be saved, I shall seek salvation in my own way, and go about to establish a righteousness of my own. Whatever it may be, whether it be by ceremonies, or by good works, or by feelings, or what not, I shall, in some way or other, set up a way of salvation other than that which God has appointed through Christ Jesus. God's love to Christ is supreme, and he will not endure that a rival should be set up in opposition to him. Another way of salvation is Antichrist, and this provokes the Lord to jealousy. If you are labouring to be saved in one way, while God declares that through his Son is the only way of salvation, you· are acting in distinct opposition to the Lord in a matter which does not admit of any compromise. Rejectors of Christ are enemies to God. If you pretend that you are God's servants, you are convicted of falsehood if you refuse to honour his Son by trusting in him. If you believe in Christ, whom he has sent, you work the work of God; and not else. Self-righteousness is an insult to Christ, and a distinct revolt from God. He who has no faith seeks salvation by a way that is derogatory to the Lord Jesus, and it is impossible for him to please God.

We must be at variance with God if we are without faith; for it is a solemn truth that "He that believeth not God hath made him a liar; because he believeth not the record that God gave of his Son." This is the crime of the unbeliever: so is it stated by the Holy Spirit speaking by the beloved John. Could you take any pleasure in a man who made you out to be a liar? Perhaps with great patience you could bear with him, but you could not be pleased with him: that would be out of the question. Does a man daily, by the mode of his life, and by the evident drift of his actions, give you the lie?— how can he talk of giving you pleasure? Nothing he could do would please you while he calls you a liar. He that makes God to be a liar, makes him to be no God; to the best of his ability he undeifies the Deity; he uncrowns the Lord of all, and even stabs at the heart of the Eternal. To ⊦alk of being well-pleasing to God in such a case is absurd.

Let me conclude this point by asking, *by what means can we hope to please God, apart from faith in him?* By keeping all the commandments? Alas! you have not done so. You have already broken those commands; and what is more, you still break them, and are in a chronic state of disobedience. If you do not believe in him you are not obedient to him; for true obedience commands the understanding as well as every other power and faculty. We are bound to obey with the mind by believing, as well as with the hand by acting. The spiritual part of our being is in revolt against God until we believe; and, while the very life and glory of our being is in revolt, how can we please God?

But what will you bring to the Lord wherewith to please him? Do you propose to bribe him with your money? Surely you are not so foolish! Is the Lord to be bought with a row of almshouses, or a chapel, or a cathedral? To most of you it would be impossible to try the plan for lack of means; but if you were wealthy enough to lavish gold out of the bag, would this please him? The silver and the gold are his, and the cattle on a thousand hills. If he were hungry, he would not tell you. What can you give to him to whom all things belong? Truly, you can assist in an ornate worship, or build a gorgeous church, or embroider the furniture of an altar, or emblazon the windows of a church. But are you so weak as to believe that such trifles as these can cause any delight to the mind of the Infinite? Solomon built him a house, but "the Most High dwelleth not in temples made with hands." To what shall I liken the most glorious erections of human genius but to the ant-hills of the tropics, which are wonderful as the fabrication of ants, even as our cathedrals are marvellous as the handicraft of men. But what are ant-hills or cathedrals when measured with the Infinite? What are all our works to the Lord? He who with a single arch has spanned the world, cares little for our carved capitals and groined arches. The prettinesses of architecture are as much beneath the glory of Jehovah as the dolls and boxes of bricks of our children would be beneath the dignity of a Solomon. God is not a man that he should take delight in these things. "Will the Lord be pleased with thousands of rams, or with ten thousands of rivers of oil? shall I give my firstborn for my transgression, the fruit of my body for the sin of my soul?" It is not this that he asks of you, but to walk humbly with him, never daring arrogantly to doubt his truth and mistrust his faithfulness. Go not about by a thousand inventions to aim at what you will never compass, but believe your God, and be established. So much upon that painful point. Remember the impossibility of pleasing the Lord without faith, and do not dash your ship upon this iron-bound coast.

II. Now, secondly, THE APOSTLE MENTIONS TWO ESSENTIAL POINTS OF FAITH.

He begins by saying, "He that cometh to God must believe that he is." Note the key-word "*must*": it is an immovable, insatiable necessity. Before we can walk with God, it is clear that we must *come to God*. Naturally, we are at a distance from him, and we must end that distance by coming to him, or else we cannot walk with him, nor be pleasing to him. That we may come to him, we must first believe that there is a God to come to. More; we must not only believe that there is a God—for only a fool doubts *that*: "The fool hath said in his heart, There is no God"—but we must believe that Jehovah is God, and God alone. This was Enoch's faith: he believed that

Jehovah was the living and true God. You are to believe, and must believe in order to be pleasing with God, that he is God, that he is the only God, and that there can be none other than he. You must also accept Jehovah as he reveals himself. You are not to have a God of your own making, nor a God reasoned out, but a God such as he has been pleased to reveal himself to you. Believe that Jehovah is, whoever else may be or may not be.

But the devils believe and tremble, and yet they are not pleasing to God, for more is wanted. Believe that God *is* in reference to yourself; that he has to do with your life, and your ways. Many believe that there is a hazy, imaginary power which they call God ; but they never think of him as a person, nor do they suspect that he thinks of them, or that his existence is of any consequence to them one way or another. Believe that God *is* as truly as you are ; and let him be real to you. Let the consideration of him enter into everything that concerns you. Believe that he is approachable by yourself, and is to be pleased or displeased by you. Believe in him as you believe in your wife or your child whom you try to please. Believe in God beyond everything, that "he is" in a sense more sure than that in which anyone else exists. Believe that he is to be approached, to be realized, to be, in fact, the great practical factor of your life.

Hold this as the primary truth, that God is most influential upon you ; and then believe that it is your business to come to him. But there is only one way of coming to him, and you must have faith to use that way. He that died and lives for ever saith, "I am the way. No man cometh unto the Father, but by me." He that cometh to God must believe in God as he is revealed, and must come to God as God reveals the way of approach ; and this is an exertion of faith. Faith as to this point is essential. You cannot come to him in whom you do not believe. Are not many hearers of the Word really as far from God as infidels ? Let me ask you, how many atheists are now in this house ? Perhaps not a single one of you would accept the title, and yet, if you live from Monday morning to Saturday night in the same way as you would live if there were no God, you are practical atheists ; and as actions speak more loudly than words, you are more atheists than those doctrinal unbelievers who disavow God with their mouths, and, after all, are secretly afraid of him. A life without God is as bad as a creed without God. You cannot come to God unless you believe in him as the All-in-all, the Lord God beside whom there is none else.

Yet all this would be nothing without the second point of belief. We must believe that "He is the rewarder of them that diligently seek him." How do we *seek him*, then ? Well, we seek him, first, when we begin by prayer, by trusting to Jesus, and by calling upon the sacred name, to seek salvation. "Whosoever shall call upon the name of the Lord shall be saved." That is a grand promise, and it teaches how we come to God ; namely, by calling upon his name. Afterwards we seek God by aiming at his glory, by making him the great object for which we live. One man seeks money, another seeks reputation, another seeks pleasure ; but he that is pleasing to God seeks God as his object and end. "Seek ye first the kingdom of God, and his righteousness ; and all these things shall be added unto you."

The man with whom God is pleased, is pleased with God; he sets the Lord always before him, and seeks to live for him. This he would not do, unless he believed that God would reward him in so doing. Take this as a certainty, that we must believe that "God is the rewarder of them that diligently seek him," or we shall not seek him. We are sure that, somehow or other, it will be to our highest benefit to honour the Lord and trust on him. Albeit we deserve nothing at his hands but wrath, yet we perceive from the gospel that if we seek him through his Son, we shall be so well-pleasing to him as to get a reward from his hands. This must be of grace —free, sovereign grace! And what a reward it is! Free pardon, graciously bestowed; a change of heart, graciously wrought; perseverance graciously maintained, comfort graciously poured in, and privilege graciously awarded. The reward of godliness, even in this world, is immeasurable, and in the world to come it is infinite. We may have respect unto the recompence of the reward; indeed, we should have respect to it, and therefore boldly seek God, and seek nothing else.

The Lord is "a rewarder of them that diligently seek him." That is not quite an exact translation: the Greek word means not only seek him, but "seek him out"; that is, seek him till they find him, and seek him above all others. It is a very strong word; we hardly know how to transfer its meaning into English, for though it does not say "diligently," it implies it. We must seek, and seek out; that is, seek till we really find. Those who with their hearts follow after God, shall not be losers if they believe that he will reward them. You have to believe God so as to seek his glory. Even when you do not obtain any present reward for it, you are to say, "I shall have a reward ultimately, even if I am for a while a loser through his service. If I lose money, respect, friendship, or even life from following God, yet still he will be a rewarder, and I shall be repaid ten thousandfold, not of debt, but according to his grace." He, then, that would please God, must first believe that he is; and then, dedicating himself to God, must be firmly assured that this is the right, the wise, the prudent thing to do. Be certain that to serve God is in itself gain: it is wealth to be holy; it is happiness to be pleasing to God. To us it is life to live to God—to know him, to adore him, to commune with him, to become like him. It is glory to us to make him glorious among the sons of men. For us to live is Christ. This, we are persuaded, is the best pursuit for us; in fact, it is the only one which can satisfy our hearts. God is our shield, and our exceeding great reward; and in the teeth of everything that happens we hold to this, that to serve God is gain. If God helps us to trust him, and therefore to live unto him and seek to be well-pleasing in his sight, we shall succeed in pleasing him. We cannot conceive that the heavenly Father sees, without pleasure, a man struggling against sin, battling against evil, enduring sorrow contentedly through a simple faith, and labouring daily to draw nearer and nearer to him. God is not displeased with those who, by faith, live to please him, and are content to take their reward from his hand. He must be pleased with the work of his own grace. The desire to come to God, the way to come to God, the power to come to God, the actual coming to God—these are all gifts of sovereign grace. Coming to God, however feebly we come, and seeking him, however much else we miss, must be well-pleasing in his sight; for it is the result of his own purpose and grace which he gave us in Christ Jesus before the world began. But all this hangs upon faith. Without faith there is no coming to God who is, and no seeking of God who is a rewarder; and therefore without faith it is impossible to please God.

III. WE WILL NOW GATHER A FEW LESSONS FROM WHAT THE APOSTLE HAS TAUGHT US. Help us, O gracious Spirit!

First, then, the apostle teaches us here by implication that *God is pleased with those that have faith.* The negative is often the plainest way of suggesting the positive. If we are so carefully warned that without faith it is impossible to please God, we infer that with faith it is possible to please God. If you believe that he is, and that he is a rewarder of them that diligently seek him; if you are willing to believe all that he teaches you because he teaches it, and are really a believer in himself and in all that he is pleased to reveal, then are you pleasing to him. He that believes in God believes in all the words that God speaks, and he surrenders himself to all that God does; and such a man must be pleasing to God. We believe in one God, and in one Mediator between God and man, the man Christ Jesus; and we trust in the Lord as he thus draws near to us: thus are we in the way of pleasing God. By faith we ourselves have become pleasing to God, and our actions performed with a view to his honour are pleasing to him. What a joy is this! It is bliss to think that I, who, in my unregenerate state, grieved the Holy Spirit, and vexed him day by day, am now the object of pleasure to him. I, whose actions were contrary to the law of God, and the bent of whose mind was against the gospel of Christ, I, even I, who was once obnoxious to Divine anger, an heir of wrath, even as others, have now, through faith, become to God an object of his complacency. This is very wonderful. If the Holy Spirit leads you to feel the full sweetness of this truth, you will rejoice with joy unspeakable. I feel like singing rather than preaching. Oh, guilty one, wilt thou not now believe thy God? This is the way to come back to him. When the prodigal said, "In my father's house there is bread enough and to spare," he believed in his father's power to supply all his needs. When he thought in his heart that his father would receive him, then he said, "I will arise and go to my father, and will say unto him, Father, I have sinned." You must have so much belief in God as to believe him to have the heart of a father towards you, or you will never come back to him; but when you begin to trust your God your face is already towards the heavenly home, and before long your head will be in your Father's bosom. If faith can make the vilest and guiltiest pleasing to God, will they not believe in him? What a transformation this would work in them! Oh, that this morning all of us may stand out in the clear sunlight of Jehovah's good pleasure, and know ourselves to be well-pleasing to him through Jesus Christ!

Learn, next, that *those who have faith make it the great object of their life to please God.* Am I speaking the truth? Will each one ask whether it is true about himself? Do I, as a believer, live to please God? We need personal heart-searching on this point. The believer in the invisible God delights to act as in his sight, and in secret to serve him. I take a choice pleasure in rendering to my God a service unknown to others, not done for the sake of my fellows, but distinctly that I may do something for my Lord's own self. It is sweet to give or do simply to please *him*, without respect to the public eye. Even such actions as must come under the gaze of others are not to be done with the view of winning their approbation, but only to please God. The doing of such actions is a singular fountain of strength to a man's mind. It is ennobling to feel that you have only one Master, and that you live to please *him*, even God. To please men is poor work. To live to follow everybody's whim is slavery. If you let one man pull you by the ear in his direction, another will tug at you from another direction, and you will have very long ears before long. Happy is he who, pleasing God, feels that he has risen above seeking to please men. It is grand to say, "This is what God would have me do, and I will do it in happy fellowship with others, or alone by myself, as the case may be; but do it I must." This gives a man backbone, and at the same time removes the selfishness which is greedy of popular applause. It is a grand thing to be no longer looking down for cheer, but to be distinctly looking up for it. The man who truly believes in God makes small account of men. Put them together, they are vanity; heap them up in their thousands, they are altogether lighter than vanity. Nations upon nations, what are they but as grasshoppers! The lands in which they live, what are they before God! "He taketh up the isles as a very little thing." To please God even a little is infinitely greater than to have the acclamations of all our race throughout the centuries. The true believer feels that God is, and that there is none beside him; none that needs to be thought of in comparison with him. The theology of the present aims at the deification of man, but the truth of all time magnifies God. We shall stand by the old paths, wherein we hear a voice which bids us worship Jehovah, our God, and serve him alone. He shall be all in all. Only as we see men loved of him can we live for men; we seek their good in God, and for his glory, and regard them as capable of being made mirrors to reflect the glory of the Lord.

Note, next, the apostle teaches us here that *they that have faith in God are always coming to God;* for he speaks of the believer as "He that cometh to God." If you once learn to believe God, and to please him, you are coming to him day by day. You not only come to him, and go away from him, as in acts of prayer and praise; but you are always coming; your life is a march towards him. The way of the believer is toward God; by his faith he comes ever nearer and yet nearer to the eternal throne. What is his reward? Why, he that sitteth on the throne will say, "Come, ye blessed of my Father, inherit the kingdom prepared for you from the foundation of the world." Come! Come on! You have been coming, keep on coming for ever. There is a gentle, constant, perpetual progress of the believer's heart and mind nearer and closer to God. I could not wonder at Enoch being translated after walking with God hundreds of years; for it is such a small step from close communion with God on earth to perfect communion with God in heaven. A thin partition divides us which a sigh will remove. The breaking of a blood-vessel, the snapping of a cord, the staying of the breath, and he that had God with him shall be with God. Sometimes he could not tell whether he was in the body or out of the body, but had to leave that question with God; he will soon be able to answer the question for himself, and know that he is absent from the body, and present with the Lord. O beloved, please God, please God; and as you please him by your simple confidence and childlike trust, you are coming nearer to him.

The next lesson is one I have already spoken of: *God will see that those who practise faith in him shall have a reward.* I say, God will see to it, for the text says, "*He is* a rewarder of them that diligently seek him." The Lord will not leave the reward of faith to the choicest angel: he himself will adjudge the recompence. Here we may get but scant reward from those whom we benefit: indeed, they usually return us base ingratitude. Joseph was a faithful servant to Potiphar; but Potiphar put him in prison on a groundless charge. Joseph helped the butler, and interpreted his dream, yet he remembered not Joseph, but forgat him. You may not reckon upon due returns from your fellow-men, or you will be disappointed. Like David, you may guard Nabal's sheep, and when the sheep-shearing comes you may hope to be remembered, and he will insult you with a churlish answer. Expect little from men and much from God, for by nature and by office he is a rewarder. No work done for him will go unrewarded. In his service the wages are sure. Rise into the Abrahamic life which stays itself upon the Lord's word, "Fear not, Abraham: I am thy shield and thy exceeding great reward." It is enough reward to have such a God to be our God. What if he gives us neither vineyards nor olive gardens, neither sheep nor oxen; he himself is ours, and this is a greater reward than if he gave us all the world. God himself is enough for the believer. If his faith be true and deep, and intelligent, he cries, "Whom have I in heaven but thee? and there is none upon earth that I desire beside thee."

The last lesson we gather from it is this: *those who have no faith are in a fearful case.* I speak not of the heathen, but of unbelievers who reject the gospel. "Without faith it is impossible to please God." Some of you are always fashioning fresh nets of doubt for your own entanglement. You invent snares for your own feet, and are greedy to lay more and more of them. You are mariners who seek the rocks, soldiers who court the point of the bayonet. It is an unprofitable business. Practically, morally, mentally, spiritually, doubting is an evil trade. You are like a smith, wearing out his arm in making chains with which to bind himself. Doubt is sterile, a desert without water. Doubt discovers difficulties which it never solves: it creates hesitancy, despondency, despair. Its progress is the decay of comfort, the death of peace. "Believe!" is the word which speaks life into a man; but doubt nails down his coffin. If thou canst believe, O guilty one, that Jesus Christ bore the guilt of sin upon the cross, and by his death has made atonement to the insulted government of God; if thou canst so believe in him as to cast thyself just as thou art at his dear feet, thou shalt be pleasing to God. I entreat thee to look up and see the pierced hands, and feet, and side of the dear Redeemer, and read eternal mercy there; read full forgiveness there, and then go thou away in peace, for thou art well-pleasing to God. The sinner who believes God's testimony concerning his Son has begun to please him, and is himself well-pleasing to the Lord. Oh that you would now trust him who justifieth the ungodly and passeth by the iniquities of sinful men! He will receive you graciously and love you freely. Oh, come to him, for he is a rewarder of them that diligently seek him. God help you to do so at once. But without faith you cannot please him. Do what you may, feel what you like, you will labour as in the very fire, and nothing will come of it but eternal despair. The Lord help you to believe and live. Amen.

10. Scriptural Salvation

"For the scripture saith, Whosoever believeth on him shall not be ashamed."—Romans x. 11.

THE shepherd on the hill is most of all anxious about his sheep: he cares for his cottage, he trains the woodbine around his porch, sows flowers before his door, and digs his little plot of garden ground; but, since he is a shepherd, his chief thought follows his flock, and especially any of the sheep that are wandering, or the lambs that are tender. Even so I feel that my main business is the saving of souls. I may fitly preach to you upon any scriptural subject, and I may minister to the delight of the family of the redeemed, and lead them into the deep things of God; but my principal business must always be watching for souls. This one thing I do.

When a city is to be stored for a siege, it will be well for those who attend to the commissariat to lay in a proportion of everything that is necessary for human comfort, and even a measure of certain luxuries; but it will be of first importance to bring in great quantities of corn. The necessaries of life must be the chief provision. These we place in store-houses by tons, whereas in other articles pounds may suffice: if there be a failure of bread, what will the people do? For this reason, I feel I must preach over and over again the plain gospel of salvation by grace through faith in Christ Jesus. While I would withhold nothing that may minister to edification, to comfort, to growth, or to the perfecting of the saints; yet, first and foremost in abundance, even to overflowing, I must gather for you the bread of life, and set forth Christ crucified as the sinner's only hope. Faith must be urged upon you; for without it there is no salvation. Paul, in this case, was acting upon this safe principle, as he always did; for he is speaking of salvation in the plainest terms. His heart's desire and prayer for Israel was, that they might be saved, and he proved the truth of that desire by setting forth that which would save them: he keeps to faith in Christ, and hammers upon that nail to fasten it surely.

I. I shall begin my sermon this morning by reminding you that, HERE IS AN OLD-FASHIONED WAY OF PROOF: "The Scripture saith."

113

In this enlightened age little is made of Scripture; the tendency is to undermine men's faith in the Bible, and persuade them to rest on something else. It is not so with us, as it certainly was not so with Paul. He enforced and substantiated his teaching by declaring, "The Scripture saith."

In this he follows the manner of Christ Jesus, our Lord. Though quite able to speak of himself, our Lord continually referred to Holy Scripture. His first public sermon was founded upon the Book of the prophet Isaiah. All along to the very end he was always quoting the Old Testament. So did his apostles. One is struck with their continual reference to Moses and the prophets. While they set the truth in a fresh light, they fell back continually upon the old revelation. "As saith the Scripture," "According to the Scriptures"—these are phrases constantly repeated. Paul declared that he spent his life "witnessing both to small and great, saying none other things than those which the prophets and Moses did say should come."

Evidently *they regarded the statements of Scripture as conclusive.* They took counsel of the Scriptures, and so they ended the matter. "It is written," was to them proof positive and indisputable. "Thus saith the Lord," was the final word: enough for their mind and heart, enough for their conscience and understanding. To go behind Scripture did not occur to the first teachers of our faith: they heard the Oracle of divine testimony, and bowed their heads in reverence. So it ought to be with us: we have erred from the faith, and we shall pierce ourselves through with many sorrows, unless we feel that if the Scripture saith it, it is even so. "Holy men of God spake as they were moved by the Holy Ghost," and therefore they spake not erroneously, nor even dubiously.

In the passage before us we have an instance of *inspiration endorsing inspiration, and building thereon.* Paul wrote by the direction of the Holy Spirit; he was himself a fully inspired man, and he had no lack of original speech; yet he falls back upon the Scripture. He calls the Old Testament to bear witness to the doctrine of the New, and in the same act expresses the agreement of the New with the Old. How far have they diverged from the Christian spirit, who begin to question the authenticity and authority of the books of Moses and the prophets! Brethren, had Paul been without inspiration, he was so great a saint and so eminent a confessor, that his reverence for the Old Testament would have been a lesson to us; but since we believe this epistle to have been inspired of the Holy Ghost, we are bound, as by divine law, to treat the ancient Scriptures as the great apostle treated them, namely, with absolute deference, regarding them as the sure Word of the Lord. To us it matters not what critics may say to shake faith in Holy Writ; their efforts will be all in vain if we are intimate with the Author of these books, and by his Holy Spirit possess a personal sense of his truth, his wisdom, and his faithfulness. After God has spoken, it little concerns us what the wise men of the world may have to say. They have always spoken against the Word of the Lord; but they have always spoken in vain, and so will they speak, even to the world's end.

Paul, in saying here, "For the Scripture saith," is referring, I think, to the general sense of Scripture, rather than to any one passage. There are several texts from which it may be gathered that believers shall not be put to shame; such as, "They looked unto him, and were lightened: and their faces were not ashamed." But if the apostle is referring to any one passage of the Old Testament, he is not quoting it verbatim, but he is expounding it, and giving its general sense. Assuming that he refers to Isaiah xxviii. 16, I am glad of the lesson which he affords us in a kind of instructive criticism. When the Spirit of God himself deals with inspired Scripture, we can gather from his example how we may deal with it. It is best as far as possible to quote the very words of Scripture, lest we should err; but we have here a permit to quote the clear and evident sense, and we are allowed to regard that sense as equally authoritative with the exact words. Paul quotes, if he quotes at all, from the Septuagint translation rather than from the Hebrew, thus sanctioning a translation. Let us read the words in Isaiah xxviii. 16. "Therefore thus saith the Lord God, Behold, I lay in Zion for a foundation a stone, a tried stone, a precious corner stone, a sure foundation: he that believeth shall not make haste." You see at once the difference between the text as Paul gives it to us, and the original Hebrew.

Observe, first, that under the guidance of the Holy Spirit, *Paul reads the passage in its largest sense.* The original text is, "He that believeth"; but Paul makes it, "Whosoever believeth." That is the true meaning. "He that believeth," means any "he" that believeth; and to make this fact clear, Paul says, "Whosoever believeth." We ought to take the promises of Holy Scripture in their widest possible application. When we meet with a passage distinctly referring to one person only, we are allowed to remember that no Scripture is exhausted by one fulfilment. You, being like that person, and in similar circumstances to him, may quote the promise as made to you; for it is intended for the whole class of persons of whom that one person is the representative. "He that believeth," is in Paul's judgment, nay, in the judgment of the Holy Ghost, tantamount to "Whosoever believeth." A promise made by man will legally be interpreted in its narrowest sense; but a promise made by God may always be taken in its major sense, since God's thoughts are higher than our thoughts, and his ways than our ways. Everything it will honestly bear you may pile upon the back of a divine promise. God loves to see faith taking him at his word, and he will do for it exceeding abundantly above what we ask or even think.

Next, note that *Paul reads the verse with the context.* In the Hebrew it is, "He that believeth"; but Paul reads it, "Whosoever believeth *on him.*" Did he do right to supply the "on him"? Certainly, since he thus gives the sense of the quotation as it stands in the prophet. I said before that Paul is not quoting *verbatim et literatim,* he aims at giving the sense of the passage; and, therefore, paraphrases it so as to remind you of its connection. "On him" is necessary to a perfect quotation of the passage as it stands. Let us read again: "Behold, I lay in Zion for a foundation a stone, a tried stone, a precious corner stone, a sure foundation: he that believeth"—evidently it is, "He that believeth" in this foundation "shall not make haste." That

115

foundation is not "it," but "Him"; for it refers to Christ. Expressions separated from that which comes before them, and follows after them, may not express the writer's mind; and, therefore, when we quote from Holy Scripture we should endeavour not merely to give the words which are actually in the text, but to add such words as duly set forth the context. This lesson is worth learning.

Once more, *the apostle gives us the true and plain meaning* of the text. He leaves the figure which was suitable for Isaiah, but might have been misunderstood by the Romans, and he gives the sense intended by Isaiah in plainer language. The prophet said, "He that believeth shall not make haste." That "making haste," means being fluttered and alarmed, and so being led to run from the foundation. Such a person fled in haste because he was ashamed of his hope. Paul puts aside the drapery of the metaphor to let the uncovered sense stand out boldly. He expounds the Scripture under infallible guidance, and gives its meaning to us in this form, "Whosoever believeth on him shall not be ashamed."

The true sense of the passage our apostle uses by way of argument: he enforces the promise of the gospel by the teaching of the prophet. Dear friend, when you go to win souls, go with a clear understanding of the Scriptures, and then quote those Scriptures frequently, if you would have power over the minds of men. Do not think to convince sinners by your own fine phrases, but use the words which the Holy Ghost teacheth. If you want to bring souls to faith in Christ, remember that faith is begotten by the Word; for "faith cometh by hearing, and hearing by the word of God." The more of the true sense of the Word of God we can compress into our exhortations, the more likely shall we be to succeed in our gracious design. This is Paul's mode of argument, "the Scripture saith"; and we know no better.

II. And now, secondly, we have before us A SIMPLE STATEMENT OF THE WAY OF SALVATION: "The Scripture saith, Whosoever believeth on him shall not be ashamed." The way of salvation is to believe on Christ, whom God has laid in Zion for a foundation.

What is believing on him? It is *trusting in him.* The language is not "Believe him,"—such belief is a part of faith, but not the whole. We believe everything which the Lord Jesus has taught, but we must go a step further, and trust him. It is not even enough to believe in him, as being the Son of God, and the anointed of the Lord; but we must believe *on* him, just as in the building (for that is the figure used by Isaiah) the builder takes his stone and lays it *on* the foundation. There it rests with all its weight, there it abides. The faith that saves is not believing certain truths, nor even believing that Jesus is a Saviour; but it is resting *on* him, depending *on* him, lying with all your weight on Christ as the foundation of your hope. Believe that he can save you; believe that he will save you; at any rate leave the whole matter of your salvation with him in unquestioning confidence. Depend upon him without fear as to your present and eternal salvation. This is the faith which saves the soul.

Notice, next, that this faith is *believing on a Person:* "He that believeth on "—*it?* No! On "HIM." Our faith is not based on a doctrine, or a ceremony, or an experience: but on "Him!" Our Lord

Jesus Christ is God; he is also man : he is the appointed and anointed Saviour. In his death, he is the propitiation for sin; in his resurrection, he is the justification of his people; and in his intercession, he is the eternal guarantee of their preservation. Believe "*on him*." Our faith fixes herself upon the Person of the Lord Jesus as seen in his sufferings, his offices, and his achievements. "Whosoever believeth on him shall not be ashamed."

The text refers to *the truth of the trusting*. The apostle does not say, "Whosoever believeth on him with full assurance, or with a high degree of confidence, shall not be ashamed." No; it is not the *measure* of our faith, but the *sincerity* of our faith which is the great question. If we believe on him at all, we shall not be ashamed. Our faith may be very trembling, and this will cause us sorrow; but a trembling faith will save. The greater your faith, the more comfortable for you; but if your faith is small as a grain of mustard-seed, it will save you. If your faith can only touch the hem of the Saviour's garment behind him, it will heal your soul; for "Whosoever believeth on him shall not be ashamed." Is there not blessed comfort about this assurance?

Observe, again, that all depends upon *the presence of this trusting*. and not upon the age of it. "He that believeth on him" : this relates to the immediate present. Perhaps the truster has only believed on Jesus during the last five minutes. Very well, he does believe on him, and he shall not be ashamed. Some of us are glad to remember that we were built on the sure foundation more than forty years ago. But the length of years during which we have believed does not enter into the essence of the matter: believers are saved whether their faith has lasted through half a century or half an hour. "Whosoever believeth on him," takes in the convert of this morning as well as the hero of a thousand fights. My newly-believing friend, I am sorry you have put off faith so long; but, still, I am greatly glad that you have believed at all; for your faith shall not be put to shame.

One other remark needs to be made before I leave this point. Note *the soleness of the object of faith*. "Whosoever believeth *on him*." Nothing else is mentioned in connection with the Lord Jesus, who is the sole foundation. It is not written, "He that believeth on Jesus nine parts out of ten, and on himself for the other tenth." No! "Whosoever believeth *on him*"—on him alone. Jesus will never be a part Saviour. We must not rest in part upon what we hope to do in the future, nor in part upon the efficacy of an outward ceremony. No! The faith must be "*on him*." Both feet must be on the Rock of Ages. The whole stone must rest on the foundation. Take Christ to be the sole Saviour of your soul. I saw written at the foot of a Cross in France, "SPES UNICA"—Jesus is the lone hope of men. There is but one star in your sky, sinner, and that star is the Star of Bethlehem! There is but one light for the tempest-tost mariner on the stormy sea of conviction of sin, and that light is the Pharos of the Cross. Look there! Look there! Only there; "For the Scripture saith, Whosoever believeth on him shall not be ashamed."

Now if any soul here perishes, it will not be my fault. However feebly I may preach this morning, I shall go home satisfied that I have set before you enough for your salvation, if you be willing and obedient. I have most plainly set before you the way of salvation. What more can I do? I can bring the horse to water, but I cannot make him drink; I can set the water of life before you, but I can do no more if you turn away from it. If you accept of the Lord Jesus and believe on him, you shall not be ashamed; but if you put him far from you, you will die in your sins, and your blood will be upon your own heads.

III. So I pass on to the third point: THE GLORIOUS PROMISE TO THOSE WHO OBEY THE GOSPEL. "The Scripture saith, Whosoever believeth on him *shall not be ashamed.*"

Take the Hebrew form of it first: "*shall not make haste.*" When a man builds his hope upon the Lord Christ, he is not driven into worry and hurry. He quietly walks with God, and does not haste through fear. They say that the floods are out, that the winds are howling, that the rains are descending: he that trusts in a refuge of lies may well make haste to flee; but he that has built his house upon the rock, quietly answers, "The flood is coming; I supposed it would. The rains are falling; I expected that they would. The winds are blowing; I was forewarned of the tempest, and I am prepared for it by being on the rock!" His house will stand. He will never be ashamed of its foundation. In patience he possesses his soul.

> "Calm 'mid the bewildering cry;
> Confident of victory."

The Holy Spirit's reading of the Holy Spirit's Word in the Old Testament is, "He shall not be ashamed," and this means that *he shall not be ashamed at any time by discovering that he has been deluded.* Men are ashamed when their hopes fail. If a man has an expectation of eternal life, and on a sudden he sees his hope dashed to shivers, is he not ashamed? If on his dying bed his confidence should turn out to be based on a falsehood, how ashamed he will be! He will then say, "I am ashamed to think I did not take more care. I am ashamed that I followed my own judgment instead of God's Word." They shall lie down in sorrow who find their hope to be as a spider's web. It will be a awful thing in our last moments, when we most need comfort, to be driven to despair by the wreck of our confidence. If any of you are trusting in your gold, it will turn out to be a poor confidence when you are called upon to leave all earthly things. I have heard of one who, on his death-bed, laid bags of money to his heart; but he was forced to lay them away, and cry, "These will not do! These will not do!" It will be a sorry business if we have been trusting in our good temper, our charity, our patriotism, our courage, or our honesty, and when we come to die shall be made to feel that these cannot satisfy the claims of divine justice, or give us a passport to the skies. How sad to see robes turn to rags, and comeliness into corruption! How wretched to regard one's self as covered with a garment fit for Christ's great wedding-feast, and then to wake out of a dream and find one's self naked? You will never have this vexation of spirit if you take Christ Jesus to be your confidence. So far from being ashamed, you will boast in the crucified

Saviour; yea, you will vow with Paul, "God forbid that I should glory, save in the cross of our Lord Jesus Christ."

Furthermore, dear friends, he that believes on Christ *shall not be ashamed to own his faith.* This is a sharp saying, and it cuts as a razor. I wish it would make a great gash in cowardly spirits. "Whosoever believeth on him shall not be ashamed." Some think they believe on Christ, and yet they are ashamed to own their faith in the Lord's appointed way; or, indeed, in any way. If they are in ungodly company, they do with their faith as they do with their dog when a friend comes in: they say, "Lie down, sir." Because it is inconvenient to be known to be a believer, they treat the Lord Christ as they would treat a dog. Some of you have never made a confession of your Lord: what will become of you? "Oh," say you, "do not say hard things!" I do not say them out of my own head: let me read the passage to you from verse ten: "For with the heart man believeth unto righteousness; and with the mouth confession is made unto salvation. For the Scripture saith, Whosoever believeth on him shall not be ashamed." What is the meaning of the whole passage? I cannot shut my eyes to the truth, that it speaks of confessing Christ, and declares that he who really believes on him will not be ashamed of it. If you, my hearer, are ashamed of your Lord, your faith is not real; or, to say the least of it, you have cause to suspect that it is not. If you are ashamed, you are an unbeliever; for, "Whosoever believeth on him shall not be ashamed." The Christian's song is—

> "I'm not ashamed to own my Lord,
>   Or to defend his cause;
> Maintain the honour of his Word,
>   The glory of his cross."

For my own part, I have often said, and I cannot help repeating it yet again—

> "E'er since by faith I saw the stream
>   His flowing wounds supply,
> Redeeming love has been my theme,
>   And shall be till I die."

I am not ashamed of my hope; I love to state it, to glory in it, and to make it widely known. I heard of a "modern-thought" minister of some repute, that a person asked him, "Sir, what is your theory of the atonement?" He replied, "My dear sir, I have never told *that* to any living person, although I have been a preacher for years, and I am not going to commit myself now." He seemed to think that this was rather a wise thing. My course runs in the opposite direction: I believe in the vicarious sacrifice of Christ, and I am not ashamed of the old-fashioned doctrine. "He loved me, and gave himself for me"; why should I be ashamed to own it? I will not believe anything that I dare not preach. I have a grave suspicion that it will go ill at last with the man who has one faith for the public and another for himself. We should be ashamed at being ashamed of Christ and his truth.

Still, this is not all the meaning of our text: *the believer shall have no cause to be ashamed.* Let me try to illustrate this assertion.

We shall not be ashamed because our faith is proved to be unreasonable. When a man is convicted of believing an absurdity, he is ashamed. But there is nothing unreasonable in the truth that "God so loved the world, that he gave his only begotten Son, that whosoever believeth in him should not perish, but have everlasting life." I will not say that reason teaches this grand fact; for reason could not reach so high. This truth is above reason, but it is not contrary to reason. When you get some idea of the infinite goodness and justice of God, it will not seem unreasonable that he should be willing to forgive sinners, nor unreasonable that he should devise a way by which he can do this without injury to his moral government. There is a sweet reasonableness in the provision of a Substitute for guilty men, and a still sweeter reasonableness in the salvation of those who believe in the Lamb of God. In fact, the gospel system is so blessedly reasonable, that when it comes home to the enlightened understanding it carries the mind by storm. I have seen love at first sight with many a man who, for the first time, has heard how God is "just, and the justifier of him which believeth in Jesus." It has seemed so Godlike a method, that the man has accepted it at once: it bore its proof in its face.

Next, we are not ashamed because our faith has been disproved; for it has never been disproved. No man has been able to prove that the Son of God was not here on earth, and that he did not die on the Cross, the "just for the unjust, to bring us to God." The resurrection has never been disproved, nor the ascension, nor the descent of the Holy Ghost. Nothing has overthrown apostolic testimony. To cavil at a statement is not to disprove it. To make it a matter of coarse jest is not to disprove it. The apostles and their companions bore public witness; and died because of their solemn conviction of the truth of their testimony. They were simple men, who could not have invented the gospel story if they would; and they were good men, who would not have invented it if they could. Until men can prove that there was no Christ, and no propitiation for sin, we shall not be ashamed to believe on him.

We shall never be ashamed of believing on Jesus, because by experience we shall find it to be unsatisfactory to our conscience. No, no. We are more than content with the ground of our trust in this respect. Well do I remember when I first gripped the thought that Jesus suffered in my place and stead, and that I, looking to him, was saved. I felt a peace like a river, ever flowing, ever deepening, ever widening. My former trouble had arisen from the question— how could God, as a righteous judge, pass by my violation of his holy law? Sin is not to be viewed as a personal offence to God, as a Being, but a rebellion against his laws as the Judge of all the earth, who must do right. How could he wink at sin? How could he treat the guilty as the innocent? When I saw that he did not wink at sin, but that Jesus came to vindicate the divine law by suffering in our place, I rested with all confidence on that blessed fact. My heart said, "It is enough," and to-day it cries, "It is enough." My conscience has never raised a question about the security furnished by the ransom of the Lord Jesus. My heart remains perfectly at ease now she knows that "He his own self bare our sins in his own body on the tree." If the nature of God had not required an atonement for sin, the conscience of the sinner might have needed it. The righteous apprehension of conscience as to wrath to come demands a vindication of the law. Because we have this vindication in Christ we are not ashamed.

We are not ashamed of the gospel of salvation by faith in Christ because it proves inoperative upon our lives. I remember the witty Sidney Smith, who by mistake figured as a clergyman, managed to come into collision with the Methodists, and he charged them with so much preaching faith that good works were at a discount. Surely he never heard Mr. Wesley. I venture to say that the Methodists produced more good works than Mr. Smith's preaching ever did. If any say to us, "This faith of yours takes you off from trusting in works "; we answer, "It does; but it does not take us off from practising them." Faith is the mother of holiness and the nurse of virtue. The lives of the Puritans who taught the gospel of faith in Christ were infinitely preferable to the lives of those Cavaliers who believed in human merit. The fact is, that men who believe in the Lord Jesus Christ have even been ridiculed for being righteous over much, and rated for a sort of moroseness of morality; but history has never afforded the least support to the charge that they were indifferent to morality. Indifferent to morality? We never knew what holiness was until we believed in Jesus. We had no aspirations after purity till we were saved by him. The spiritual effect of faith in Jesus is of the noblest. Oh, that we could display more of it!

We are not ashamed to challenge investigation as to the philanthropic effect of faith in the gospel. If anyone should sneer, and say, "You believers think yourselves saved, and so you are comfortably unconcerned as to what becomes of others." I should answer, "What a lie!" We love the souls of men, and we have proved it in our ministry, and in our incessant efforts to save them. We have gone with breaking heart and bowed head because certain of our hearers remain in unbelief. I can appeal to you all, that my ministry has been full of earnest expostulations, affectionate appeals, and tearful entreaties. God is our witness how truly we can say, our heart's desire and prayer to God for others is, that they may be saved. We are not ashamed to say that the ministry of those who believe alone in Christ, and who know assuredly that they are saved by grace, has about it, as a rule, a greater power to win souls than the ministry of those who preach other gospels. We say no more, lest we become fools in glorying. We are not ashamed of our hope on this ground.

We are never ashamed of it, again, as to its operation upon others. When I look back through my life, having preached nothing in this place but faith in Christ as the way of salvation, I can, without any effort of memory, remember many drunkards made sober, harlots made chaste, lovers of pleasure made lovers of God. Many have been reclaimed from among the poorest and most degraded, and some from the rich and vicious. We have seen what faith in God has done by lifting them from the level of selfishness to the heights of grace. If we had to go down into the worst slum of London we would not wish for anything better to preach than Christ crucified; and if we had to visit the gayest hells of the West End, we would not wish for any theme more powerful than the Cross of our Lord Jesus. "Believe and live" is still a charm most potent. We have no cause to be ashamed of what the truth of God has done in ages past, and is doing even at this day.

I will tell you when we should be ashamed of our hope, and that would be if we saw it repudiated by dying saints. It is all very well to be a believer when you are young, and in health, and can go about your business; but how will it fare with men and women, when they are called to go upstairs and suffer, and never to come down again till carried to their long home? How does the gospel serve them when they know that they cannot live another week? What is the condition of believers on the brink of the grave? Those who believe in Jesus are calm and happy; frequently they are exultant, and the bed can scarcely hold them because of their supreme joy in the prospect of being with their Lord. I am not telling you idle tales, brothers and sisters. Many of you know that I speak the truth; for it is of your own relatives that I am speaking now. Our people die well. We have no occasion to be ashamed. Tested by the dying of our fellow-believers, we are not ashamed of the gospel.

We might be ashamed, once more, if we could be outbidden in our prospects by some other system. What form of religion offers more to the believer than the system of grace and simple faith in Jesus? Nowhere in the world, that I know of, is there any other system of religion which promises sure salvation to its followers. The Roman Catholic system does not at all provide for present and everlasting salvation. What does it provide for? For your getting out of purgatory in due time, and no more. When I was in the Church of St. John Lateran, at Rome, I read a request for prayer for the repose of the soul of his Eminence, Cardinal Wiseman. Now Cardinal Wiseman was a great man, a prince of the church, but yet he is somewhere in the other world, where he is not in repose: so this request indicates. There must be a very poor outlook for an ordinary Catholic. For my part I would give up so cheerless a hope, and become a believer in the Lord Jesus Christ, and go to heaven. "Whosoever believeth on him shall not be ashamed." When the best Catholic finds himself in purgatory he will be ashamed, and will say, "Oh, that I had taken to the way of trust in the all-sufficient merit of the Lord Jesus; for then I should have been covered with his righteousness, and should have been with him where he is." Beloved friends, our rivals do not outbid us. Our gospel brings immediate pardon for every sin, a gracious change of nature, the regeneration of the heart, and the preservation of the soul to Christ's eternal kingdom and glory. Hallelujah!

IV. I have done, when I say to you, lastly, that in my text we see A WIDE DOOR OF HOPE FOR THE SEEKER. Read that word, "whosoever," whosoever, whosoever. I must keep on ringing that silver bell. It rings in the thirteenth verse—"Whosoever shall call upon the name of the Lord shall be saved." It rings in the text—"Whosoever believeth on him shall not be ashamed."

No secret decree has ever been made to shut out any soul that believeth on him. God has not spoken in secret in a dark place of the earth, and said, "Such a man may believe in Christ, and yet he shall be lost." Do not be afraid of this; for it is impossible.

No measure of sin in your past life can deprive you of this promise. "Whosoever believeth on him," though he had been a murderer, or a thief, or a drunkard, or an adulterer, or a liar, or a blasphemer, shall find his faith removing his sins through the blood of Jesus, and renewing his heart by the Holy Spirit. " *Whosoever* believeth on him shall not be ashamed." Says one, "I shall always be ashamed that I have so greatly transgressed." Yes, I know; but still you shall be so perfectly pardoned that your sin shall be blotted out, and you shall not remember the shame of your youth.

"But I do not feel as I ought," says one. You shall feel aright if you will believe on him. You shall not be shut out of the promise through any want of sensitiveness. It is not said, "Whosoever believeth on him and is sensitive to a high degree shall be saved." No : "Whosoever believeth on him." You ought to be sensitive, you ought to be tender, you ought to be grieved for sin, and you shall be if you believe on him. If you believe on Jesus, he will give you true repentance and deep self-abhorrence; but you must come to Jesus for these things, and not try to find them in your own depraved hearts. Nothing limits this "whosoever" : "Whosoever believeth on him shall not be ashamed."

"Alas," cries one, "I have a strong besetting sin, I have a hot temper, or fierce lusts, or a desperate thirst for drink." Yes, I know; but if you believe on him you shall not be ashamed; for these shall be conquered and destroyed. You shall be helped to fight against them until you get a complete victory, and so you shall never be ashamed.

'Ah," says one, "but I once made a profession, and I have gone back." Yes; but, "whosoever" does not shut out the wanderer. Backsliding is a great and bitter evil, but he that believeth is justified from every sin. "Though your sins be as scarlet, they shall be as white as snow; though they be red like crimson, they shall ⁃be as wool." Come, then, with your heaped up sins and be unburdened. Come, though seven devils dwell within you : come to have them driven out, and yourself made white in the blood of the Lamb. Come, for you shall not be ashamed. Let no man stand back and say, "I dare not come." Remember, the word of the Saviour, "Him that cometh to me I will in no wise cast out." "In no wise," that is, for no possible reason. "Oh, but my birth was shameful." I may be speaking to one who is illegitimate. This is no barrier; for children of shame may be made heirs of glory. The Lord rejects none, however uneducated, coarse, or dull they may be. Neither does race offer hindrance. Be you an Englishman or a Chinaman, there is no difference. White, black, brown, red, or blue, still does the promise stand, "Whosoever believeth on him shall not be ashamed." There is no distinction as to rank, name, class, or reputation. "Oh, but look at my profession." I am sorry if it is an ill profession : get out of it, and do something honest; but whatever you may be by trade, come

to Jesus and believe on him; for, "Whosoever believeth on him shall
not be ashamed." "Alas, I am too old!" says another. What are
you? Two hundred? "No, not so old as that." Then, you are
under age as yet. Never mind how old you are; "Whosoever
believeth on him shall not be ashamed." If you have one foot in the
grave, faith may put both feet on the Rock of Ages. You are yet on
praying ground and pleading terms with God, therefore come to
Jesus; for he hath said, "Him that cometh to me I will in no wise
cast out." Come with your little faith, and your trembling hope, and
believe on the Lord Jesus, and you shall not be ashamed.

Lastly, in that day when the earth and heaven shall melt, and
nothing shall be seen but Christ upon the throne, judging all the
earth, *those who have not believed in him will be ashamed*. They will
have no excuse to offer: they have none even now. They will then
be ashamed that they did not take the counsel of their godly friends,
and heed the pleadings of their minister. They will be ashamed to
think how they put off thoughts of Christ, and lingered until they
found themselves in hell. The face of the Lord Jesus will be terrible
to unbelievers to the last degree. One young person, in great trouble
of soul, said to me the other day, "When I am lost, I shall always
see your face; it will accuse and condemn me." She will not be lost.
Dear girl, I trust she will soon find peace with God through Jesus
Christ. It will be terrible to those who refuse the gospel even to
remember the preacher of it; but infinitely more so to see the face of
him who bled and died, and loved unto the uttermost. Oh, to think,
"I would not have him! I would not be saved by him! I preferred
to trust to myself, or not to think at all, and now here I am."
Assuredly, the flames of hell will be more tolerable than a sight of
his face. The bitterest wail of Tophet is this—"Hide us from the
face of him that sitteth upon the throne!" Ye sinners, seek his face,
whose wrath ye cannot bear. God help you to seek it now. Before
you leave this house may you seek it and find it. He saith, "Seek ye
my face." May God the Holy Spirit lead you to obey the call. Amen.

11. The Hold-Fasts of Faith

"Who is the father of us all, (as it is written, I have made thee a father of many nations,) before him whom he believed, even God, who quickeneth the dead, and calleth those things which be not as though they were."—Romans iv. 16, 17.

ABRAHAM had received an assurance from the Lord that he was to be the father of many nations. His faith in this promise underwent great trials. Where there is the sweet honey of promise, there the wasps of doubt will be gathered together. A promise calls for faith; but through our natural depravity, it awakens unbelief; and there is a struggle around the sacred promise, such as that represented in the prayer, "Lord, I believe: help thou mine unbelief."

Satan, with slimy flattery, decoys men into a belief of his lie; but the God of truth gives us his bare promise, and bids us believe it; and when questions suggest themselves, he does not relax his claim, but bids us still believe. True faith, as the work of God, is not a thing to be put down: it is a conquering grace, and makes a brave fight against wicked unbelief.

While doing so, faith has her eyes open, and she, in due season, spies out grounds of confidence. She looks at God himself; she considers the days of old; she remembers her own experience of the right hand of the Most High; and thus she lifts her eyes to the hills, whence cometh her help. When faith has discovered a helpful truth she makes immediate use of it as a holdfast, even as Abraham did in the case now before us.

The great difficulty with Abraham was *death*. Death was around him on every side. God had promised him life, and life more abundantly; for he was to be the father of many nations, and have a seed as many as the stars of heaven for multitude; but as to all possibility of his being a father, his body was now dead. He was a hundred years old, and withered with age: how could he become a father of nations? Sarah, also, as to being a mother, was practically dead, for she was

---

* The preacher begs the reader, before perusing the sermon, to read the two portions of Scripture which were used in the public service. They are set down at the end of the sermon.

ninety years old. How should she bear sons unto Abraham? Further on the Lord bade him, when Isaac was miraculously born, to offer him as a sacrifice, and Abraham was willing to do even that at God's command. He believed that in Isaac should his seed be called, and therefore he looked that God should " raise him up, even from the dead ; from whence also he received him in a figure." The patriarch's faith settled down upon *God's power to quicken the dead,* and he found in that unquestioned truth a foundation for the firmest confidence. The truth of God's power to quicken the dead met all the difficulties of Abraham's position. He argued : What if my body be dead ? God can quicken it. What if my wife be, in this matter, as one dead ? By God's power she can receive strength. What if my son, when growing up, should be dead on the altar ? He that made me the promise can raise him up from the dead ; for what he has promised he is able to perform. Abraham's faith was a nail fastened in a sure place. He knew Jehovah as " God, who quickeneth the dead " ; and that resurrection word was, to his faith, a shout of victory.

Abraham had a second holdfast in *the creating power of God.* The Lord had spoken to him concerning his seed as though it existed, and had said, " I have made thee a father of many nations." As though these nations were already born, he had changed his name from Abram to Abraham, which means " father of a multitude." Yet, when he entered his tent, no child fondly climbed his knee, no babe smiled from the arms of Sarah ! " To me thou hast given no seed," was the humble statement of the believing patriarch. He felt that Jehovah could call forth from non-existence a people as many as the stars of heaven, for he had said, " so shall thy seed be." You know what it is to call a servant. You say "Mary," and there she is. You have called one who is, and she appears at your call. But God calls the things that are not as though they were, and lo, they appear at his bidding ! He says, " Light be," and light was. He says, " Let there be a firmament," and the blue sky overarches the whole earth. When he calls for fish or fowl, for plant or beast, they answer to the call. So Abraham argues : If God calls for descendants for me, they will come. Though there be no sign of my being a father, and, speaking after the flesh, it is impossible ; yet God, who calls everything out of nothing, can call for a numerous progeny for me, and that progeny will come.

Thus, you see, in the hour of trial, Abraham's faith fell back upon the two facts of resurrection and creation, and there it rested in peace.

I desire, at this time, without wisdom of words, in great simplicity, to teach this one lesson. It is a very plain lesson, but if it be well learned, it will be a well of strength and solace to you. God raiseth the dead, and createth out of nothing, and therefore he can carry out the promises of his gospel. Get this worked into your own souls, and you will be strong in faith. Once strong in faith you are strong everywhere, for as a man's faith is, so is he. If your faith shall learn to stay herself upon eternal principles, and find her rest in the omnipotence of God, you will become like Abraham, a prince among men ; and this service will bring you a life-long blessing.

Before I plunge into the sermon, let me speak a word to anxious men and women who are not yet saved, but who long to be partakers of life in Christ Jesus our Lord. You are in a conflict of soul just now. The Lord has set before you the promise, " He that believeth on the Son hath everlasting life." This you would fain believe, but you are staggered by the greatness of the mercy. How is God able to justify the ungodly? How can he have fellowship with you, for you are defiled with sin? You seem to yourself to have been such a monster of unbelief and enmity against God that you can never be put among the children. "How can these things be?" is the inquiry of your trembling spirit. Can a lion become a lamb? a sinner be turned into a saint? Can the leopard lie down with the kid? a rebel become a companion of those who fear the Lord? Can a man who merits the fiercest wrath of God yet live in his love, and delight himself in his favour? Is it not beyond belief that one steeped in evil should, at last, be found without fault before the throne of God? God promises eternal life to all who believe on his Son Jesus; but how can it be fulfilled? Here is the struggle. I want you, dear friend, before I go fully into my subject, to pick up at once the thread of it, and say, "I see where the preacher is driving. He wants me to believe that God can do anything which he has promised to do, seeing that he can raise the dead, and call the things that are not as though they were." Get this one thought into your mind, and I hope it will be a help to you in the hour of conflict between faith and feeling.

First, let me try and show *the time for the exercise of such a faith;* or, when shall we rest on resurrection and creation? Secondly, let us look upon *the basis of this faith;* and then, thirdly, let us sum up *the outcome of such a faith.* If we really get such a faith, it will be fruitful in abundant blessing.

I. THE TIME FOR SUCH A FAITH AS THIS. To believe God unstaggeringly in the teeth of appearances—when is the best time for this? This duty is not at its best when all goes well with us; for when we walk by sight, we scarcely walk by faith. When the soul is full of joy, there is wide space for gratitude, but narrower room for faith. "What a man seeth, why doth he yet hope for?" The light of fleeting day is not for perceptions which deal with eternity: faith's hour of prime is midnight. Even a horror of great darkness affords her a better opportunity for communion with the covenant God. Faith beholds her visions in the night: she wants not earthly light. A blind man loses nothing by the set of sun, and faith loses nothing by the removal of outward evidences. Faith has wrought many of her greatest deeds in hours which seemed least suitable for her undertakings. Like David's hero, she slays her lion in the pit in the time of snow. Like Jacob, she wrestles with the angel, and wins the victory, when night has fallen on all the world. Sunshine-faith comes and goes; true faith stands sentry at all hours. Fair-weather faith is poor stuff; give me winter-faith, which has warmth within it when the blasts from the north freeze flesh and blood, even to the bone.

First, *as to trusting God on account of the resurrection*, we shall find it greatly in season *when our soul is at first made to feel its spiritual death*. I am addressing some who mournfully cry, " How can I be saved? I am as dead as the earth I stand upon. I feel nothing.

> 'I hear, but seem to hear in vain,
>   Insensible as steel;
> If aught is felt, 'tis only pain
>   To find I cannot feel.'

My heart is as iron hardened in the forges of hell. I am without God, and without hope; and yet I do not mourn over my sin, nor feel my awful position as I ought to do. I fear I am dead in trespasses and sins, and I ask with the prophet, 'Can these dry bones live?'" Now is a special time, poor sinner, for believing in God that quickeneth the dead. Now is thy choice opportunity for testing the resurrection power of the Lord Jesus, who said, "I am the resurrection and the life." God can keep his promise of grace to thee, even to thee, if thou believest; for he quickeneth the dead. Thou believest that all the dead shall rise at the last day; canst thou not believe that, though thou art spiritually dead, God can quicken thee? Canst thou not believe in the power of the Lord to carry out his word? If resurrection has been wrought by him, all things are possible with him. If thou art as a dead man, as stiff and cold to heavenly things as though thou wert a corpse, yet God can quicken thee into newness of life. Is not this plain enough? Believest thou this? If thou canst believe it, thou art on the way to salvation. If thou canst trust God in Christ to make thee live, man, thou livest! The very fact that thou dost trust in Christ Jesus for eternal life proves that thou hast eternal life; for Jesus said, "He that believeth in me hath everlasting life." Even now, while conscious of so much death, believe in God, who quickeneth the dead.

Next, there is another notable occasion for faith, when the child of God is *in apprehension of death through soul trouble.* He is crying, like David in the eighty-eighth psalm, "My soul is full of troubles, and my life draweth nigh unto the grave." Though not absolutely dead as to spiritual things, yet the little life which remains is weak, faint, slumbering, and lethargic. I think I hear you cry, "I am counted with them that go down into the pit: I am as a man that hath no strength: free among the dead, like the slain that lie in the grave, whom thou rememberest no more: and they are cut off from thy hand." Now is the season to glorify God by believing the promise. You have the sentence of death in yourself, that you may not trust in yourself, but in the Lord alone. Your old sins rise up and accuse you: your present evil tendencies, like a rotting body of death, surround you; you find no comfort or joy in life. It seems as though God had given you up, and left you to perish. Though once you rejoiced before him, you are forced to sigh as one forsaken of his God, shut up for destruction. Now, even now, you are on a vantage-ground for glorifying the Lord by faith. It may be that, at this time, you enjoy nothing when you go up to religious services, and in reading or praying at home the chill of death makes every godly exercise a burden. You are so harassed with fears, so worried with cares, so tortured with regrets, and so tried with temptations that you are forced to cry, "My God, my God, why hast thou forsaken me?" Come, my brother, look to the strong for strength! Thou canst do nothing, it is clear; therefore cast thyself on him who is able to quicken the dead. Is there not foothold here? To thee, even to thee, though thou be moaning out, "O wretched man that I am! who shall deliver me from the body of this death?" to thee, I say, comes this brave hope, "The Lord is risen indeed," and he that believes in him, though he were dead, yet shall he live! Believe thou that word, "I will never leave thee, nor forsake thee"; and that other, "I give unto my sheep eternal life; and they shall never perish, neither shall any man pluck them out of my hand." Surely, if thou rememberest that God quickens the dead, thou canst believe that he will preserve thy soul when heart and flesh fail thee!

To another character is a like opportunity offered. *When death threatens to reach us through temporal trouble,* then may we believe in him that quickeneth the dead. It may be that the arrows of death have slain your dearest and best, and, at the same time, you have suffered crushing losses in business, sickness of body, and crosses in your family circle. You think you could truly say with David, "All thy waves and thy billows have gone over me." If God does not soon interfere, you will either be dead, or worse than dead. You cry, "I am afflicted, and ready to die, from my youth up." Listen, my brother, listen hopefully. Thou believest that the trumpet shall sound, and the dead shall be raised. Surely, he that can raise the myriads of the dead, can deliver thee out of thy killing troubles. He can bring thee through the valley of the shadow of death, and give thee beauty for ashes. I know he can, and so dost thou know it. Doubt no longer, but rest thou in the life-giving God, and he will deliver thee. "Many are the afflictions of the righteous: but the Lord delivereth him out of them all;" and so he will deliver you.

One more case occurs to me. This is a very sad one to my own heart. *When death crushes down the church,* and there seems no sign of revival, then should we believe in the God of resurrection. The carnal man cares nothing for the condition of the church of God; but the spiritual man takes pleasure in her stones, and favours the dust thereof. Some of us would sooner suffer personal calamity than see the cause of God and truth in a low condition. It may be that, in the church of which you are a member, you pine under a blight. Little prayer, no Christian fellowship, very few conversions, very little desire to win souls: your heart sinks within you, for death is all around. You look abroad, and there is the same state of things. We are sweltering in false doctrine and suffocating in worldliness. In many quarters, religion itself seems dead, and buried beneath a mound of rubbishing entertainments. What then? Where shall we turn for comfort? There are a few good, faithful men left; but it will be vain to trust in them; what can they do? We resolve to hold fast by the faith ourselves; but we dare not trust to resolves, for a witchery is abroad which would fascinate the very elect. Here is our mainstay: God is able to quicken the dead. Of the stones of Jordan's river, he is able to raise up children unto Abraham. The Lord God is able, from the slums and dens of London, to call a people that shall maintain his truth. God that quickeneth the dead can either work the seven-fold miracle of arousing his dead church, and making it a power to bless the world; or he can set existing churches on one side, and call them a people that were not a people, and her beloved that was not beloved. Have faith in God that quickeneth the dead that none of his promises or purposes will fall to the ground.

I turn now to the other ground of Abraham's hope. He had no child, and yet God tells him that he shall have a seed as numerous as the stars of heaven. How is the man of God to believe this? *His second holdfast is the creating power of God :* He calleth the things which be not as though they were. He can create as well as quicken. When can we use this fact as a reason for faith?

Friend, look to this, *when necessary graces are lacking in thy heart.* Though thou canst not find one of the saving graces within thy soul, yet believe in the promise of the Lord. What if within thy bosom at present there seems to be neither repentance, nor faith, nor hope, nor love, yet the Lord can create them all within thee. He can call the things that are not, and they will appear. Those of us who carry about with us a body of flesh and blood, are sometimes horribly cast down. When we look within, even by the candle of the Word, there are times when we cannot find in our own souls anything which we would wish to find : peace has fled, love is languishing, holiness is grieving, joy is banished : we are not fruitful, nor useful, nor happy; and yet we cannot give up our faith, but would fain have it strengthened. Then let us believe in him who maketh all things new. He will create in us the new heart and the right spirit, and call out graces which are not ours as yet.

"Well," cries a child of God, "I think I can find faith, and a little love; but what shall I do *when joy and peace are gone?* I have lost the rest I once enjoyed. I cannot sing as once I did, when I thought I could out-sing the seraphim, because my indebtedness to infinite love was greater than theirs." Ah, well, dear friend! God can create joy and peace, and put them in your soul, as new gifts from heaven; for he "calleth those things which be not as though they were." Believe for faith, believe for hope, believe for peace, believe for joy. These graces are set upon lower graces: "grace for grace." You rise not on stepping-stones of your dead selves, but on the ladder of the creating God, who has said, "I create the fruit of the lips; peace, peace to him that is far off, and to him that is near, saith the Lord; and I will heal him."

I spoke just now in reference to temporal troubles; there is a grand platform for faith *when no help is visible.* When you cannot see any friend who will assist you, nor any way in which you can help yourself, then trust in the Creator, who can make a way. Our friends, like swallows, soon quit us when our summer is over, but God's promise is not dependent upon man's faithfulness. We do not see how we can be delivered; but then the Lord's way is in the sea, and his footsteps are not known. My dear friend, do you not believe in God, your Maker, who calleth things that are not as though they were? He can deliver you by means unknown to yourself. Lean hard upon the creating arm. Trust in God, though the fig-tree do not blossom, though there be no herd in the stall, nor flock in the fold, nor corn in the barn. Trust in the promise, "Thou shalt dwell in the land, and verily thou shalt be fed." The Lord that made heaven and earth can set bread on thy table, and put clothes on thy back.

Once again let me speak of *the church in evil days.* Let us trust the Creator concerning his new creation. You bemoan yourself because you are not clothed with power from on high to bring sinners to Jesus. When you get into your class, you feel yourself to be as a dry tree, and not as Aaron's rod, which budded, and brought forth almonds. If you preach, you feel unfit for the hallowed employ. What is worse, the same weakness is almost everywhere. Few seem raised up to preach with power, and to lead on the hosts of God to victory. This is very sad : but suppose death to be everywhere, death in the pew, and death in the pulpit, death among the prophets, and death among the people; yet the Lord, who calleth things that are not as though they were, has but to give the word, and great will be the company of them that publish it. Our royal Leader has hidden forces at his command. Sir Walter Scott speaks of the highland chieftain, in the lone glen, who gave his whistle shrill, and straightway an army arose where none had been seen before—

> " From shingles gray their lances start,
> The bracken-bush sends forth the dart,
> The rushes and the willow-wand
> Are bristling into axe and brand,
> And every tuft of broom gives life
> To plaided warrior armed for strife."

Thus can our Lord garrison his church in a moment. In her desolation he can people her with such multitudes that she shall ask, " Who hath begotten me these ? " The Lord can send martyrs if they be wanted, confessors, preachers, writers, and consecrated men and women of every sort. Let us have no timorous thoughts; but let us glorify God by firm faith.

Thus have I set before you the fact that our times of deadness and discontent are grand seasons for believing in him that quickens the dead, and calls all things into being.

II. Secondly, we will observe upon how these things are manifest to us, even resurrection and creation. We shall speak of THE BASIS OF THIS FAITH.

If our faith is to be based on resurrection, what do we know about it ? Paul seems to pass over every other resurrection, and to dwell only upon *the resurrection of our Lord*. See the closing verses of this chapter : "If we believe on him that raised up Jesus our Lord from the dead ; who was delivered for our offences, and was raised again for our justification." Brethren, you believe that our Lord was crucified, pierced to the heart, dead and buried. A stone was rolled to the mouth of the grave, and that stone was sealed and guarded lest the body should be stolen; but yet he rose from the dead. It glads my heart to hear a great multitude sing—

> " Death cannot keep his prey—
> Jesus, my Saviour !
> He tore the bars away—
> Jesus, my Lord '

131

> Up from the grave he arose,
> With a mighty triumph o'er his foes;
> He arose a Victor from the dark domain,
> And he lives for ever with his saints to reign.
> He arose! He arose!
> Hallelujah! Christ arose!"

Realize that resurrection more and more, for there lies your hope. Hear this! Our Lord "was delivered for our offences." God gave him up to justice, as if he had said, "Take him away: I have laid on him the transgressions of my people—take him to the place of chastisement. Condemn him, scourge him, crucify him; for he is made a curse for my people. I have delivered him up, I have left him, and forsaken him." See the soldiers lead him through the streets of Jerusalem! See, they fasten his hands and feet with nails to the cruel cross! Behold him lifted up to die in agony extreme! He dies: they take down those precious limbs, wrap them in white linen, and place them in the sepulchre. He is delivered unto the grave for our offences. There went all my sin, and the sins of all believers: he made an end of sin in his death. The wrath of God was spent upon him for those sins which were made to meet in the person of the Well-Beloved, and now those sins are gone for ever. How do we know? We know that it is so because our Surety is set free. To meet our debt he was put in prison. When he paid the debt, he would be liberated, but not till then. When he was raised again it was because our justification was accomplished. A public declaration was given that the debt was discharged, and the everlasting righteousness was brought in. Right well do we sing—

> "He bore on the tree the sentence for me,
> And now both the Surety and sinner are free."

If Christ be raised from the dead, believers are no more guilty before God, for their guilt must have been put away, or else their Representative would not have risen. If God has let our Representative and Substitute go we are free. What a glorious rock this is! Cannot you get upon it—the resurrection of your blessed Lord? This is a fact proved beyond any other fact in history, and means this to us, that he has completed the work by which his people are saved. Hallelujah!

> "If Jesus had not paid the debt
> He ne'er had been at freedom set";

but in the prison of the grave he would have been incarcerated to this hour. God, who has raised his Son, and thereby set free his people, may well be trusted to fulfil every promise. To this I add that we know that all the dead will rise; and surely on this ground we may rest in the Almighty God. We have seen others spiritually quickened, and made to live unto God; yea, more, in the case of many of us, we, who were dead in trespasses and sins, have been quickened; and therefore, knowing of a surety that God quickeneth the dead, we are persuaded that what he has promised he is able to perform. We are eternally secure in a risen Saviour, because all the promises are in him yea and amen; and the fact of his rising proves that he can do all things for us.

If you desire another basis for your faith—and we hardly think you do—there is *creation*. If you wish to strengthen your faith, behold creation, and you have not far to go: your own body is full of wonders. See the fields with their ripe harvest; wander in the woods and forests, mark the hills and valleys, the rippling brooks and flowing streams, and the wide expansive ocean. Look up to the sun, the clouds, the sky. Go out at night, and watch the moon and stars. Who made all these? Who leadeth them out in their order? Who built the unpillared arch, which covers all things? Who created everything, from the tiniest atom up to the greatest world? Who but God? Surely he that made all these can make me a new creature in Christ Jesus. He that made all these things can make me meet to be a partaker with the saints in light. If he chooses to be a potter, as he does, he can make me revolve upon his wheel, and with every touch of his finger he can impart beauty to me till he has made me symmetrical in holiness, and fit for the Master's use. We, seeing the works of his hand all around us, ought to believe in him without a doubt. Mungo Park, the African traveller, lost his way in the wilds, and there and then was cheered by viewing a tiny moss, and marking its singular beauty. He saw the finger of God in that small object, and felt sure that the great God would take care of him. So may we be taught faith by every created thing: the Creator can do all things.

When you have looked at creation, remember providence, which is a prolongation of the creative act. The power which made all things upholds them. The Lord keeps them in their places, or they could not remain. They tell us nowadays that the universe stands because of law. Is there any power about a mere law? No, my friends: law requires the almighty power of the living God! Nowadays, philosophers are quick to claim for men freedom of action; but the Lord, who made man, is spoken of as if he were no free agent, but the mere slave of laws. Everybody is now to be a free agent save only the living God. Is this philosophy? Is this reason? Is God the captive of his own laws? I know no such God. He doeth all things. Natural laws are but the summary of God's usual way of working; but the laws neither hinder God in anything, nor perform anything, as of themselves. He himself causeth everything to abide, or to change, as seemeth him good. As you see everything upheld by the word of his power, surely you have good ground for believing in his power to keep his promise to you.

Meanwhile, a creation work of grace is going on around you. If you do not feel it in yourself, my brother, you can soon see it in others. Speak to the people of God, and they will tell you; and to new converts, and they will show you. The story of what free grace has done is ever telling, yet untold. One will tell you, "I was a drunkard, and the Lord converted me." Another will confess, "My feet had almost gone, but the Lord preserved me." Another will declare, "I was in the furnace, and the Son of man walked in the fire with me." Another will testify, "I was brought low, and he helped me." You will have abundant evidence that grace-creation is going on continually, and that God is working great wonders in the midst of his people ; wherefore, be of good courage, and put your trust in the God of the new creation.

I wish the grace of God would bring every one of you as far as we have now come, namely, to believe that he who raises the dead, and creates out of nothing, can do for us what we need. We have an Almighty God to deal with : and his grace is linked with his omnipotence, and his love is as large as his power. I want you to trust him. Oh, if you have never done so, do it now ! God help you ! If you are holding on to anything but God in Christ Jesus, let it go— let it go at once ! You will not hurt by falling into the unseen arms. I have heard of one who, wandering in the night, came to what he thought to be an awful precipice ; and as he was about to fall, in sheer desperation he caught the root of a tree, and held there for dear life. His arms were weary ; his hands were ready to fail him ; but he held on with a death-grip. At last he was obliged to give up his hold, and when he had done so, down he fell ; and you expect me to add that he was dashed to pieces. No, he only fell a few inches upon a soft bed of moss, for he was not near a precipice after all. When you let go all other trusts, you think it an awful thing to fall into your Saviour's arms ; but it is not so : it is not a dangerous venture, but a wise reliance. If faith falls, she falls upon the bosom of her God. If you trust him who loved you unto death, you are safe and happy. Give up all earthly confidence, all human hope, and repose in Jesus crucified, and you shall find rest unto your souls.

III. But now, let us review THE OUTCOME OF THIS FAITH. May we all see the same results in ourselves through the Holy Ghost !

Abraham believed, and *looked at things from God's standpoint.* " As it is written, I have made thee a father of many nations, before him whom he believed, even God." Abraham looked at the promise as Abraham, and he could not see how it could be. He had no child, and his wife was old. But God calls him by the name which signified "Father of a multitude," because he viewed him as such, and the Lord talked to him about his household after him, about their number, and about their being strangers in a strange land. To God's foreseeing eye Abraham was what he was to become : he calls the things that are not as though they were. Now, faith has the wonderful property of becoming like the God in whom it trusts, and of looking at things as God sees them. How I wish, my dear, tried brother, you could see your troubles as God sees them—namely, as means to your advancement in grace ! Look at affliction to-day as a process that is enriching you. Sinner, when you believe in Jesus, God looks at you as saved, justified, forgiven, and quickened into eternal life. If you believe in Jesus, see yourself as God sees you. It is a great thing for a sinner, dead in himself, to say, " And yet I live ; " but assuredly he may say it. It is a great thing for one consciously guilty to say, " And yet I am justified : " still, it is true, and it is no presumption to believe it. Oh, this is a grand art, to look at things from God's point of view ! Faith takes the omnipotence of God, and girds herself with his almighty power ; and then she takes the foresight of God ; and though it doth not yet appear what we shall be, faith perceives that in Christ the poor, trembling, and guilty soul is made pure, spotless, and glorious before God. Believer in Jesus, know yourself to be what the gospel says you are, and hold on to that knowledge. However desperate the tug may be, never let go your conviction that God's view of you in Christ is the true one. God sees the truth of things, and teaches faith to see the same. Justification by faith is no fiction; it is a fact that the believer is just, is saved, is complete in Christ Jesus. God give us to see this fact, even as he sees it, and then, being justified by faith, we may have peace with God.

Next, you see that Abraham *considered his body now dead*. Our Authorized Version runs thus:—"He considered *not* his own body now dead." The Revised Version has : "He considered his own body now as good as dead." It is a curious fact that among the ancient manuscripts there are two readings of almost equal value : one with the "not," and one without it. I think both mean the same thing. You say, "How is that?" He considered his own body to be dead, but he did not make any consideration of that fact, but believed in God all the same. He considered it so far as to be fully aware of it ; but he did not consider it so as to raise a question about the fulfilment of the promise. He considered it to be true that he was past having a son in the strength of nature, but he considered that he should have a son through the power of the promise. God could work out his purpose as well with Abraham and Sarah in old age as in their youth. O poor seeking soul, listen to this! Know yourself to be spiritually dead. Think as badly of yourself as ever you like, for you are worse than you think you are; but after you have considered the fearful fact of your lost estate, do not go on to consider it as any hindrance to God in the work of his grace. Jesus is able to save you over the head of all your death, and guilt, and corruption. If you have been a thief, a Sabbath-breaker, a liar, a swearer, a murderer, yet he can forgive you; and if to-day you feel so dead that you can do nothing towards your own salvation, yet if you will believe his promise, he that can raise the dead can save you from the guilt and power of sin. Do not consider your helpless state to be any barrier to free grace, for the love of God will triumph over all your loathsomeness and death.

Abraham, as the outcome of his faith, *obeyed God in all things*—a very essential point, this. Believing God, he left his estates in Ur of the Chaldees, and came to Canaan, to live in tents, and wander about like a gipsy, that he might dwell where the Lord had called him to sojourn alone, a stranger in a strange land. If you believe the promise of the gospel, you will come out from the world, you will come out from sin, and you will become one of those strangers who follow Jesus whithersoever he goeth. God will be your Leader, Christ will be your Commander ; and though *in* the world you will not be *of* the world. All true believers, like Abraham, obey. Obedience is faith in action. You are to walk in the steps of the faith of father Abraham. His faith did not sit still, it took steps; and you must take these steps also by obeying God because you believe him. That faith which has no works with it is a dead faith, and will justify no one. How should a dead thing justify? Faith, knowing a thing to be true, acts upon that truth, and is thus itself justified, or proved to be justly called faith.

And then the result was that *Abraham enjoyed the promise.* I have often thought of the old man laughing at the thought of the birth of a son to him in his hundredth year. Two people may do the same thing, and in the one it may be right, and in the other it may be wrong. Sarah laughed because she thought it absurd, and could not believe it; but Abraham laughed because he did believe it, and realized it. He knew it would be so, and he began to laugh with joy and gladness. Oh, for more of such laughing! He believed himself to be the father of many nations, and the old man laughed, and laughed again; it seemed such a fountain of happiness to him. If you believe, you will laugh too. We have too much crying among us. Oh, for a little more filling of the mouth with laughter, and the tongue with singing, for the Lord hath done great things for us, whereof we are glad! It is not a fiction, it is a fact. The Lord has given us eternal life in his Son, Jesus Christ our Lord. Let us laugh and laugh again, for an unutterable joy of heart floods our spirit. Bunyan pictures Christiana as saying to Mercy, "What was the matter that you did laugh in your sleep to-night?" And Mercy said, "But are you sure I laughed?" When she told her dream, Christiana said, "Laugh! ay, well you might to see yourself so well." She laughed because she dreamed she had been welcomed into glory. To faith this is no dream. We have had many dreams of this sort, and we know that we are saved by grace, adopted of the Father, united to the Son, indwelt by the Holy Ghost—visions most true; and these have made us laugh with an inward, inexpressible delight. The more steadfastly we believe, the more of this rapturous joy we shall experience.

Best of all, because of this, *Abraham was accounted righteous.* And who accounted him righteous? Well, not the sons of men; they knew him as righteous only by his outward character; but God accounted him righteous because he had faith. The moment you believe in his risen Son, God counts you righteous; and as you keep on believing, God accounts you righteous. "Oh, but I am a poor, imperfect creature!" God counts you righteous. "I strive after holiness, but I am not what I want to be." God counts you righteous. God never makes mistakes; he never mis-counts. If he counts a man righteous, that man is righteous, depend upon it—righteous in such a way that he may stand before the judgment-seat of God at the last, and none shall be able to lay anything to his charge.

> " Bold shall I stand in that great day,
> For who aught to my charge shall lay?
> While through thy blood absolved I am
> From sin's tremendous curse and shame."

Believe, and you shall be accounted righteous. The Lord help you, for Jesus' sake! Amen.

12. Three Texts, But One Subject – Faith

" In the shadow of thy wings will I make my refuge."—Psalm lvii. 1.
" Cast thy burden upon the LORD, and he shall sustain thee."—Psalm lv. 22.
" Let him trust in the name of the LORD, and stay upon his God."—Isaiah l. 10.

IT is the preacher's business to endeavour to make plain to the people the meaning of the word FAITH. Inasmuch as salvation comes by believing, it is most important that men should know what believing is; and though we have to preach upon many topics, and take the whole range of the Word of God, yet it often behoveth the minister of Christ to dwell especially upon the way whereby men are savèd, and to explain what is that step by which they enter into eternal life.

You may think that it is very easy to explain faith, and so it is; but it is easier still to confound people with your explanation. There is nothing simpler in the world than to believe in Christ Jesus; yet probably there is nothing more difficult than to explain to a man what it is to believe in the Lord Jesus; not that the thing itself is difficult, but the explaining of it is not so easy. You remember the story, perhaps, of Mr. Thomas Scott, a very excellent commentator, who brought out an edition of John Bunyan's *Pilgrim's Progress*, to which he has written very excellent, and, I think that I must add, very dull notes. On going round his parish, he called on an aged person, and found her studying the book. " Well, my good woman," said he, " I see that you are reading Bunyan's *Pilgrim's Progress*." " Yes, sir," she replied, " I always enjoy that book." " And, pray, do you understand it?" " Yes, sir, I understand it very well; and I think that, by the grace of God, I shall one day understand your explanation of it," which was not very complimentary to Mr. Scott. So, I have no doubt that there are many who better understand what faith is without our explanations. It is so easy to darken counsel by words without knowledge, and to give illustrations which themselves need to be illustrated, and definitions which need to be defined. I am afraid of doing that to-night; I see my difficulty, and I cry to God to help me to put faith very plainly before every sinner here, that you may all know what it is, and may at once exercise it.

I have met with a large number of persons, who have believed in Christ, who were accustomed to hear the gospel preached, and to have faith explained to them; but in almost every case they have told me that they did not know what faith was till they themselves believed, and, although they were told, a hundred times over, that it was simply trusting in Christ, they still did not get a hold of the right idea, they still entertained the thought that there was something to be felt, something to be done, something to be endured, something or other more than the simple casting of themselves upon Christ for eternal salvation. I have also noticed how, when I have tried to use illustrations, the friend to whom I have spoken has not been affected by them, and has not understood my illustrations. Speaking to a young man once, I quoted to him that verse of Dr. Watts which begins,—

> " A guilty, weak, and helpless worm,
>   On thy kind arms I fall."

" But," said he, " I cannot fall." " Oh! my dear friend," I replied, " you do not catch the idea at all, because it is not a thing that a man can do. He falls because he cannot help it; there is no effort in falling, it is cessation from effort." Still, though I put it, as I thought, so that he ought to understand it, he did not comprehend it then. It was some time after, when the Holy Spirit revealed it to him, that he came to understand what faith was. Perhaps you ask, " Are we such dolts that we do not even understand plain Saxon language when it has to do with spiritual things?" Ah, my hearers, sin has made fools of us! Sin has so befooled us, that even God's Word itself does not convey God's meaning to our stupid minds until the Spirit of God comes, and teaches our reason, reason, and takes the film from our eyes, and helps us to see what is, in itself, plain as a pikestaff, but is not plain to us by reason of our sinful and corrupt nature. Before I try, then, to preach about what faith is, may I ask you to pray the Holy Ghost to come, and open men's eyes, that they may see what faith is? For truly, as we know not what we should pray for as we ought, we know not how to believe as we ought; and we make mistakes on this simplest of all subjects until the Holy Spirit sets us right. Divine Spirit, we believe in thee, but we do not believe in ourselves! We see, in some measure, how stupid, how ignorant we are. Come, we pray thee, and teach us even the first lesson of the doctrines of Christ, teach us to believe in Jesus!

If you want to cut a diamond, you must cut it with a diamond; so, if you want to explain Scripture, you must explain it with Scripture. I thought, therefore, that I would take three expressions from the Old Testament, which may help to set forth what faith really is.

I. The first expression you will find in the fifty-seventh Psalm, and the first verse. It shows that faith is HIDING IN GOD : " Be merciful unto me, O God, be merciful unto me: for my soul trusteth in thee : yea, in the shadow of thy wings will I make my refuge."

See then, trusting in God, that is, faith, is the same thing as hiding under the shadow of God's wings by way of refuge. Let me explain that figure, first, as relating to *birds beneath their mother's wing*. There is a hawk in the sky, the hen sees it, she begins to give her warning "cluck"; the little chickens hardly know what the danger is, but they understand the mother's call, and they see her crouching down on the ground. Have you never seen her close to the earth, with her wings outspread, and calling and calling again till every one of her birdlets comes and hides beneath the mother's wing? They are out of sight of the bird of prey; if that hawk comes down at all, it will have to attack the hen, and kill her before it can reach her chicks. The pecks of its bill, the tearing of its talons, will have to be first upon the mother-bird, for her little ones are all hidden beneath the covert of her wings.

Now, that hiding is an illustration of faith. Here is Christ, the Saviour, and I hide myself under him. The justice of God must smite the sinner, or One who is able and willing to suffer in the sinner's stead. It is imperative, as a first law of the universe, that sin cannot go unpunished. As justice approaches, with drawn sword, I find Christ coming, and interposing between me and the sentence of the law; and if the avenger seeks me, I hide away under Christ, and all the blows must be dealt upon him. You know how he was wounded, rent, torn, that you and I, hiding beneath him, might escape. It sometimes happens, on the sides of the Alps, that a mountain goat or a wild gazelle may be feeding there, and an eagle spies out a kid close by its mother, and the powerful bird thinks to devour that kid, and down it flies; but the little creature crouches as low as it can at its mother's side, and there stands the mother with horns ready to meet the eagle, and to fight against it for the life of her beloved little one. So the little kid is hidden away behind its mother, and she valorously contends for it. In that way we must hide behind the Saviour. We sang just now,—

> "Rock of Ages, cleft for me,
> Let me hide myself in thee!"

I put myself behind my Saviour; I say to God, "Deal not with me; deal with my dying Saviour. My God, I interpose between thy wrath and my guilty head the sacrifice which he presented on the cross, when he bowed his head, and said, 'It is finished.'"

The act of the chickens hiding away beneath the hen's wings is a very good description of the act of faith.

It may be further illustrated by *travellers hiding beneath a rock*. Journeying through hot countries, they find towards noon that the air is very sultry, and that the sandy soil beneath them reflects the heat of the sun; they seem to be travelling in a hot bath, and they feel faint and weary. But yonder there is a great rock cropping out of the soil, and under its shadow the heat is not felt. I have often been struck with the singular coolness that there is just by the side of a great rock. I have myself sometimes stood out in the sunshine in the South of France, and it has been so hot that I have felt ready to faint, and I have just stepped back within the shadow of a rock, and found it almost as chilly as a vault. Refreshing indeed has it been to get into the cooler atmosphere. Well, now, Christ is the shadow of a great Rock in a weary land; and if you and I come to him, and let his shadow come between us and the burning heat of the sun of divine justice, the heat will fall on the rock, not on us. We shall be safe and refreshed, and the Rock will screen us from all evil. Come and put Christ between you and God. He is the Interposer between God and man; and that is true faith which gets to the side of the Rock Christ, and hides away beneath his sheltering shade.

Take another Biblical metaphor, that of *the manslayer hiding in the city of refuge.* That was a part of the law, you remember. If one had killed a man inadvertently, and not of malice, the next of kin of the man killed would seek revenge; and he followed up the manslayer, and the poor man's only hope of life was to hurry away as quickly as ever he could to a refuge city belonging to the priests. If he could once pass through the gate of a city of refuge, he was sure of a fair trial, and could not be put to death by the avenger of blood. Oh, how he hurried! How his feet seemed to fly over the soil, especially if he saw the avenger at some little distance following him with hot foot! But once let the city gate be shut, within the sacred streets he breathed freely, he was safe. Come, guilty souls, and fly away to Christ, as the manslayer fled away to the city of refuge; and once safe in him, with Jesus as the great gate between you and the avenger of blood, you are perfectly safe. Do you comprehend and catch the thought? t is hiding away in Christ from the pursuit of vengeance, from the ighteous wrath of God, that brings safety.

Another illustration comes in here, it is that of *the conies hiding in the rocks:* "The conies are but a feeble folk, yet make they their houses in the rocks." A coney was not exactly like a rabbit; a rabbit hardly dwells among rocks, but this creature was always found in holes and crannies of the rocks. Poor little coney, a dog is after it, and the sportsman seeks to destroy it; but there is an opening in the rock, and he slips in there, and is perfectly safe. The dog barks, and the coney s little heart beats fast; but barking will not kill conies. The sportsman looks up and down, but he cannot see the coney; he can see the rock, but he cannot see the coney within the rock. The coney has hidden right away from the keenest sight of the man who would destroy him. Now, just hide in that way in Christ, who died for guilty men. Trust him; believe him; believe that he will save you. Hide yourself in the Rock of Ages, and then, though you may feel some fears, you will have no need of any. Once safe in Christ, all is well with you. You know that, when a ship has been driven by a storm, and the winds are out, the mariners hasten to the harbour. When they get into port, down goes the anchor. The rattle of the chains is one of the pleasantest sounds ever heard when one is sea-sick, and worn out with a tempest-tossed voyage. Down goes the anchor; well, but after that the motion of the ship still keeps on, she rocks to and fro; yes, but the anchor is down, the fear is all over; no matter how the vessel rocks, the winds cannot drive her out of the harbour; she is safe in port, and the anchor is down, all is well with her. Oh, if to-night you can let the anchor go right down into the deeps, and trust Christ, get a grip of Christ, and hold on to Christ, you may have some

140

tears, and there may be some tossings for you yet to endure, but all is well! As the ship hides itself in the harbour, so do you hide away in Christ, saying with David, "In the shadow of thy wings will I make my refuge." This is faith.

I cannot preach as I would. I have been learning to preach for ever so many years, but I cannot do it as I want to; but I wish that, instead of my preaching to you, you would practise what I bid you, and hide away under the shadow of Christ's wings.

> "Come, guilty souls, and flee away
> Like doves to Jesu's wounds;
> This is the welcome gospel-day,
> Wherein free grace abounds."

I remember when I first hid away in that Rock. I have been tempted many times to come out; but I never will. I cannot fight the hawk, I cannot kill the eagle, but I can squeeze myself further back into my Rock, and hide away there; and even—

> "When my eye-strings break in death,
> When I soar through tracks unknown,"

and see Christ on his judgment-throne, I hope still to shelter in the Rock of Ages. Do the same, dear sister. Do the same, dear brother. May the Holy Ghost lead you to do it now! Remember that you have to believe for yourself; the Holy Ghost will not believe for you, he cannot believe for you. How can he? He has nothing to believe. It is you who have to believe; and though he worketh in you to will and to do, he works, but you believe. It is only personal faith that saves; it could not be the faith of the Holy Ghost, it must be the sinner's own faith though it is wrought in him by the Spirit of God. Therefore, believe thou, and live thou unto God.

II. Having dwelt on that illustration long enough, I ask you now to notice another expression in Psalm fifty-five, verse twenty-two: "Cast thy burden upon the Lord, and he shall sustain thee." This passage sets forth faith as ROLLING OUR BURDEN UPON GOD.

I believe that this text might be rendered, "Roll thy burden upon the Lord." The similar passage in Psalm thirty-seven, verse five, "Commit thy way unto the Lord," is in the margin, "Roll thy way upon the Lord."

Faith, then, is *the leaving of our burdens with God*. When a man believes in Christ, he shifts his burden from his own shoulders on to the shoulders of Christ.

> "My soul looks back to see
> The burdens thou didst bear,
> When hanging on the cursèd tree,
> And hopes her guilt was there."

There you are, stooping down beneath a crushing load, heavy as that which Atlas was supposed to bear when the whole world was on his back, and Christ comes in, and says, "Roll thy burden from off thy shoulders on to mine; let me bear it for you."

Well, then, if the burden be laid upon Christ, then *we have not to bear it ourselves.* Notice that. Some will say, "We trust Christ, but yet we are not at ease." How is that? If you have trusted Christ, you have rolled your burden upon him; it is no longer upon you. I do not know whether there are still, near Ludgate Hill, as there used to be, certain rests for burden-bearers. You might have seen the porter come toiling up to that spot, and as he shifted his burden on to the rest, he was himself relieved of the load. I have often looked at one of those rests at Mentone, and seen the women come along the road, with huge baskets of lemons or oranges on their heads, and as soon as they have reached this kind of table, they have put their burden on it, and sat down, and rested a while. Now, when they put their basket of oranges there, it is not on their head, is it? There is the beauty of rolling your burden upon Christ; when he takes it, it is not on you any longer. A thing cannot be in two places at one time; and when, by faith, I lay my burden down at Jesus' feet, I have not got it. If my sin is laid on him, it does not any longer lie on me. Come, poor soul, here is the act of faith, to take the mighty burden, that will crush thee lower than the lowest hell, and lay it on Christ thy Saviour.

When the burden is on him, and not on us, *the burden is not ours to take up again.* I have heard that some of our rests in London were done away with, because porters were known to come and put their loads on them, and sit down a while, and afterwards get up and go home without them. You would hardly believe they could be so forgetful; but people do strange things. However, that is a mistake that I want you to make with regard to Christ, for there is no mistake in it. Lay your sin on him by an act of faith; but do not take it up again. I never can believe, as some do, in God forgiving our sin, and afterwards laying it to our account. I do believe that, in the day when our sin was laid on Christ, it was all laid there, and taken away from his people never to be charged against them again. "As far as the east is from the west, so far hath he removed our transgressions from us." How far is the East from the West? If you could travel, like a ray of light, as far eastward as you pleased, while another went as far westward as he could desire, you might go on for ever and for ever, and yet not meet. The distance, so far as created things can be, is infinite; and so far hath the Lord removed our transgressions from us. If we, by faith, lay our sins upon Christ, God himself forgets them, and casts them behind his back, so that he says that, if they are searched for, they shall not be found any more for ever.

And here is one of the greatest mercies of all, that *the burden is not even on Christ now.* Roll thy burden upon him; and if thou dost, that burden is not on him now. He died on the cross, and they laid him in the sepulchre. Thy sin rolls into his sepulchre, it is buried; Christ has left it as a dead and buried thing, and he has risen from among the dead. He took your debt upon himself; but when he paid that debt, it was not any more due from him, neither was it due from you; therefore, we rightly sing,—

"Now both the Surety and sinner are free."

The atoning sacrifice of Christ is so complete a satisfaction to the Lord, that even the sin that was laid on the Lamb of God is gone for ever. It has ceased even to be, so that a believer in Christ may indeed rejoice with joy unspeakable and full of glory.

Now then, roll your burden upon the Lord. I really think that, if a number of friends all stood here to-night, groaning under a great load, and I said, "Just roll your burdens off," they would understand me. What a lot of rolling off would be done very soon! That is all that is required with your sin. Jesus is willing to take it; Jesus is willing to obliterate all the black record against you; let it go to him. Tell the devil that you have been answering him long enough, and you are not going to talk to him any longer, for you have an Advocate, in whose hands you are going to leave your case. When a man has an advocate, he does not go and do his legal business himself; he refers everybody to his advocate. "Go and settle with him," says he; and to-night, when the devil says, "You are a sinner," I reply, "I know I am; and so are you." "Ah!" says he, "but you deserve death." "Yes," I answer, "but there is One who stood in my stead; go and settle my account with him. He undertook my business, and he said that he would see me through with it if I would but trust him, and I do trust him; I must refer you to my Advocate, he can settle with you; I cannot." Do that, I pray you. Roll your burden upon the Lord. Trust in him; to roll your burden upon him, is to trust him; I do not know a better figure by which to set faith forth. Oh, that God the Holy Spirit may use it to-night to the unburdening of many poor souls!

III. I said that we would have three of these Old Testament diamonds; the third is found in the fiftieth chapter of Isaiah, and the tenth verse, where faith is likened to STAYING UPON GOD. I read it to you just now, but we will read the verse again: "Who is among you that feareth the Lord, that obeyeth the voice of his servant, that walketh in darkness, and hath no light? Let him trust in the name of the Lord, and" (here is the same thing as trusting in the name of the Lord, the explanation of it) "ay upon his God."

The word "stay" means "lean." If I cannot stand, if I feel giddy, I naturally put out my hand; and if I feel faint, I lean upon some support; and the more faint I am, the more I lean. At this moment, I lean my whole weight upon this platform rail, just *so*. If this rail gives way, I must go down. I am leaning, staying myself wholly here. Now that is what you have to do with Christ, lean on him; with all your weight of sin and sorrow, lean on Jesus Christ, and lean hard. Do not try to hold yourself up now; throw yourself right on him, lean on him, rest on him, let him bear the whole of your weight. Stay yourself upon him.

In order to do that, you must *believe that the Lord Jesus Christ is able to bear you up*. Do you not believe it? He is God as well as Man; he has offered an all-sufficient atonement to God; he is well-pleasing to the Father; he is the Lord strong and mighty, a Saviour, and a great One. Lean on him, and lean hard. Did anyone say, "I am afraid to trust Christ, lest he may not be able to bear me up"? Oh, dear friend, do not talk so! It does seem so absurd. I remember a good old lady, who would never go over the Saltash bridge at Plymouth. She looked up at it, and said that she did not believe that it would ever bear her weight. There were great luggage trains that went rolling over it, but still she always said that it would not bear her. You smile, do you? Now, just think that you are that old woman; you are doing a more foolish thing than she did, if you cannot trust Christ with your weight, Christ who is omnipotent to save. How foolish you must be! He is able to save you. He is able to save unto the uttermost them that come unto God by him; therefore stay yourself upon him.

Then, *lean all your weight on him;* if you do that, you no longer have to support yourself. The sinner says, "I do not think that I could ever get to heaven." Lean upon Christ to get you there. "Oh, but if I were to leave my sins, I am afraid that I should go back to them!" Lean upon Christ to keep you from going back. "Oh, but if I lived here many years, I should be tempted, and I might fall!" Lean upon Christ to preserve you from falling. "Ah, but you do not know what a temper I have!" Lean upon Christ to conquer your temper. "But, sir, I have gone back so many times." Lean upon Christ to keep you from going back any more; stay yourself upon him. I cannot possibly mention all your weaknesses, and all your doubts, and all your fears; but whatever they are, lean upon Christ, lean hard on him, like one of our female missionaries, when sustained by one of her converts in the hour of death. The convert said, "Lean on me, missionary; lean on me, sister;" and as she thought that the missionary had a delicacy in resting all her weight, she said, "If you love me, lean hard; for the harder you lean, the more I shall feel that you love me." And Christ says to you, "Sinner, if you love me, lean hard." Lean hard on him, and he will bear you up. You do not need strength for leaning on Christ.

" True belief and true repentance,"

perseverance, and every grace that you want to make you meet to be a partaker of the inheritance of the saints in light, Christ will give it all to you. Depend upon him for it all. You will never have ease of mind, you will never know what full salvation means, till you just give yourself up, as though you were dead, that he might be your life. Resign yourself to Christ, as a wandering sheep has to do to the shepherd, when he takes it by the legs, and throws it on his shoulders, and carries it home rejoicing. Christ can save; he will save; therefore, stay yourself upon him.

If you do, *you shall have perfect peace.* "Thou wilt keep him in perfect peace, whose mind is stayed on thee: because he trusteth in thee." I should like to begin preaching again with that for my text, "Thou wilt keep him in perfect peace, whose mind is stayed on thee: because he trusteth in thee." If you have not perfect peace, it is because you are not staying yourself on God as you ought to do. There is no other way of coming to a perfect rest but by a perfect leaning upon Christ. Will you do that to-night? If a man were to get one foot on a rock, he might stand very well. Suppose that he puts the other foot on the sand, the sea comes up, the sand is treacherous, and his foot begins to sink. I should recommend him to get wholly on that bit of rock, and to stand there. Do so, then; stay yourself wholly upon Christ. Have no confidence in yourself, in baptism, in sacraments, in prayers, in good works, in anything but the finished work of Christ; and when you get there, you are on a foundation that never can be moved.

I would like to say, as I finish, that I have now served the Lord Jesus Christ for about forty years, and I have preached his gospel, I can say, with all my heart, neither have I cared for anything but to win souls to my Lord Jesus: but when I came to him at first, I had no hope but in his blood and merits, and I have no more hope now, apart from his blood and merits, than I had at the beginning. I stand on the same foundation as I stood upon then. I have heard of a good man, who said, as he was dying, that he was sorting over his life, putting his good works in one bundle, and his bad ones in the other. At last he said to his wife, "It is no use sorting them out, for the good ones are so bad that I think that I will fling them all away, and cling to Christ alone." There was a famous cardinal, in Luther's day, who fought tremendously against the Reformer; but he said, in the course of the discussion, that, seeing that there is much in our good works that is faulty, and no man can be quite sure that he has done enough good works to save him, upon the whole it is better to trust only to the merits of Christ. Well, the best of everything always suits me; and if that is the best, I will let other people have the second best, and just trust in Christ, and trust in Christ alone. Oh, that you would all do so to-night! Have done with yourself, have done with your good works, have done with your bad ones, have done with any reliance upon self whatever; and just come as you are, and trust Christ, who died for the guilty and undeserving. O bankrupt sinner, O sinner without a hope, come thou and just stay thyself upon the immovable foundation of the atoning sacrifice of Christ, and thou shalt find eternal life to-night, yea, even to-night! God grant it, for Jesus' sake! Amen.

Exposition by C. H. Spurgeon.

ISAIAH L.

Verse 1. *Thus saith the LORD,*

There is always something weighty coming when you have this preface. If God speaks, we ought to hear with reverence, with attention.

1. *Where is the bill of your mother's divorcement. whom I have put away? or which of my creditors is it to whom I have sold you?*

God is here addressing his ancient people; they had been given up, as it were, left, forsaken. They compared themselves to a wife who had been divorced by her husband, or to children who had been sold by their father because of his extreme poverty. The Lord says, "Now, tell me, have I really put away my chosen people as a man in a pet puts away his wife? Have I really sold you to profit by you? What benefit is it to me that you are carried away captive, and that you are left without comfort?"

1. *Behold, for your iniquities have ye sold yourselves, and for your transgressions is your mother put away.*

It was not God's changeableness, but their own sinfulness that had brought upon them all their sufferings. The Jews might have remained a nation in possession of their own land to this day, if they had not turned aside unto idols. It was not that God cast away his people whom he did foreknow; but they cast him off, they sold themselves. Now, if any child of God has fallen into trouble of heart, and has lost his comfort, let him not blame God; his sorrow is caused by his own act and deed. And if any man or woman here should be in deep trouble brought on by sin, let them not set it down to their destiny, let them not call God unkind; but let them take the blame to themselves: "For your iniquities have ye sold yourselves, and for your transgressions is your mother put away."

2. *Wherefore, when I came, was there no man? when I called, was there none to answer?*

It is Christ who is speaking here by the mouth of the prophet. When he came, there was "no man." He could not find in all the nation any faithful one to help him in his great redemptive work. "He came unto his own, and his own received him not." He preached repentance and faith throughout the land; but they cried, "Crucify him! Crucify him!" They loved darkness rather than light, because their deeds were evil.

2. *Is my hand shortened at all, that it cannot redeem? or have I no power to deliver?*

If you are in the worst plight in which you can be, God can still help you. Despair of yourself; but do not despair of him. If you have come to the very bottom of all things, and the last ray of hope is quenched in midnight darkness, God is still the same. Hear what he says to you, "Is my hand shortened at all, that it cannot redeem? or have I no power to deliver?" Can he not break the bonds of drunkenness? Can he not deliver the unchaste from their vile passions? Can he not pick up from the dunghill the outcast and the offcast? Is anything too hard for the Lord? Is the salvation of the greatest sinners impossible for him to accomplish? That can never be, for he is "mighty to save."

2. *Behold, at my rebuke I dry up the sea, I make the rivers a wilderness: their fish stinketh, because there is no water, and dieth for thirst.*

God divided the Red Sea, he parted the Jordan asunder, and made a way for his people to pass over. He who has done this can do anything. When God takes up the case, impossibility is not in the dictionary. However great your sorrow, however deep your misfortune, or however grievous your sin, if God comes to deal with it, he will make short work of all your troubles, and all your despair.

3, 4. *I clothe the heavens with blackness, and I make sackcloth their covering. The Lord GOD hath given me the tongue of the learned, that I should know how to speak a word in season to him that is weary: he wakeneth morning by morning, he wakeneth mine ear to hear as the learned.*

This is Christ speaking again. When he came here, though he found no man able to help him, none to come and join him in the redemption of his people, yet he gave himself up to the tremendous task. He became instructed of the Father. He was taught to speak a word to weary ones. "Never man spake like this Man." There is no gospel like his gospel, no doctrine like his doctrine. · He went to God in private "morning by morning." He received his message from his Father, and he came and delivered it to the people. Oh, what a glorious Christ we have!

5. *The Lord GOD hath opened mine ear, and I was not rebellious, neither turned away back.*

He had his ear bored, as slaves had when they would not go out free, but meant to remain with their master. Christ had a bored ear, an opened ear. He never rebelled against God's will. He was obedient to the Father, even unto death. If you want to know how obedient he was, hear me read the next verse :—

6. *I gave my back to the smiters, and my cheeks to them that plucked off the hair : I hid not my face from shame and spitting.*

Now let me go back a little, and read again the third verse : "I clothe the heavens with blackness, and I make sackcloth their covering." "I gave my back to the smiters, and my cheeks to them that plucked off the hair." It is the same divine Person, who musters the hosts of heaven till the very skies are blackened with the artillery of God, who here says, "I gave my back to the smiters, bowing down to the brutal Roman scourge, and my cheeks to them that plucked off the hair." You remember the scene that I pictured last Sunday night, the whole band of soldiers mocking Christ, and even spitting upon him.* That was the fulfilment of these words, "I hid not my face from shame and spitting." That same Christ, without whom was not anything made that was made, whose face is the sun of heaven, whose glory is matchless and unsearchable, says, "I hid not my face from shame and spitting." Do not say, then, that God has no love to you. Do not say that he has cast you away as a husband divorces his wife. Talk no more as if there were no help for you, no means of your deliverance. Behold how low your Saviour stooped, how gracious he was to suffer so much for guilty men, and be encouraged to trust him. He who gave his back to the smiters says to you, "The chastisement of your peace was upon me, and with my stripes you are healed."

7. *For the Lord* GOD *will help me ;*

This is Christ still speaking. Though God himself, yet as the God-Man, looking to his Father for help in the dread struggle through which he went to save us, he declared, "The Lord God will help me."

7. *Therefore shall I not be confounded : therefore have I set my face like a flint, and I know that I shall not be ashamed.*

And he was not ; he went through with all that he had undertaken. He drank our bitter cup till none of the dregs remained. He bore the terrible wrath of God, which else would have rested on us for ever ; God helped him, and he bore it all.

8, 9. *He is near that justifieth me ; who will contend with me ? let us stand together : who is mine adversary ? let him come near to me. Behold, the Lord* GOD *will help me ; who is he that shall condemn me ? lo, they all shall wax old as a garment ; the moth shall eat them up.*

Will any now come to battle against Christ, and hope to conquer him ? Voltaire used to say, "Crush the Wretch !" but where is Voltaire now ? And those who agreed with Voltaire, where are they now ? But Jesus ever liveth and reigneth, and God is with him. He who shall once come to battle with our glorious Lord shall soon know the power of Christ's weakness, and the omnipotence of his death.

10. *Who is among you—*

Here is a very blessed question. Christ, having passed through all the trouble that could be passed through, and having come out of it triumphant, now looks round on all his followers, on all the children of God, and he says, "Who is among you"—

10. *That feareth the* LORD, *that obeyeth the voice of his servant, that walketh in darkness, and hath no light? let him trust in the name of the* LORD, *and stay upon his God.*

Do you see the drift of it ? Our Saviour trusted, and he was not con-

---

* See the *Metropolitan Tabernacle Pulpit*, No. 2,333, "The Whole Band against Christ."

founded. He stayed himself upon God even when he said, "My God, my God, why hast thou forsaken me?" and he came off a conqueror. Trust you in God, and you also will be victorious. Let your strength be drawn from that strong and mighty One who is pledged to help all who trust him, and you shall triumph even as Jesus did.

Do you refuse to trust God? Then listen to this :—

11. *Behold, all ye that kindle a fire, that compass yourselves about with sparks : walk in the light of your fire, and in the sparks that ye have kindled.*

If you think to make yourselves happy in sin, go and do it. If you fancy that your own righteousness will save you, go and try it.

11. *This shall ye have of mine hand; ye shall lie down in sorrow.*

Your fire shall not warm you; your sparks shall not enlighten you; you will have to lie down to die, and you shall lie down in sorrow. O my dear hearers, the time will come when every one of us must put off this body, and lie down to die! God grant that we may none of us have to lie down in sorrow; but instead thereof, having trusted in God, may he light our candle for us in the last moment, that we may fall asleep in Jesus, and wake up in his likeness in the everlasting glory!

May God bless to us the reading of his Word! Amen.